David Hare was educated at Oundle School, studied French at St Andrews University, and has worked as a strawberry picker, curry deliverer, pizza maker, university lecturer and a PR director. He is now a freelance writer, trainer and mindset coach with private and corporate clients across the world. David has been practising Nichiren Buddhism as a member of Soka Gakkai International (SGI) since 1985, and lives with his family in Leicestershire, UK.

www.thankingthespoon.com
Twitter: @DavidHareCoach

Praise for
The Buddha in Me, the Buddha in You:

'An inspiration to anyone who wants to make fast and forever changes in their lives with relevant and powerful insights about life, love, leadership and the challenges faced by today's world. It will even help you discover who you really are.'

David Taylor, author of *The Naked Leader*

'An inspiring, compelling and enchanting book. All the way through I kept saying to myself: "That is so true!" I was left feeling intrigued and uplifted. Full of warmth, wit and wisdom, it highlights that anything is possible in life.'

Leigh Ferrani, author, playwright and literary consultant

'A powerful and important message for a time of turbulence and confusion ... with verve, wit and plenty of practical, doable tips.'

Eddy Canfor-Dumas, author of *The Buddha, Geoff and Me*

'Let your inner Buddha be your buddy ... Packed with inspiration and timeless wisdom; chanting optional.'

Andy Cope, author of *Be Brilliant Every Day*

'A call to action and so full of empowering words of wisdom, you could fill a stadium with sticky notes! ... Get your highlighter out and dog ear more pages than you ever thought possible.'

James DuMont, actor

A modern GPS guide for navigating the road to real happiness in this lifetime. David Hare distils thousands of years of Buddhist concepts into actionable steps, filled with the same wit and compassion that made his Thanking The Spoon blog such a treasure.'

Justin Simien, award-winning Hollywood filmmaker and author

'Much to offer to anyone prepared to ask fundamental questions about their life, and where it's going.'

William Woollard, author of *The Reluctant Buddhist*

'Took my thoughts and, more importantly, my emotions to a depth that I found truly challenging and incredibly inspirational ... I am in awe of this book.'

Richard Jackson MBE, Co-founder of Mancroft International

'The whole point of your life is to become happy and to unlock the potential that already exists within you. This book will show you how.'

Duncan Pow, actor and author of *In Between Jobs*

'Written with warmth and humour ... practical exercises and affirmations for people who want to access Buddhist wisdom, but aren't necessarily into chanting, incense and bells! Approach with caution ... it may just remove all your excuses for unhappiness and underperformance!'

Steve Miller, TV hypnotherapist

'Shows us how even a non-Buddhist can apply the wisest principles of Buddhism to enhance their life in profound ways ... offers us a path to a happier life.'

Alex Lickerman, author of *The Undefeated Mind*

THE
BUDDHA
IN ME,
THE BUDDHA
IN YOU

A handbook for happiness

David Hare

LONDON · SYDNEY · AUCKLAND · JOHANNESBURG

1 3 5 7 9 10 8 6 4 2

Rider, an imprint of Ebury Publishing,
20 Vauxhall Bridge Road,
London SW1V 2SA

Rider is part of the Penguin Random House group of companies whose
addresses can be found at global.penguinrandomhouse.com

First published by Rider in 2019

www.eburypublishing.co.uk

A CIP catalogue record for this book is available from the British Library

ISBN 9781846046247

Printed and bound in Great Britain by Clays Ltd, Elcograf S.p.A.

Penguin Random House is committed to a sustainable future for our
business, our readers and our planet. This book is made from Forest
Stewardship Council® certified paper.

Note: These pages reflect the author's own understanding and interpretation of Nichiren Buddhist teachings as practised by members of
Soka Gakkai International (SGI), a socially engaged, worldwide Buddhist
movement inspired by the Buddhism of Nichiren Daishonin (1222–1282).
Although a number of inspirational SGI leaders have been quoted and have
shown strong support for the book, this is not an official SGI publication.

For Anna, Zofia and Leon,
my treasures of the heart.

'The Lotus Sutra has the drama of fighting for justice against evil. It has a warmth that comforts the weary. It has a vibrant, pulsing courage that drives away fear. It has a chorus of joy at attaining absolute freedom throughout the three existences. It has the soaring flight of liberty. It has brilliant light, flowers, greenery, music, paintings, vivid stories. It offers unsurpassed lessons on psychology, the workings of the human heart; lessons on life; lessons on happiness; and lessons on peace. It maps out the basic rules for good health. It awakens us to the universal truth that a change in one's heart, or attitude, can transform everything.'

Daisaku Ikeda, third President of Soka Gakkai
International, in *The Wisdom of the Lotus Sutra*

'I will teach you how to become a Buddha easily.'

Nichiren Daishonin, in his letter
'The Wealthy Man Sudatta'

CONTENTS

Introduction xi

1 What's it all about? 1

2 Life is precious 7

3 Happiness is the soundtrack of your mind 13

4 The Ten Worlds – Buddhism's model of
   the mind 41

5 Karma – your whole life in your hands 63

6 Everyone's a Buddha 82

7 You have a problem? Congratulations! 94

8 Beyond the survival mentality 108

9 Cultivate the treasures of the heart 121

10 Living in the moment – happiness here
    and now 139

11 Determination through the ups and downs 153

12 Become the master of your mind 169

13 **How to choose a great mentor** 197

14 **Small self, big self** 204

15 **Beyond the OK society** 229

The Buddha's Invitation 237

Notes 239

Glossary 244

About Soka Gakkai International (SGI) 249

Select Bibliography 251

Acknowledgements 254

Index 256

INTRODUCTION

An accidental Buddhist

I first bumped into Buddhism in Paris in the summer of 1983, after leaving home at the age of seventeen with plans to work my way across Europe. I came from a loving family but was bursting to break free from the sheltered life of my single-sex public school. Studying French at university could wait for a year. It was time to lose my inhibitions and find some excitement in the real world, beyond the dreamy yet claustrophobic cloisters where I had spent the last seven years. I arrived at Stalingrad coach station (now long gone) in the north-east of Paris at dawn, after a fourteen-hour journey from London. I had my rucksack, a basic map of the French capital, twenty Silk Cut, a packet of Polos and £400 that I had saved from working as a hotel barman in my hometown of Peterborough.

Most of the money, the inhibitions and the plans to see Europe evaporated within a short time of my checking into the utterly charming Hôtel de Nesle, a quirky, bohemian Latin Quarter hostel that was a *de rigueur* first stop for solo travellers on a tight budget. I was immediately seduced by the breakfast of warm croissants and hot chocolate, followed by a roll-up from a fellow new arrival. We all sat at a big table under bouquets of dried flowers that hung from the rafters in reception. The place was owned by a large, warm and redoubtable matriarch called Renée, who had the air of a Romany fortune teller and called everyone *chéri*.

Of Camus and Camembert

In this pre-internet age, the Hôtel de Nesle was the place to network. A warm and welcoming sanctuary where you could get drunk, get high and, if you wanted to, get into brief, no-strings relationships. We were a friendly ragtag bunch of drifters, buskers, EFL teachers, artists and gap-year students, mainly from the USA, UK, Germany and Scandinavia. Our late-night conversations about Sylvia Plath, Jim Morrison or Albert Camus were fuelled by red wine, baguettes and Camembert (which in those days did not settle quite so immediately around my waistline). And before bedtime, the guitars and tarot cards would usually make an appearance. These new experiences ignited a spark within me. Paris was a place that promised adventure and the chance to rebel against my loving but sheltered childhood. I wouldn't need to travel across Europe after all.

I soon made friends with a New Yorker called Ken. The deal was that he would show me round Paris and I would help him learn French. Little did I know that this chance encounter would spark a sequence of events that would change the course of my whole life. Ken had taken a shine to a young Finnish lady called Mina, who was renting a room in an apartment in the 19th arrondissement, in those days one of the less salubrious parts of the capital. As Mina was heading home to Helsinki, she threw a leaving party, to which Ken and I were invited. At the party, we met her landlady, Christiane Alix, who now had a spare room to rent. I knew Christiane was a Buddhist because she told me straightaway and in her lounge she had a strange altar with a scroll in it. But we didn't let her weird religion put us off. Ken and I moved in a couple of days later.

Destiny and dominoes

So ... the Hôtel de Nesle, meeting Ken, his Finnish love-interest, her leaving party, my first sight of a Buddhist altar, a cheap spare room to rent ... Did this series of dominoes fall in some preordained sequence? Was it fate? Cosmic coincidence? Karma? At the time, it seemed like none of the above. I had absolutely no intentions of becoming a Buddhist, despite Christiane's earnest endeavours. Firstly, I was a devout (if increasingly sceptical) Catholic. And secondly, although I found the philosophy intriguing, the practice was just a bit too 'far out'. In Christiane's altar, there was a scroll with some Chinese-looking characters on it that she chanted in front of (sometimes for one or more hours at a time), as well as candles, incense, a gong, prayer beads and fruit. My first impressions were that this scroll and its central mantra – Nam-myoho-renge-kyo – were at best weird and at worst sinister.

Over time, I learned that Christiane and many of her friends practised something called Nichiren Buddhism, which had been founded by a revolutionary Japanese monk called Nichiren Daishonin (1222–1282). He based his philosophy on the Lotus Sutra, the ultimate teaching preached in India 3,000 years ago by the first Buddha, Siddhartha Gautama, also known as Shakyamuni.

In a nutshell, Nichiren, who described himself as 'merely the son of a commoner from a remote province', believed in the Buddha in me and the Buddha in you. He believed in everyone's innate wisdom, courage and compassion (the three main qualities of 'Buddhahood') and taught his followers how to access these qualities, a full 700 years before positive psychology, 'New Age' affirmations, life coaching, NLP or modern-day CBT had been invented.

Nichiren boiled down the essence of Buddhahood into a formula that people could use to improve their daily lives – particularly through chanting the mantra 'Nam-myoho-renge-kyo', which we'll explore in Chapter 3. Many of his writings (nearly all of them in the guise of personal letters – known as 'gosho' in Japanese – to his followers, and published today in two volumes under the title *The Writings of Nichiren Daishonin*) were sent to women and the working classes, telling them the unusually good news that enlightenment was available to them in this lifetime. This was a radical teaching in the militaristic and hierarchical society of thirteenth-century feudal Japan. And totally typical of this daring and charismatic man, this maverick on a mission, this bold reformer of Buddhism. Little wonder the government repeatedly exiled this rebel monk and tried to chop his head off (his decapitation being thwarted only by the timely appearance of a passing comet that blinded his would-be executioner).

But at the time none of this felt relevant to me and I spent ages debating with Christiane about our different religions. All my philosophical points made perfect sense to me, though somewhere deep inside I did feel moved by her heart, by her compassion and also by her anger about the injustices of the world in her disadvantaged corner of Paris. I was profoundly sceptical and yet I was also seeking answers to age-old questions such as 'what's it all about?', and 'why am I here?' Christiane assured me that, through chanting, I could find all those answers within. But I would religiously leave her apartment as soon as the Buddhists turned up to chant (partly because I did not like the noise they made) and would head off to the peace of the local park or, if I was feeling spiritual, to Notre Dame or Sacré Coeur.

Thanking the spoon

However, this wise and perceptive lady could sense that I was struggling. She saw straight through my intellectual arrogance to all the confusion and insecurity it hid. Despite her own deep sufferings, lack of cash and bad luck in love, Christiane was a 'surrogate mum' to almost any waif or stray that happened to wander across her threshold. By this stage I still had no job, was down to my last few francs and was in a relationship with a beautiful artist who was dabbling in Buddhism to beat a serious heroin addiction. Of course, some people would have taken all of this in their stride, but I did not have the emotional resilience to do so. I was on the verge of giving up and heading back to England. It was at this point that Christiane shared some Buddhist guidance from second Soka Gakkai President Josei Toda (1900–1958), an educator and peace activist who did more than anyone to bring Nichiren Buddhism to the masses in the nuclear devastation of post-war Japan: 'When we are upset, it's easy to blame others. However, the true cause of our feelings is within us. For example, imagine yourself as a glass of water. Now, imagine past negative experiences as sediment at the bottom of your glass. Next, think of others as spoons. When one stirs, the sediment clouds your water. It may appear that the spoon caused the water to cloud – but if there were no sediment, the water would remain clear no matter what. The key, then, is to identify our sediment and actively work to remove it.'

Christiane's point was that if you take ownership of your problems, if you 'thank the spoon' rather than resenting others for what is happening to you, you can become the creator of your own future and develop the inner resources to transform your life.

Biting the strawberry

This was not what I wanted to hear – subconsciously I was quite happy being an angry victim, thank you very much. In the end, with some exasperation, Christiane tried one more analogy: 'Look, I can spend all day explaining what a strawberry tastes like, but unless you actually try it, you will never know.' I hate strawberries, but the analogy is still valid. You only know what it's like to chant when you give it a go. And so, a few days later, on 3 July 1983, after more fruitless attempts to find work and a happy relationship, I 'bit the strawberry'. I figured I had nothing left to lose. I decided to categorise Buddhism as a philosophy or therapy, not a religion, even though Christiane was – and still is – a passionate member of a religious movement called SGI (Soka Gakkai International). That way I could square it with my Catholic faith and not feel guilty. I was encouraged to chant for 'actual proof' and for 'benefits', such as a job and a happy relationship. With my then shallow understanding of the teachings, I found this emphasis on 'proof' rather unsavoury and unspiritual, however ... I didn't want to go back to Peterborough. Not yet anyway. After learning the basic chant from Christiane at her home in Paris, I began chanting to a blank wall and a candle in the bedsit I had moved to. I used a teaspoon and a glass instead of a proper gong. I had a set of beads and a prayer book given to me by an SGI member. I gradually built up my 'altar' over the next couple of months.

But when I quickly found a job (as a chef in an Italian takeaway) and when my girlfriend beat heroin, I dismissed both as mere coincidence. I then went to university in Scotland for the next two years, where I completely forgot about Buddhism, pizzas, spoons and strawberries. Going to church did not cross my mind and neither did chanting – I'd boxed Buddhism off as just one of many 'exotic' experiences in Paris. And university was an easy place to be a cool agnostic. My earnest practice only began when I returned to Paris in 1985 for a mid-degree teaching placement and noticed that most of those annoying Buddhists who came to Christiane's flat had moved forward in their lives.

They reported a whole range of tangible and intangible benefits from their spiritual practice. One had a happier marriage, while another had unearthed the courage to leave a violent relationship. One had a better-paid job, another had found a new career with less money but more meaning. One had overcome a major health challenge, and another had discovered her artistic talent, realised she was gay and made a whole new set of friends. Some had rediscovered a sense of hope or freedom or confidence, while others were kinder, less angry, more energetic, or less anxious. And some were still struggling, but with more hope and determination than before, thanks to the warm encouragement of their fellow Buddhists. All of this had more impact on me than any doctrinal theory: these people were leading meaningful lives through a philosophy that actually seemed to work. I began to think there might be something in this Buddhist practice after all. That it might provide a powerful and practical tool for living. By contrast, the soundtrack of my own mind, after a very tough second year at university, was much less joyful and positive than before. And so began my thirty-year adventure ...

Everything is easy, everything is difficult

My memories of those early days of my practice in 1985 are that chanting was quite an emotional experience and that I had lots of 'epiphanies', not all of them welcome (to begin with). I felt like my whole life was being thrown up in the air but that when the pieces came back down I would be stronger and happier – which is what gradually happened (and indeed it has happened several times since). The chanting produced a powerful mixture of feelings. It was both unsettling and uplifting. As actor and SGI Buddhist Duncan Pow writes in his novel *In Between Jobs*: 'I have found something else, something inside me that I was not aware I had. It makes everything easy. It makes everything difficult.' Although my new practice brought a lot of buried stuff to the surface of my life, I also felt that I was absolutely on the right path, which was exciting. I felt fully alive again, with little bursts of joy peeping through.

Since then, just like those Parisian Buddhists, I have received lots of tangible and intangible benefits from the practice. And lots of challenges too. Two spells of unemployment and three different and fulfilling careers; difficult relationships faced and transformed; new friendships and passions discovered and explored. A home filled with fun, warmth and laughter thanks to a wonderful wife and two amazing children. When my Buddhist practice is strong, I see life's problems as a joyful combat, rather than a painful ordeal. I also have the joy of supporting 200 other Buddhists in the area where I live.

And I have been inspired on numerous occasions by the writings of Daisaku Ikeda, the third and current President of Soka Gakkai International (SGI), who since 1958 has pioneered the worldwide spread of Nichiren Buddhism, fighting relentlessly and with utter determination for human beings everywhere to become absolutely happy. For this reason, his words of wisdom appear in several places in this book.

In short, I am immeasurably happier, wiser and more grateful than the confused and self-centred young man who bumped into Buddhism in 1983. Looking back, I can see that in those days my personality was a fairly toxic blend of low self-esteem combined with a high sense of entitlement! Today, I have a much stronger sense of purpose and understand in my heart that life is precious. The soundtrack of my mind is, most days, more upbeat, proactive and optimistic. And I feel that, through my practice, I can face with courage and joy the challenges that come my way, and that through sharing Buddhism and through my work as a life coach, I can help others to do the same.

Answers as unique as you

I came across coaching in 2004, shortly after losing a well-paid, high-status job as global PR director for a big multinational. One minute I was in a private jet flying to a board meeting, and the next I was scraping around for bits of freelance copywriting work and spending my way too quickly through my severance money. My Buddhist practice had been quite weak and self-centred for a few years – climbing the corporate ladder had gradually become my new 'religion'. Suitably chastened by this crash back to earth, I was chanting about what to do next and, surfing the internet one day, took up the offer of a free telephone coaching session from a college that was advertising a one-year coaching qualification. I found the conversation incredibly helpful. The lady listened to me with compassion and wisdom, asked me some great incisive questions, did not once tell me what to do and sparked some fantastic 'light-bulb' moments. She said that I would find all the answers inside me and just needed to trust my own wisdom. Now then ... where had I heard that before?

Needless to say, I signed up for the course and since then have developed my own very fulfilling coaching practice, helping many people across the world to achieve breakthroughs in their lives. Clients come to me with all sorts of challenges. Sometimes they feel they have 'lost their mojo' (it's in there somewhere), or feel confused or trapped or stressed or overwhelmed. Sometimes the problem is more specific – career direction, relationships, body image, public speaking or work-life balance, to name just a few. But in almost every case, underneath the problem they first mention, people are really striving to discover their true voice and to create a beautiful and authentic life with more meaning, excitement and fulfilment.

Buddhism without the bells?

I started writing this book in 2009 while struggling with an unexpected bout of depression and wrestling again with questions about happiness: what is it, is it really achievable and how can each of us develop more of it while living harmoniously together? As a Buddhist life coach, I wanted to work out where personal development ends and religion begins. Are they compatible? Do they share the same goals? Is one more effective than the other? I'd also noticed coaching clients and delegates on courses asking me more often about Buddhism, perhaps because mindfulness has now gone mainstream, with books, workshops and even the UK's National Health Service promoting its benefits, while comparisons have also being drawn between Buddhist practice and Cognitive Behavioural Therapy.

So I wondered whether you can take powerful Buddhist principles, which I know have worked for thousands of practitioners, wrap them in personal development techniques and then do without the chanting and the ceremonies? Do you have to be spiritual to profoundly change your life, or are interventions such as coaching and hypnotherapy enough? I also found myself wondering if religion really can provide answers to the turbulent issues and injustices of our times. We live in an age where materialism isn't working. We have mostly lost trust in politicians. Science does not have all the answers. And Emotional Intelligence (EQ) teachings are liberating and enlightening but risk creating a self-centred culture of entitlement.

Happiness for self and others

Since 2004, to improve my skills as a coach and trainer, I have attended and have run many personal development courses, and devoured the excellent books that go with them. They've taught me that I can fulfil more of my potential, that I deserve to succeed, that nobody can make me feel mad, bad or sad, that limiting beliefs sometimes hold me back, that I can set more exciting goals for myself, that some powerful affirmations can boost my self-esteem ... in short, that I am pretty darned amazing. I have shared such books with friends and clients who have likewise revelled in their new-found awesomeness. But what none of these courses tend to emphasise is that, if I am amazing, everyone else must be as well. And if we could all draw out more of each other's wondrous potential, what difference might that make to our troubled world? So, this book will share with you ten of the most powerful lessons taught by Nichiren:

1. Life itself is precious. Its essence, its energy. My life, your life, all life. And, on a level that even our subconscious cannot perceive, it is interconnected. A Buddha is one who perceives this truth and loves the fact of just being alive.

2. To reveal the joy, life force, wisdom, courage, gratitude and compassion needed for a happy life requires great effort and gritty determination. It means recognising, fighting and defeating what a life coach would call your 'gremlins' and what Nichiren Buddhists call your 'Fundamental Darkness' – or 'FD' for short. It means going deeper than the limits of

your conscious and subconscious mind, and trusting the original enlightened core of your being.

3. Buddhahood is absolutely not some superhuman or divine state, but something very real and practical that is attainable by all of us, in this lifetime. It is the respect in your voice and the warmth in your heart. It includes profound feelings of joy, wisdom, courage, compassion, gratitude and optimism that produce a sparkle in your eye and a dance in your smile, and both of these and more in other people too.

4. You and everyone else can become happy and enlightened: the sports star, the soldier, the postman, the newsagent, the tramp, the supermodel, the noisy neighbour, your mother-in-law and you. When Nichiren began teaching this philosophy, he upset powerful rulers who were using the established religions of the day to keep people in their place.

5. All the answers you'll ever need are inside you, none of them require prayers of supplication to God or Buddha or Allah. Neither do you need a guru or a priest or a master to act as a middle-man between you and your own enlightenment. The answers are as unique as you.

6. There is no actual heaven. There is no hell. Neither is a physical place that you go to. Both exist in your heart. Your heart counts most of all.

7. You do not need faith to start practising. Buddhism is empirical: you test it out in the real world and see what happens. Although Nichiren drew heavily on Buddhist scripture (what he called 'documentary evidence'), he mainly encouraged his followers to set goals and chant to achieve them, to test the practice, to see if it works.

8. Because of the Mystic Law of cause and effect, you are responsible not only for everything that you think, feel, say and do but also for what happens to you. How hard to believe – in the West anyway – yet how empowering when viewed from the perspective that you can start to change what you attract from this moment on. Most personal development teachings say you're only responsible for how you react to events 'outside your control', though it is interesting to see books such as *The Secret* explain this 'Law of Attraction'.

9. The purpose of life is to grasp what happiness is and to achieve it, for yourself and for others – in the process transforming our planet's terrible tendency towards war and destruction.

10. Finally, life is eternal. You get to come back over and over again, with some periods in between to enjoy a refreshing nap. (This nap is known by most of us as 'death' and to some people the word has negative connotations ...)

These are the main principles taught by Nichiren. It is worth stating at this point that, as they might say on the BBC, 'other schools of Buddhism are available'; and indeed if you're wondering why there's no mention in the above list of vegetarianism, nirvana, the Dalai Lama, meditation or mindfulness, it's because Nichiren Buddhism is very different from the Tibetan and Zen traditions more commonly encountered in the West. For example, Nichiren Buddhists, for reasons explained later, do not worship a statue of a Buddha on their altars. Quite a few are meat-eaters and more than a few are partial to a drink or two.

All the chapters that follow are based on the ten core principles sketched above. My aim is to give non-Buddhists some bite-size chunks of practical wisdom and advice to use amidst the realities of everyday life. Practising Buddhists will also find this book useful. In fact, Nichiren's provocative insights into how life works can inspire anyone who's serious about self-development and/or wants to make a valuable contribution to society. People who, amidst the challenges of daily life, understand just how precious life is and fight to reveal its dignity.

How do we achieve this, then?

It is an obvious truth to state that the world could benefit from more people who are committed to being positive, joyful, resourceful, respectful, brave and compassionate. Indeed, many of these values have been taught by personal development authors, by other religions and by leaders on conference platforms right across the political spectrum. The much more challenging question is: *how* do we achieve this, then? How can we attain this breadth and depth of character? What's the most efficient and effective tool? Is there one? Is there anything that actually *works*? The Nichiren Buddhist answer includes study, dialogue and engaging in a daily practice of chanting the mantra 'Nam-myoho-renge-kyo'. As mentioned, Chapter 3 will explain in detail what these words mean, but in a nutshell they represent:

- the voice of the Buddha in you
- the rhythm of life
- the vibration of the Universe.

I believe that this prayer is the deepest and most powerful 'how to' technique for achieving individual happiness and world peace. For Nichiren Buddhists, the mantra Nam-myoho-renge-kyo is the mother of all affirmations. It turns up the volume on the good stuff in your mind. In positive psychology jargon, it generates your highest level of esteem (for self and others), your most resourceful state and your ultimate life purpose, all rolled into one simple mantra. It takes the complex and profound philosophy of Buddhism and helps you make it real in your everyday life.

That said, many readers, for many different reasons, will feel that a twice-daily Buddhist practice is not for them (or not right now anyway). After all, it took me two years to acquire a taste for it, after that initial encounter in Paris. Likewise, I have close friends and relatives who have a strong seeking spirit and an open mind, but do not see themselves as 'spiritual' or do not want to belong to a religious movement.

For all these reasons and for just such readers, each chapter in this book ends with a set of affirmations and suggested journal exercises as additional practical resources. Affirmations are a sort of 'positive brainwashing' and are commonly used in coaching sessions. They describe the kind of person you most aspire to become – for example, 'I am a loving and attentive father', or, 'I treasure my body by eating healthily every day'. You can say them in your head or out loud (if the latter, I would recommend the privacy of your own home, rather than the high street or an open-plan office). You can even recite them into a mirror if you like. They are especially powerful when recited just before you go to sleep, because your subconscious mind is more receptive then, but you can use them in all sorts of different situations. Affirmations help you 'rewire' your beliefs and they programme your subconscious mind to expect and achieve more happiness. During that dose of the blues in 2009, I would listen to a recording of about 50 different affirmations while driving up and down the motorway to London. Slowly, they made an enormous difference, alongside my Buddhist practice.

As for the journal exercises at the ends of chapters, they are an opportunity for self-reflection (ideally in a personal diary/notebook) or discussion with friends, and include the types of questions I often ask when coaching my own clients. SGI members reading this book may also find the questions useful, particularly as potential topics or as prompts for monthly discussion meetings. Either way, I hope they will give you food for thought and exciting insights that help move your life forward. Both the affirmations and exercises can be used with or without a Buddhist practice.

I also hope that through reading this book you will discover a deeper wisdom about how life works and feel a fluttering in your belly that says daily life is wonderful and worth waking up for. I hope you will connect with even more of your brilliance and live with more courage, more meaning and more joy. I hope this book will help you find the positive aspect in all emotions, even anger and despair, for the beautiful lotus flower of Buddhahood grows only in the muddy pond of daily life. It's my wish that, after reading this book, you feel so bouncy and excited just to be alive that random strangers come up to you in the street, squeeze your (possibly) chubby cheeks and declare: 'Wow, you are bursting with joy and scrumptiousness, thank you for being in the world!' Admittedly this doesn't happen every day in my part of Leicestershire. Yet.

So, let's begin the journey by finding out what a Buddha is and why you might want to be one …

CHAPTER 1

WHAT'S IT ALL ABOUT?

The word 'Buddha' simply means someone who is 'awakened'. So at its most basic level, Nichiren Buddhism is a deep insight into how life works. How to get the most from it. How to give your all to it. How to be happy. How to create value in society. How to find the Buddha in me and the Buddha in you.

Nichiren believed that we are born to reveal our infinite courage, wisdom, life force and compassion, all of which could be compared to the virtues taught by Plato or the signature strengths identified by the father of positive psychology, Professor Martin Seligman. These Buddha virtues are latent in *all of us*, not just in a select élite, and anything that stops us revealing them is an illusion. In other words, a misconception about how fundamentally incredible we all are and how life works. Illusions are the totally transparent and invisible windows through which we view the world, yet which determine our perspective on it. And illusions masquerade so eloquently as truth because they are created from deeply held beliefs that once served us well.

Get over yourself!

From one perspective, the core of Nichiren's message is a strict yet compassionate exhortation to 'get over yourself'! However, he's not saying 'pull yourself together', rather that you need to get over your smaller self – in short, smash through your illusions or limiting beliefs (to use coaching jargon) and live a big, fantastic, fully connected life. Or as author and coach Joe Vitale would say, 'get clear'. In Nichiren Buddhism we call this process 'human revolution' and we believe it is the only route to lasting world peace.

That often means getting over some of your 'tribal attachments' (for example, to race, education, class or religion), many of which seek to separate you from the universal human race and are anchored in what I call our Survival-Obsessed Self ('S-O-S') or small ego. I think the two deepest illusions we have, that are at the root of pretty much all suffering, are the notions that:

a) Life ends with death (admittedly it looks that way);
b) We are fundamentally separate from each other
   (admittedly it looks that way).

More on each of these and on our over-used S-O-S in later pages ...

Illusions come seductively packaged

What makes a teaching powerful? What holds people back from making progress in their lives? The most beneficial teachings – such as the Buddha's Lotus Sutra – are the ones that cause real paradigm shifts within individuals and society. The ones that shatter our illusions, bulldoze our comfort zones and remove our subconscious and karmic excuses for being unhappy and/or disrespectful to others. Poems such as 'The Invitation' by Oriah Mountain Dreamer, books such as *The Alchemist* by Paulo Coelho, *The Celestine Prophecy* by James Redfield, and *Loving What Is* by Byron Katie. Movements such as SGI.

Unfortunately, our illusions do not dock up with a stark health warning stamped on them; they come instead seductively packaged and full of whispered promises. Or full of consolation. They do not admit to you that they will ultimately produce a life of joyless frustration. They arrive with the best of intentions and, within their limits, work well – for a while at least. The familiar witty comfort of the cynic. The coping strategy that gets you through another crisis. Delicious but destructive addictions. The belief that it is your wife or husband's job to make you happy. Or your role to make them happy. Hiding away under the comfortable duvet of failure, or slumbering on the mattress of mediocrity in the midst of an 'OK society'. The belief that longer pleasures equal deeper happiness. Casual, devil-may-care bravado. Illusions that may have served us well in childhood, or further back, in our caveman days, when our S-O-S (Survival-Obsessed Self) meant everything.

And we are still hardwired to survive – by 14 million years of primate evolution. Striving and thriving do not yet come naturally, though I believe they are the natural next stage of our evolution as a species. Even though I have written this book from the most sincere place in my heart, there are moments when I struggle to believe its message, let alone put it into practice. Just like the people I coach, I occasionally get a blue day, when my old illusions drown out the volume of the good stuff in my head. As Nichiren wrote:

> We ordinary people can see neither our own eyelashes, which are so close, nor the heavens in the distance. Likewise we do not see that the Buddha exists in our own hearts.[1]

And Shakyamuni, the founder of Buddhism, said himself that the Lotus Sutra, his ultimate teaching, was the 'most difficult to understand and to believe'.

Go deeper than your subconscious mind

When I first met this practice, I was, to quote the title of a book by my fellow SGI member William Woollard (of *Top Gear* fame), a rather 'Reluctant Buddhist'. Indeed, I began chanting partly to prove that it was a load of nonsense and would never work for me. And there have been periods of my life where I have, for a time, put more faith in coaching and in self-help books than in Buddhism. But after thirty years of testing this practice, my deep initial scepticism has given way to a growing belief that Nichiren's teachings are not only complete, profound and practical, but that they also go deeper than the subconscious level of the mind.

Nichiren Buddhism is more profound than popular personal development teachings because it:

- explains that much of what happens in your current lifetime was 'chosen' by you in your previous lives ('karma');
- reveals that at a fundamental level we are connected with every other human being and that therefore true individual fulfilment is inextricably linked with other people's happiness;
- provides powerful and practical tools so that you can access your most resourceful state on a daily basis.

Hollywood actress and SGI member Cathryn de Prume, who has chanted for thirty years and has appeared in major box office movies such as *Wild* with Reese Witherspoon, once shared with me how she dealt with rejection when movie auditions did not work out: 'To me, the key difference between Nichiren Buddhism and popular self-help practices is that they're focused solely on one's self. But when I'm not busy working as an actress, instead of focusing on an unsuccessful audition, I'll go and chant with someone in their home, which is a strong tradition in SGI. By supporting someone else, I grow my own life. Our movement and this practice give me the opportunity to nurture other people, therefore cultivating my compassion, giving me a broader perspective that includes my family, community, society and the world.'

There's a Buddha in me and a Buddha in you

Nichiren was adamant that *everyone without exception* has Buddhahood. This teaching has some potentially spectacular implications for society. In fact, Nichiren Buddhists make a vow to relentlessly perform their own individual human revolutions and support others with their own personal transformations of the heart so that we can build a more vibrant, respectful and peaceful world. As singer-songwriter and SGI member Howard Jones comments: 'This is a very active type of Buddhism, it's about getting stuck into the world and making a contribution.'

World peace (known as 'Kosen-Rufu' in Nichiren Buddhism) isn't some hippie-Sixties-utopian fantasy. It's much tougher than that, because the practice of revealing your brilliance means making the effort to clean out your own unique mucky stuff, with a goal to raise the life state of the whole planet. Every day. And Nichiren Buddhism asserts quite simply that if more people sort their own stuff out, then the world will *inevitably* become a better place. That we'll have a dynamic society based on deep respect for everyone's Buddhahood, irrespective of factors such as race, religion, nationality and sexual orientation ... All of these labels originate in our S-O-S mentality and are no more than powerful illusions that seek to separate us from each other.

Powerful illusions prevent us remembering what Buddhists believe is the most important truth of all: despite our apparent differences, ultimately we are all made from the same stardust, we all share the same universal life force, and we are all – in the core of our beings – enlightened Buddhas.

Mindset mantras for realising happiness is possible

I open my heart to the deep well of happiness inside me.

I release the illusions of my smaller self and connect with my bigger self instead.

I realise I can be more and achieve more.

I see the Buddha in me and in others.

CHAPTER 2

LIFE IS PRECIOUS

Life is precious. The rest of this book will make much more sense if part of you already knows this (or is at least willing to imagine it might be so). It took me twenty-four years of Buddhist practice and a serious dollop of depression to begin to glimpse this fundamental truth! Of course, I know many non-Buddhists who seem to have been born understanding this – feeling that every moment and every life is valuable and being grateful just to wake up every morning. May hats be doffed to you, because once we grasp this truth, there is almost no limit to what we can be, do and achieve in terms of goals and relationships.

When asked to give a split-second guess, many people on The Winning Edge personal development programme developed by Richard Jackson imagine that they will live for 200,000 days in the average lifetime of 76 years. They look pretty shocked when they realise that this number of days would mean living to the very ripe old age of 550, and that the mathematical answer is actually closer to 28,000!

But length of life isn't the main issue, it's what you do with every moment that counts. There are people of 21 years old who walk around with slumped shoulders, already looking weary of life. People in what Buddhism calls 'Hell state' who may not want to live another seven days, let alone grind their way through another 20,000. The worst kind of death is surely when your seeking spirit and self-respect die while you are still alive.

Treasure every moment and every person

My grandma died at ninety-two (a good twenty years after her death was first predicted by most family members). She was in great pain from cancer for much of her later days, and yet, and yet … she still had a twinkle in her eye to the very end, even though she could barely see. In fact, when I kissed her on the cheek five days before she passed away, she was confused, thinking I was her fit young doctor, and laughed so much when she realised I wasn't. So when, like her, you know that life is *in and of itself* truly precious, you can have a youthful spirit all the time, however grey your temples or creaky your knees. Even if you're ninety-two and just days from death.

On the other hand, when you think: Blow it, I'm going to drink too much, or start an argument over a nothing (albeit a nothing that feels all-consuming in that moment) or give up on a goal (again) or put up with an abusive relationship, you are, on a very deep level, saying to yourself and the Universe: 'Life is worthless.' This is the point at which our Fundamental Darkness or 'inner gremlin' quietly and gleefully sniggers, knowing that it has beaten our positive intentions.

If …

… you knew in your heart that life was precious and worthy of the deepest respect, why would you ever beat yourself up, neglect your health, hurt others, ignore your loved ones, settle for second best or give up on your dreams? Might you naturally be more determined, more respectful and more grateful?

Would you make sure you had more things to look forward to? Might you succumb less often to laziness and procrastination – after all, every time you say 'I can't be bothered', you're telling the Universe that life is not precious. And might you never again catch yourself 'killing time'? (Boy do I hate that expression – though pleading guilty to doing it now and again myself.) Would you enjoy every moment more? Would you find a partner who deeply respected you, just as you are? Might you work harder, look after your customers better or study more? Might you inspire yourself and your colleagues or team a bit more every day? Might you finally start that novel you've always wanted to write? Or take up that musical instrument you promised yourself years ago? And, if you really believed in the dignity of *all* life (not just yours), why would you damage the environment, start a war or feel envious of others?

Many of my clients come to coaching because they suddenly realise they're drifting through an aimless life of mediocrity. Very often this feeling is caused by a lack of exciting and meaningful goals, especially during the so-called mid-life crisis. I recently heard of a man approaching the end of his life with many regrets – mostly about things he had not dared to do – comparing his life to a 'ball in a pinball machine bouncing around off the flippers and buzzers and then falling through the hole in the bottom'. This is much less likely to happen if you feel your life is precious and if you have an exciting vision for the future. My first responsibility as a coach is to treasure the life of each new client.

If all the people in your street, community, school, hospital, company, town and country loved the fact of *just being alive*, might we have more respect, more gratitude and less violence? Might we focus on what we have in common, rather than on our perceived differences?

All the people who've changed the world for the better – Shakyamuni, Nichiren, Jesus, Mandela, Gandhi, and of course my grandmother – instinctively got this basic truth about the dignity of life. Without it they would never have dug up the resilience and determination to achieve what they did, time and time again, often against all the odds.

Talking of slim chances, I feel inspired every time I look at a small ash tree growing on the chimney pot of a house two doors down from me. Of course, I'm vaguely aware that it may be causing serious structural damage and that, as we live in a terrace, it could affect my roof one day, causing complicated insurance claims that I would possibly not enjoy. Yet I marvel at how tenacious and determined Life is to manifest in such conditions, at how a three-foot sapling can actually be alive and well eighty feet off the ground, dealing with all sorts of weather that it shouldn't be big or clever enough to handle!

How precious Life is!

Interestingly, Nichiren's life hung by a thread on numerous occasions as the authorities and rival Buddhist sects sought to rid Japan of this troublesome priest. As he once wrote:

> ... for a period of more than twenty years, [...] I have been expelled from temples or driven out of various places, have had my relatives harassed, have been subject to night attack, confronted in battle, and countless times showered with abuse. I have been beaten, wounded in the hand, and my disciples have been killed. I have nearly been beheaded and twice have been condemned to exile. [...] I have known not an hour, not an instant of peace or safety.[1]

Despite all this, he lived to the relatively ripe age of sixty-one, long enough to establish his teachings and build a small but solid following. As I said, it took me twenty-four years of Buddhist practice just to glimpse this principle – that Life is precious. In fact, there's no way I'd have even spotted that ash tree a couple of years ago. But I believe that the ongoing journey of our human revolution is nothing more or less than understanding and celebrating the fundamental truth that Life itself is the greatest treasure. It seems to underpin everything that Nichiren Daishonin taught. It is impossible to fake the feeling that Life is precious and worthy of the deepest respect, but it is an awareness that grows and grows the more you invest in your personal and spiritual growth.

If this sounds like some ridiculous utopia, then the simple

message from your own Buddhahood is 'get over yourself'. You already know people who understand in their hearts that Life is a treasure to be revered. It could be your own grandmother, it could be someone who's had a premature brush with death, it could be a neighbour or friend or teacher or figure in your local community. Someone who's lost a loved one in tragic circumstances, or had a life-threatening illness or been involved in a serious accident. If they can do it, what's stopping you? Or anyone else? And what if the ripples spread?

Mindset mantras for cherishing your life

Every moment is precious and I am grateful for every moment I am alive.

I can be more and do more.

From now on, I dig up great determination to achieve my full potential.

I find it in my heart to treasure at least one thing about every person I meet.

I am in the moment yet I look forward to tomorrow as well.

I love and treasure the very essence of Life itself.

Journal exercises

1. Work out how many days you have lived for so far.

2. Go back through the years and write a list of people whom you feel grateful to, and why. This can include 'enemies' as well as friends. Then pick up the phone and say thank you!

3. Write a list of events that you are grateful for.

4. List your own reasons why you feel life is precious.

5. Spend time with people who are grateful to be alive and ask them what they give thanks for.

6. Think about the different areas of your life that are important to you (such as family, career, health etc ...). For each one, ask yourself: 'On a scale of 1 to 10, how much am I treasuring it? Enough to fulfil my potential? Or could I do more?'

7. Ask yourself: 'Where am I settling for second best in my life?'

8. Ask yourself: 'How can I inspire myself and other people every day, based on an ever deeper understanding that every moment and every life is precious?'

9. Work out how many of your 28,000 days you have left.

10. Now make a list of what you are looking forward to doing with the rest of your life, for yourself, your loved ones and the wider community.

CHAPTER 3

HAPPINESS IS THE SOUNDTRACK OF YOUR MIND

This is a book about happiness. In Nichiren Buddhism, we can define happiness as:

1. the soundtrack of your mind (if you so choose)

2. the purpose of your life

3. creating value from every situation

4. feeling grateful for your 'problems'

5. little to do with money

6. little to do with time or place either

7. being 'neither elated by prosperity, nor grieved by decline'

8. knowing that nobody can ever 'make you feel' anything

9. living in the moment

10. comparing yourself to your own potential (rather than to other people)

11. your right and also your responsibility

12. having the compassion and courage to fight for other people's happiness as well.

Stop and listen to the music of your mind

So, happiness is the soundtrack of your mind – when you're happy, obviously! The point is that you always have a soundtrack playing in your subconscious. A kind of background mood music. Stop and listen (how often do we take the time to do that?): is it excitement, hope, love? Or anxiety, regret and frustration? Is it well-being, amusement or compassion? Impatience, cynicism or boredom? A mixture of all the above? Something else altogether? Something you could not describe in words very easily at all? When I first start coaching a new client, this 'soundtrack' is one of the main things I listen out for because often one of my jobs is to help someone change their mood music before they can take action to achieve a specific goal. Whatever your soundtrack, the essential point is that it determines how you process the world around you, it influences your reactions to situations and conversations, it guides your decision-making and it will influence how you interpret this or any other book ... but more important than any of that, at its deepest level your karmic soundtrack also decides what happens to you, what you attract (or don't attract) into your life. Chapter 5 explains more about how you shape your own karma or destiny.

Compose a new soundtrack for your mind

All these different 'tunes' (and many more besides) are available to you all of the time. And the good news is that you are both the composer and the orchestra. And the entire Universe is on hand to give you a standing ovation. Or a boo or two. We all have a dominant soundtrack and this determines the kind of person we are – what we think, say and do – and therefore what we achieve (or don't) and who we become.

But we tend to assume that sadness and happiness are always and only triggered by outside events; hence our instinctive avoidance of problems. As William Woollard points out: 'We are conditioned in all sorts of ways, pretty much from our earliest childhood, to respond to problems and difficulties negatively, to be avoided almost whatever the cost.' Presumably when we lived in caves and survival was the main aim, it would not have made much sense to go looking for extra problems!

We have an equally strong tendency to pursue joy via material wealth, fame, job promotions, relationships, status, food and holidays. Achieving these goals can certainly bring a rush of sat- isfaction, but if we get obsessed with these temporary pleasures, it's a fragile kind of happiness: money can disappear, fame too, positions get made redundant and partners (how dare they...) change from the people they were when we first got together with them. Nichiren Buddhism does *not* advise against achieving these goals; on the contrary, we are taught to chant for our desires – we are material as well as spiritual beings after all. But to attach yourself too closely to such things, to build your life around what Buddhism calls 'rapture state', is not the route to lasting happiness.

The happiest people understand that life is about how you feel *here and now*, not if and when you get that job/girlfriend/house. Or if and when you get to heaven. It can be tempting to stake a lot of your happiness on two weeks a year on a beach in Bodrum. But if – say due to work or relationship difficulties – your mind is in turmoil, Bodrum won't feel like a blissful pot of paradise, no matter how brightly the sun may shine.

Such are the subtleties and apparent contradictions of the human mind. You can feel excited even if you have no money.

You can feel frustrated and empty even when you have all the trappings of success. You can feel restless in a tropical paradise. And uplifted in an inner-city slum. If outside events were *really* responsible for how we felt inside, everyone in the same place at the same time would feel exactly the same emotion to exactly the same degree for exactly the same length of time. As far as we know, this has never happened. The outside stuff does not determine how we feel (even though it often looks that way).

Joy no matter what

Buddhism makes a really useful distinction between *relative happiness* and *absolute happiness*. Relative happiness is, say, when you have built a life that's financially secure, with good relationships, satisfying work, and robust health. It's the kind of happiness achieved to the highest degree by famous footballers, actors and other celebrities. The people who are fast-tracked through airports, or have AAA backstage passes to the big shows, or are invited to the prestigious captain's table on a cruise ship while the rest of us eat at the back of the room. The people we admire or are jealous of, or are happy for, or want to chop down to size, depending on our point of view or frame of mind.

I think the main reason some people aspire to be like these role models is that they have reached the highest rung on the 'survival ladder'. In the animal kingdom, they would be the lions and lionesses. Nothing can touch or threaten them. Or so it seems. It's the kind of happiness that can look very solid from the outside, but probe a little deeper and you often find that the people concerned are constantly anxious about it evaporating, especially if their achievements are based on looks or talent that will fade over time. Or they feel empty and lonely inside. Or have become cold and hard. Or arrogant and uncaring. Or whatever other soundtrack is playing deeper in their mind. As I write this chapter, a famous TV pundit and ex-footballer, Gary Speed, has just taken his own life and everyone seems at a loss to explain it, because from the outside he seemed to 'have it all'. Sadly we will never know what bleaker soundtrack was playing in his head. Many of my clients first come to me with goals around relative happiness – such as their job, money or house – and while these are important concerns, most of them gradually come to realise that there is more to life than what you can count in hectares and horsepower.

Nichiren taught that *absolute* happiness is feeling joyful and undefeated *no matter what* is happening on the surface of your life. This, of course, is a slightly bigger ask because it is something we must find within, no matter what we might be lacking, or what might happen around us. A profound sense of joy is something that can only exist in the deepest reaches of our life, and which cannot be destroyed by any external forces. It is eternal and inexhaustible.

Buddhism does not suggest that happiness is about passively accepting injustices in your life, just sitting back and thinking, 'Everything will be OK' or putting on a brave face. We'll come back to this topic later, especially when we discuss anger, which, like any other emotion, has a positive aspect when you express it through your Buddhahood and point it in a useful direction.

The purpose of Buddhist practice is to establish this soundtrack of joy in our lives *whatever* is happening on the outside. For example, when I have man-flu, do I 'choose to' feel sorry for myself and grumpy? (Yes, probably for the first few hours!) Or do I expand my life to the point where the symptoms no longer dominate my attention? I can equate my man-flu to a drop of ink clouding a thimble of water. Or the same drop of ink can land in a huge ocean of joy and therefore make little perceptible difference to my life. I know which David my family prefer ... And of course a Buddha is also someone who fights with utter determination for all people to be absolutely happy. Rather than quite wanting some people to be a bit more cheerful, some of the time.

My fifteen-year-old son recently said: 'I often feel happy for no reason at all.' Which is, of course, the best reason of all, don't you think?

Nam-myoho-renge-kyo – the ultimate happiness soundtrack

The tool established by Nichiren for accessing this ocean of joy and revealing everyone's 'Buddha-soundtrack' is the mantra Nam-myoho-renge-kyo. When I first heard these words, perhaps because I was a languages student, my immediate question was, 'What does it mean?', whereas with hindsight I can see that the more useful question would be: 'What does it *do*?'

As explained in the introduction, this chant can be interpreted as the voice of your Buddhahood, the rhythm of life and the essential vibration of the Universe. For any readers of a very left-brained, rational or scientific disposition who feel that this explanation is a bit too far out, we will shortly be looking at the limitations of basing your life purely on a very high IQ. Anyway, the main point is that Buddhists believe that the sound and rhythm of these simple words can draw out all that is best in me and in you.

From a linguistic point of view, 'Myoho Renge Kyo' is the classical Japanese title of the Lotus Sutra and Nichiren viewed it as 'containing' all 69,384 characters of that teaching, in much the same way as one drop of the ocean contains all the rivers that flow into it. He added the Sanskrit prefix 'Nam', meaning 'devotion'. Chinese pictogram characters (Chinese traditionally being the language of Buddhist study in Japan, much as Latin was for the Church in Europe) are loaded with many more meanings than your average Western phoneme, syllable or word. That's why the following explanations of each word are multi-layered:

'Nam' means what I devote my life to. Where I pour my energy, my determination, my focus, my intention – the goals I have and the values I hold most dearly. And as any life coach will tell you, what you focus on is what you bring into your life. It also means 'to return to' and therefore has a sense of reconnecting with your 'source' and original life purpose.

'**Myo**' (pronounced like the 'yo' of 'yo-yo' with an 'm' before it) is challenging to explain in words alone, as Nichiren himself says: 'It is simply the mysterious nature of our lives from moment to moment, which the mind cannot comprehend nor words express.' Usually translated as 'mystic', it also means to 'open' and to 'revive' as well as describing our full spiritual potential.

'**Ho**' (pronounced like the garden tool 'hoe') indicates how much of our potential we are achieving, the 'manifest' rather than latent aspects of our lives. 'Ho' also means Law.

'**Renge**' (pronounced like the bird 'wren' followed by 'geh') means lotus flower, which seeds and blossoms at the same time, symbolising how every cause we make, everything we think, say and do, simultaneously creates a latent effect, like a bubble, which will surface when the external conditions are right. This stunning flower only grows in a muddy pond, and so it is also a metaphor for happiness blooming amidst the sufferings of daily life.

'**Kyo**' (pronounced like the 'kyo' in 'Tokyo') signifies sound, teaching, thread, sutra, vibration and flow of life. It also evokes the eternity of life transcending birth and death.

String all that together and you can come up with various translations of Nam-myoho-renge-kyo, which in popular psychology could be compared to affirmations, such as:

- I devote myself to the Law of Life.
- I vow to transform my destiny.
- I commit myself to revealing my full potential.
- I determine to open my Buddha-conscious mind and clear my illusions.
- I tune my life into the universal Law of cause and effect.

- I am creating my future with everything I think, say and do.
- I revere the eternal core of my life.

In a sense the 77,000 words in this book are an attempt to explain what the six syllables of Nam-myoho-renge-kyo mean. Or how they make you feel. Or more importantly, what they *do*. My personal experience is that when I am really in the zone with my chanting, it feels like I am connecting with the love and light at the source of Life – in a world that needs more of both.

The semantic meaning of Myoho Renge Kyo even seems to anticipate Quantum Physics' current model of everything, known as String Theory. This proposes that the entire multi-layered Universe, including you and me, is not made up of particles and solid matter but of minute strings of energy vibrating at different frequencies. It also suggests that cause and effect can be simultaneous rather than sequential. As a life coach exploring our inner cosmos, I wouldn't know a quark from a boson if I tripped over one in the street, so I'm writing this paragraph without an iota of scientific expertise. But it strikes me that there are strong similarities between String Theory and the title of the 3,000-year-old Lotus Sutra, which could be literally translated as: Mysterious Universal Law of Simultaneous Cause and Effect Vibrating Thread. Just saying ...

For more informed insights on Buddhist cosmology, I recommend a wonderful book called *Space and Eternal Life* by astronomer Chandra Wickramasinghe and Daisaku Ikeda (with a foreword by Sir Fred Hoyle).

Of course, prose and science are too clumsy as tools to convey the spiritual depths of this mantra, so I must resort to poetry. In particular, a poem by Buddhist musician and artist Rob Cook (1953–2013), who described his core beliefs as being 'rooted in a spiritual humanism that sees humanity and the environment as one'. Towards the end of his life, when Rob was no longer able to paint, he wrote a poem called 'The Mystic Law' to communicate his love of Buddhism. Rob's beautiful verses (reproduced here with the kind permission of his partner, Jane) do not represent a literal translation of Nam-myoho-renge-kyo, but rather a personal interpretation of what it meant to him as an artist inspired by a love of nature:

> *Nam* is that
> I take my diamond seat
> and address the gaze of being
> without doubt
> without fear
> with you in mind
>
> *Myo* is that
> the thought is all
> and the light in the garden
> never paused
> from disclosing
> our true mind
>
> *Ho* is that
> the river flows still
> and the rain falls soft
> without pausing
> from washing into
> a pure mind
>
> *Ren* is that
> the wind stirs the trees
> and the air fills the sky
> sweet and sharp
> as we breathe
> inside an unbounded mind
>
> *Ge* is that
> the earth gathers together

the life of plants
soft on the water
as we hold up
a joyful mind

Kyo is that
the ripples in the lake
reflect it all so perfectly
woven together
entwined eternally
walking in heaven here.

Buddhism and the Law of Attraction

The words 'Myoho Renge' ('Mystic Law of cause and effect', for short) are the thirteenth-century and, in my view, more complete forerunner of a concept taught in 1906 by William Walker Atkinson, the pioneer of the American New Thought movement, who wrote: 'We speak learnedly of the Law of Gravitation but ignore the equally wonderful manifestation of the "Law of Attraction" in the Thought World. We close our eyes to the mighty law that draws to us the things we desire or fear that makes or mars our lives.'

One hundred years after Atkinson's explanation, the bestselling DVD and book *The Secret* also explored the Law of Attraction (LOA), teaching that 'your thoughts and your feelings create your life', which Buddhism would agree with – after all, this idea is central to the concept of cause and effect or 'Renge'. Fans of the LOA enthuse that it has made them feel happier and also more responsible for the results they achieve in their lives; it is a teaching of great optimism and an exciting way to approach daily challenges such as relationships, health, career and money (LOA fans are often criticised for being too materialistic, by the way). *The Secret* also explains that we attract the things that happen to us (an idea that logical Western minds sometimes find difficult) and Buddhism agrees, calling this concept *esho funi* or the 'oneness of life and the environment'. The word *funi* in *esho funi* means 'two but not two', indicating that on one level our identity ends at our skin and that therefore we are separate individuals, but that at a deeper level we are inseparable from each other and from our environment.

Nichiren uses the following words: 'It is called the Mystic Law because it reveals the principle of the *mutually inclusive* relationship of a single moment of life and all phenomena.'[1]

William Woollard explains what this means: 'The Buddhist view of reality is that everything but everything is interconnected and interdependent at the most profound level. Everything is fundamentally part of the whole.' In his novel *The Buddha, Geoff and Me*, Edward Canfor-Dumas eloquently describes this Law as the 'mystical, invisible thread between the churning, inner reality of my life and the great outdoors of the rest of the world'. So far, so good, and the words 'Law of Attraction' are perhaps a simpler, clearer and more evocative description than 'Mystic Law of cause and effect'.

But critics of the LOA point out that there are practitioners who keep thinking new thoughts and feeling new emotions yet who somehow still don't manage to realise their dreams. Or that sometimes they do get what they want, but not always – so how can it be a reliable 'Law'? They then get very frustrated and give up; in fact they're unhappier than before because their expectations have been raised and then dashed. They might start to think of themselves as failures, or to doubt that the Law of Attraction exists. In response, LOA fans say that these practitioners are not trying hard enough, don't believe strongly enough or haven't changed their subconscious mind enough for the environment to respond in kind. So, who is right: the fans or the failures? From a Buddhist perspective, they both are. But they are both wrong as well.

At the heart of Nichiren Buddhism is a model of the mind known as the nine levels of consciousness, or 'layers' as I prefer to call them. The first seven layers accord exactly with what modern psychology has discovered. We have our five senses (layers 1-5), then we have a conscious mind (layer 6) that makes sense of external stimuli, and next a very powerful subconscious (layer 7) which runs our dreaming mind, drives us to work on autopilot, influences all our other habits and contains all our memories and deepest beliefs about ourselves -- from this lifetime anyway. This model matches the 'iceberg' diagram familiar to the coaching world, in which only 20 per cent of your mind is 'above the surface' while a massive 80 per cent lies below. When hypnotherapy or affirmations or books such as *The Secret* work, it's because they're rearranging our 'mental dominoes' at layer 7 – powerful stuff indeed and a wonderful way to move our lives forward.

Below the iceberg

Buddhism then goes deeper to identify a further two layers beneath the subconscious: imagine that iceberg continuing into the earth's crust (8) and then the earth's core (9) – see the diagram opposite. Number 8 is your karma or destiny – a sort of 'storehouse' of causes and effects from your previous lifetimes, bubbles of latent energy or emotion in the river of your life which surface when the time is right, influencing how you behave and attracting the stuff from your environment that happens to you (see Chapter 5 for an in-depth explanation of this).

So the concept of karma absolutely echoes the LOA teaching that our thoughts, intentions, feelings and subsequent actions do indeed create our current situation, but – and it's a big 'but' (for the typical Western mind) – the concept of karma is that you've had billions of them before, in your previous existences, and that these 'karmic habits' are still having an impact in the here and now. The Buddhist view is that when we die, our lives melt into the greater Life of the Universe and are nowhere to be seen, just as our minds are seemingly nowhere when we are asleep. And when we are reborn, it is like waking from sleep,

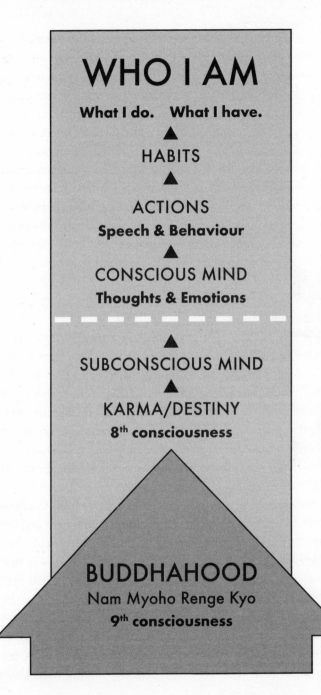

with our karma from previous lifetimes, in the same way that our minds resume their activities from the previous day when we wake up. So in the same way that we sleep and wake, we are born and die, in an eternal cycle of life.

How to change your destiny

Nichiren's emphasis was not just on reframing our thoughts and emotions at layers 6 and 7, nor on coping with difficult karma at layer 8, but on delving into the deepest layer of our lives, into our ninth consciousness, which he called Buddhahood. Layer 9 is the bit that Nichiren says is accessed by chanting Nam-myoho-renge-kyo; it is, in a sense, our heart, and when we access this deep reservoir of all that is best in us, we flush its beneficial power up through our karma and through all our other layers of consciousness.

In short, Buddhism completely agrees with the LOA in terms of 'oneness of life and environment', but goes two levels deeper, arguing that to really change our lives, we need to access the Buddha in ourselves and change our karma, the depths of our lives – not only the 'thoughts and feelings' described in *The Secret*, which lie closer to the surface. And changing our destiny can take time. Nam-myoho-renge-kyo is not a quick-fix cosmic ordering service, however much we may wish it was. Many Buddhists will admit to having one particular 'karmic Achilles heel', a situation or repeated pattern in their lives that has taken or is taking many years to transform. It could be failed relationships, work problems, addictions, money worries or health issues ...

American character-actor and SGI Buddhist James DuMont now has over a hundred film and TV credits to his name. They include *Ugly Betty*, *Dallas Buyers Club*, *Jurassic World* and *House*. He has played opposite the likes of Robin Williams, Al Pacino and Kathy Bates. James shared his own karmic Achilles heel with me in an interview for my blog: 'My father and his father made huge, detrimental mistakes that destroyed their families. The damage took years and generations to heal – and in some cases those issues have been the greatest obstacles I have faced as father and husband. Issues of infidelity, financial mistakes and more importantly issues of being present and available to set an example. This has also been my biggest benefit. I am present for my son and daughter, as best I can. I am working to be a better man, father, husband and son than the men in my family before me. In essence, my Buddhist practice is redefining the truest meaning of fatherhood in my family and all the responsibility that comes with that. This is not an easy task or mission, but it is mine.'

Buddhism without the statues

Given that Nichiren placed such emphasis on this impersonal Mystic Law of life, he actively discouraged followers from worshipping him, making statues of him or in any other way idolising his personality – and this was (and remains) a radical departure from other schools of Buddhism and 99 per cent of other religions. For an ex-Catholic like me, this concept of devotion to a Law of Life rather than to a person (or 'God') did not at first come naturally.

Instead of statues, Nichiren's legacy was a scroll, known to practitioners as a 'Gohonzon', down the middle of which he inscribed Nam-myoho-renge-kyo in big and bold calligraphy. Nichiren Buddhists chant to a Gohonzon in an altar in their homes. Long before the insights of modern Western psychology, Nichiren realised that 'what you focus on is what you bring into your life', so that is why he placed your Buddhahood and mine firmly in the middle of this scroll. Gathered around this central mantra are characters (in Chinese and Sanskrit) signifying *all* aspects of existence, including suffering, negative feelings and all our lower life states.

In itself, this scroll does not have mystical powers; it is, after all, a piece of parchment. But Buddhists believe it is a very practical tool which helps you focus on your own and other people's highest potential, a mirror reflecting your own brilliance and dignity, a reminder that you have the power within to become happier when you put Buddhahood at the centre of your life.

So there you have it. A six-syllable mantra and a scroll. Simple tools, and deliberately so, because Nichiren believed that Buddhism had become inaccessible to the mass of ordinary people. Describing the practices based on pre-Lotus Sutra teachings, Nichiren objects to the fact that:

> There are three thousand rules of conduct to be mastered. But those of us who live in this latter age can hardly be expected to abide by all these rules ...[2]

Chapter 5 goes into more detail about the reasons why Nichiren's Buddhism has no rules.

For a fuller explanation of Nam-myoho-renge-kyo than there is room to offer here, I can recommend Richard Causton's book *The Buddha in Daily Life*. Or, if you prefer fiction, *The Buddha, Geoff and Me* by Eddy Canfor-Dumas is an excellent alternative.

It takes prayer to transform a heart

I meet loads of people who say that if they had any religion at all, it would be Buddhism. That they love the 'positive thinking' aspects of the teaching, the idea that we are simultaneously free and responsible, the way it is extremely strict yet has no rules, the emphasis on being the change you want to see in the world, its pragmatic idealism ... and so on. But some of them do struggle with the idea of chanting. They might be quite happy to read books like this one, or even do affirmations into a mirror, but to actually *pray*, out loud? And not even in English? For two years after first coming across this practice, I was definitely one of those people. As my fellow SGI Buddhist William Woollard points out: 'Scepticism is a tough and resourceful fighter.

It doesn't give in easily and it is very accustomed to putting together bitter rearguard actions.'

Philosophy and affirmations and study and hypnotherapy and coaching can all change your head and improve your mindset (layer 7). But it takes prayer to transform a heart. And only transformed hearts can really change the world for the better. I think many religions have overlooked, neglected or forgotten the power of prayer and therefore most of us have not experienced the way that it can transform people's lives. Instead, we put our faith in science and logic, or in codes of conduct, or in morality, or in politicians. We are sceptical about prayer or chanting. But prayer should really be the essence of any spiritual practice. The problem is that it has often been lost along the way, wrapped up in inaccessible priestly robes and rituals, or drowned out by the corrupt power structures of some organised religions. And the people in the shiniest suits or robes don't always have the greatest wisdom. To summarise:

- Layers 1 to 5, no change.
- At layer 6, I change my thinking.
- At layer 7, I change my mindset.
- At layer 8, I change my heart.
- At layer 9, I change the world.

We are more than logical beings

I have a strong tendency to harbour the illusion that IQ is all powerful. That we are purely rational or logical beings. A couple of calls from my more intuitive clients in the last few days have put me right again and reminded me that many people are able to:

- Detect an 'atmosphere' in a room.
- Feel implausibly strong levels of rage merely when someone cuts them up at a roundabout.
- Feel moved by hearing a poem (even in a foreign language

where they don't understand the words, but just feel the rhythm and the tone).
- Shout at a tennis/cricket/golf ball (after hitting it) in the hope that it will slow down, speed up, spin left, swerve right, drop, climb or any combination of the above.

Likewise I have noticed how the best football managers can develop a noticeably strong (yet intangible and unquantifiable) 'team spirit' that enables their players to exceed what they would otherwise achieve. Interestingly, when big football clubs spend huge amounts of money on big-name players, the one ingredient their millions cannot buy is team spirit.

All of these phenomena are, to a greater or lesser extent, an illustration of 'Myo', the 'mystic' aspect of life. Nichiren says:

> There are trails in the sky where birds fly, but people cannot recognise them. There are paths in the sea along which fish swim, but people cannot perceive them.[3]

We kid ourselves when we claim that we are purely rational beings. We even kid ourselves when we think we are just rational and emotional beings. Buddhists believe that we enrich ourselves when we realise we are not only rational and emotional, but spiritual, interconnected beings too. It is perhaps the feeling that William Blake captured in these famous lines from 'Auguries of Innocence':

> To see a World in a Grain of Sand
> And a Heaven in a Wild Flower,
> Hold Infinity in the palm of your hand
> And Eternity in an hour.

In another passage touching on the mystic nature of life, Nichiren writes:

This mind is not burned in the fires at the end of a kalpa [a very long period of time], is not destroyed by the disaster of floods, cannot be severed with a sword or pierced with an arrow. One may put it inside a mustard seed and the mustard seed will not be stretched nor will the mind be cramped thereby. One may put it in the vast heavens and the heavens will not be too broad for it nor the mind too narrow to fill them.[4]

Ending the intellectual dead end

But in society and in our educational systems we tend to overrate IQ. To paraphrase the multiple intelligences theory of esteemed psychologist Howard Gardner, we measure *how clever people are* (intellectually) rather than *how they are clever* (which could include lots of other talents, such as fixing a car, playing a musical instrument or knowing how to build rapport with people). Yet there does not seem to be an especially high correlation between high IQ and happiness, any more than there is between material wealth and happiness. Or between intelligent politicians and productive, harmonious societies. We venerate clever brains when what the world needs most, to face today's challenges, is wise hearts. As spiritual teacher and author Steve Taylor asks, in his extraordinary book, *The Fall*: 'How can the most intelligent life form the world has ever known be mismanaging its own existence on this planet in such a catastrophic way? An alien observer might conclude that the whole human race has agreed to a collective suicide pact.'[5]

A friend of mine who did not fit into the school system recently said to me: 'I loved learning. I hated school.' And I know from experience that a first-class degree is no guarantee of success or happiness. In fact, if I go to university in my next lifetime I would happily trade my First for a 2:1 degree and a higher EQ. In fact, make that a 2:2 with some DIY skills thrown in as well. Better still, a Third with some EQ, DIY and a big dollop of SQ (Spiritual Intelligence), thanks very much.

I have also met some very bright (high IQ) people with major drink problems, so although they may be high-performing alcoholics at work, their personal lives often border on the hellish. At a rational level, they know that drinking too much is bad for them; at a deeper emotional level they sometimes find the resources to change their behaviour, but because their spiritual or 9th layer remains untouched, they never quite manage to change for good – they never manage to actually stop *wanting* that drink, to point their desires in a direction that says life really is precious – so why on earth would I want to self-destruct? They are 'painting over rust' rather than dealing with the corrosion itself; and so their willpower can snap at any time, especially in moments of stress.

Likewise, there are extremely clever academics who can produce piercing insights into the relationships between the characters in famous works of literature, but who then go home to miserable marriages and children who do not talk to them. And the world is run by very clever people: bankers and politicians who have Oxbridge or Harvard degrees, men and women with very high IQs – including ruthless dictators. The point is that high IQ is not all it's cracked up to be; if it was then different countries would have found a way to live in peace with each other. It might be a bright idea to stop churning out graduates, unless they are equipped with at least a basic level of emotional intelligence. Although in the longer term I believe it can only be the kind of SQ espoused by the likes of Nichiren that will mark the real end of the intellectual dead end.

As philosopher Jules Evans writes in his book *Philosophy for Life and other Dangerous Situations*: 'It's not enough to try to transform the personality through abstract philosophical reasoning, although that has its place. You need to speak to the irrational part of the psyche using maxims, songs, symbols and imagery, so that your philosophical insights really sink into the brain and become part of your nervous system.'[6]

Buddhism – a beginner's tale ...

Leigh Ferrani is a professional author and literary consultant. While training as an actress in her youth, she says she 'first discovered a love of writing and an aversion to auditions'. So she stuck with the writing and worked in journalism and advertising agencies in London before her first novel *Indigo Flats* was published. Leigh was the first person other than friends or family to read an early draft of this book, which led to her wanting to know more about Nichiren Buddhism. Three years later, out of the blue, she contacted me to say that, after being diagnosed with cancer, she had started to chant. Leigh takes up her tale:

Towards the end of 2012 I'd had three brain tumours removed, and my partner Simon and I were shattered by the news that the brain issues were secondary. I had grade III metastatic breast cancer on the right side and I'd had no idea. 'It's just one of those things,' shrugged the specialist at Bristol Haematology and Oncology Centre. We went home absolutely terrified.

Instead of enjoying my daughter Flynn's second birthday, I was booked in to start chemotherapy. Every time I looked at her little face I wanted to cry. What if I died and she had to grow up without me? I began chemo and for a while felt completely lost and powerless – suffocated by endless hospital appointments, medieval procedures and illness. I wasn't sleeping because I couldn't switch off the self-slating inner dialogue, asking what I'd done to get cancer and raking over ancient misdemeanours.

I realised that I had to find a way to battle the disease using sheer mental force, and keep my spirits up. Not an easy task but I'm a determined person. Any writer has to be stubborn if they're going to do it as a job, so I gathered together the qualities I used to build my career to fight my cancer. I also became a Buddhist.

Well, I've been chanting for six months. I am still a 'newbie' and have much to learn, but it has been a freeing experience within the confines of cancer, which chips away your control and identity.

Chanting has become part of my ever-growing 'exterminate cancer' plan. It renewed my flagging physical energy and just focusing on the words Nam-myoho-renge-kyo made me switch off from the world, concentrate on my mental strength and my breathing, and allowed me some much needed brain space which had been taken up with self-punishing negativity before. I forgave myself. Not that I had done anything wrong in the first place. People with serious diagnoses can be hard on themselves, particularly if they're used to being high achievers. I have learned to master my mind a little and be more compassionate towards myself, which has made life easier when dealing with the affliction. I now chant as much as I can manage around the demands of chemotherapy and looking after a young child.

Peace can be anyone's if they look and work hard for it. I am still battling so I can't say that I am at peace *yet* but I feel gently cloaked in something bigger and wiser than myself and my problem. Cancer may not seem like just a 'problem', however Buddhism teaches that any dilemma is a gift that gives us the opportunity to use our power within to overcome and survive. The word 'gift' might be pushing it somewhat, but imagine how I'm going to feel when I've won – and I will. I've always thrived on challenge and this is the biggest of my life.

Nichiren wrote: 'In accordance with their status, some have wives and children, relatives, fiefs, and gold and silver, while others have no treasure. Whether one has wealth or not, no treasure exceeds the one called life.'[7]

I'm not saying that I should stop chemotherapy and rely wholly on Buddhism. But it works for me, along with the many other things I do to improve my physical and mental health and wellbeing. I don't believe that every time I chant that it is curing my cancer, however it does help me to feel stronger and in the moment, especially when chanting with others. The rhythm and energy builds and eventually you can feel something tangible in the air and Nam-myoho-renge-kyo sounds like a powerful song. It's an exciting experience. And by chanting daily my Buddhahood flourishes. As it does so, hopefully my cancer will do the opposite and disappear completely.

The 'FAQs' section at the end of this chapter is dedicated to Leigh, because she suggested I add it in the first place!

Mindset mantras – affirmations to guide your thoughts or your chanting

I am the composer of the soundtrack in my mind.

I choose to be happy.

How I feel inside is more important than what I have (or don't).

Just being alive is a source of great joy.

I am a beautiful lotus flower growing in the muddy pond of daily life.

I tune my life into the rhythm of the Universe.

When I connect with my heart I find all that is best in me and in others.

I am a spiritual as well as a logical and emotional being.

Journal exercises

1. How much do you agree with the twelve definitions of happiness at the start of this chapter? Which ones strike the deepest chord, and which sit least comfortably with you?

2. What is the dominant 'soundtrack of your mind' most of the time in your daily life? Excitement, hope, love? Anxiety, regret or frustration? Something else altogether?

3. If you are not happy with this soundtrack, what 'mood music' would you like to play instead?

4. Reflect on the times when you have built relative happiness around 'external' objects or people. What can you learn from these experiences?

5. When have you confused temporary pleasures with lasting happiness?

6. How often do you feel 'in rhythm' with the world around you and that your life is 'in the zone'?

7. What patterns (good or bad) seem to repeat themselves in your life? How often do you acknowledge and feel grateful for the good stuff? What 'negative karma' would you like to change?

8. In what areas of your life do you think you are 'painting over rust' rather than tackling the root causes of an issue head on?

FAQs about the practice

What does the daily practice consist of?

We do a simple daily practice morning and evening, chanting Nam-myoho-renge-kyo as well as reciting two short chapters from the Lotus Sutra – a ceremony known as 'gongyo'. I personally chant for around ninety minutes a day; however, Nichiren simply said to chant 'to your heart's content,' so some people do more than that and some less. Breathe naturally and aim for the rhythm of a galloping horse. If you live in a flat or in close quarters with other people, make sure they are OK with the volume of your chanting!

Do I have to kneel down or sit in the Lotus position?

You can if you want to, but most Buddhists in the West sit on a conventional chair to avoid pins and needles! Sit upright – not rigid and not slumped either. Hold your hands at chest height, palms together pointing towards the Gohonzon (or a wall if you're just starting out).

Can I chant for what I want?

Definitely! Chanting is designed to help you achieve life goals and to transform suffering. Beginners are encouraged to chant to achieve their desires, whatever those may be and wherever their starting point, and to 'test the truth of Buddhism'. These desires often change as we progress in the practice. It is fine to visualise yourself achieving a goal when you chant, but don't try and work out with your rational mind exactly how it will manifest. Just listen to the sound of your own voice and then after chanting, use your wisdom to take action. Nichiren urged disciples to chant for 'actual proof' rather than just theoretical proof. At the start, I was encouraged to chant for an hour a day for a hundred days in order to fully test it. Many people start with five minutes morning and evening, build up a regular daily rhythm and then gradually begin to find more time to chant, often because by increasing their life force they find that they need less sleep. Over time, Buddhists naturally find their prayers focusing as much on the happiness of others as on their own personal goals.

Will chanting make me feel calmer?

Not necessarily – this is a benefit more commonly associated with Zen or Tibetan forms of Buddhism. If you are feeling agitated, then chanting could very well produce calmness. But if lethargy is stopping you from achieving your goals then your Buddhahood won't want to make you any calmer!

What should I think about when I chant?

It is best if you can disconnect from your everyday thoughts (and leave your mobile phone on silent!) Chanting works most powerfully when you get beneath the conscious and subconscious mind and fuse with the core of your life. It is a deeply respectful conversation with your heart or your Buddhahood. People sometimes ask me, 'How can I stop my over-active head? How can I quieten my mind?' When you ask this question, you are making it busier and noisier in that very moment. The way to stop or quieten your mind is to follow instead where your spirit yearns to take you. To try less and trust more.

So, positive imagination is fine but don't try and work out solutions to your problems with your head. Easier said than done, but it helps if you really focus on the Gohonzon (the scroll with Nam-myoho-renge-kyo inscribed down the middle) and listen to the mesmerising sound of your own voice. See if you can feel the chant go right through your body. The feeling when you connect fully is similar to 'being in the zone' when playing a sport or musical instrument. You feel focused but relaxed, as if time has stopped and you are returning to the essence of who you are by revering Life itself. Sometimes, of course, it is harder to feel this connection as we battle with the innate negativity that seeks to cut us off from our Buddhahood. Keep going anyway!

How does chanting work?

I guess this is the million-dollar question. The answer is, I don't know, I just know that it does. Equally I don't know how a tune by Ludovico Einaudi or Allegri's *Miserere* can move me to tears, but I know that they do. I don't know how the hymn 'Jerusalem' can stir in me a deep patriotic fervour but I know that it does. (By the way, I would like all these tunes played at my funeral/ celebration of my journey to my next lifetime ...) Likewise I don't know how acupuncture works, but I know that it has helped many people with severe health problems. I think all these things (and chanting) are beyond the reach of our rational minds to comprehend, for they are of the heart or spirit. I used to spend a lot of time wondering how chanting works and eventually gave up because I felt I was wasting my time and because, actually, a little bit of wonder, a little awe and mystery, feels like no bad thing in a world where we normally need everything to be analysed, measured and quantified. 'Myo' of Nam-myoho-renge-kyo means 'mystic', after all.

Does chanting have the same effect on everyone?

No. I know people who have started chanting and had amazing tangible benefits straight away (money, work, health, relationships), others who have struggled quite a lot emotionally (as I did in 1985), others whose external circumstances have not changed immediately but who have felt uplifted and more positive – and others who feel no noticeable difference at all (me in 1983). There are others again who once chanted regularly, but who just dabble occasionally now, yet who still say they feel the benefit of the practice they carried out all those years ago. Ultimately, the only way to answer this question is to give it a go and see what happens to you.

Do you practise with other Buddhists?

Yes, by attending meetings at people's homes where we chant and talk about our lives, challenges, victories and struggles. You can also go on weekend courses (for example at SGI centres in countries across the world) and there is one event per month in every part of the UK where an SGI leader gives a one-hour talk based on one of Nichiren's 406 letters (known as 'gosho') to his followers. People new to the practice are supported by a more experienced Buddhist who will give encouragement and answer any questions they may have. This is a movement of 'ordinary people leading ordinary people to enlightenment'.

Do you bring up your children as Buddhists?

No. I believe that the practice is something very personal that you choose to do or not, as and when the time is right. There are no ceremonies equivalent to baptism, communion, Bar Mitzvah or Amrit in Nichiren Buddhism. Personally I don't think any religion should be 'claiming' young people (or worse, babies) for their particular god. My fifteen-year-old son chants occasionally and I obviously I share with him my Buddhist outlook on life. My nineteen-year-old daughter showed absolutely no interest at all in the practice until very recently, when, while struggling with illness during A level exams, she finally decided to give chanting a good go! It worked, by the way. So Buddhism is in their lives, should they ever choose to explore it further, but there will never be any pressure to do so. I have known many children who do chant every day – especially where both parents are Buddhist, but they often question it in their late teenage years and stop. Many then return to the practice later on, but with a sense that it is their own, rather than a habit they have inherited from their parents.

CHAPTER 4

THE TEN WORLDS – BUDDHISM'S MODEL OF THE MIND

As a pragmatic philosophy for everyday life, Buddhism seeks to explain why different people react in unique ways to the same situation. And why the same person can respond differently to an identical situation on another day, depending on what mood they're in at the time. Why one person will lose their rag when their neighbours are arguing loudly late at night, while another remains perfectly calm (usually) and a third may be rather more concerned for their neighbours' happiness. Why one person seems to enjoy more success, luck and serenity. While another repeatedly fails and is seemingly locked in a spiral of despair and frustration.

The concept Buddhism uses to explain many of our individual differences and this constant flux in the 'soundtrack of our minds' is called 'the ten worlds' (not to be confused with the nine consciousnesses described in Chapter 3). These ten worlds are not, of course, physical planets, though it is, interestingly, becoming fashionable to ask people 'What place are you in?' rather than 'How are you?' But I digress ... The ten worlds are: Hell, Hunger, Animality, Anger, Tranquillity, Rapture (also called 'Heaven'), Learning, Realisation, Bodhisattva and Buddhahood. As Nichiren wrote:

> Neither the pure land nor hell exists outside oneself; both lie
> only within one's own heart. Awakened to this, one is called
> a Buddha; deluded about it, one is called an ordinary person.[1]

Likewise, in a different context, 400 years later, seventeenth-century English poet John Milton wrote in his epic poem *Paradise Lost*: 'The mind is its own place and in itself can make a hell of heaven, a heaven of hell.'

The most powerful reframing tool

These ten worlds within our minds are also often referred to as 'life states' and, over time, the more your mind is in a particular life state, the more your mind becomes set, creating the soundtrack of your life and deepening your karmic grooves. And, of course, the 60,000 thoughts we have every day are where it all begins, as Shakyamuni pointed out 3,000 years ago:

> The thought manifests as the word;
> The word manifests as the deed;
> The deed develops into habit;
> And habit hardens into character;
> So watch the thought and its ways with care
> And let it spring from love,
> Born out of concern for all beings ...

Buddhist practice is all about striving to spend more time in your highest life state – Buddhahood, which, because it exists at Layer 9 – below the subconscious, is seen by practitioners as the deepest powerhouse of all for reframing your thinking and thus revealing your innate Buddha nature. 'Reframing', if you haven't met this word before, is a popular personal development term that encourages people to choose a more positive and resourceful perspective for looking at difficult situations. Examples: you hit one bad tennis shot, you're still a good player, focus on the next shot. The economic climate is tough, what can you do differently to win new business? You feel scared of performing in public, but, as comedian Tommy Cooper said, 'Everyone gets butterflies, but the professionals get them to fly in the right formation!' Likewise you might feel your partner is 'constantly nagging' you but as Daisaku Ikeda explains, you can learn to compare their words to an altogether sweeter sound:

> It would be great if we could live cheerfully, enjoying life to the extent that we regard our partner's nagging as a sign of his or her good health and proof that he or she is still alive and kicking. When we develop a broad state of life, then even our partner's ranting and raving will sound like the sweet song of a bird.[2]

A client I was recently coaching said: 'My mother was a lazy optimist and my father a busy pessimist, so I blame them for my mediocre life.' She realised after a brief conversation that if she drew the best rather than the worst from her parents, she could choose to be a proactive optimist instead!

Being a pragmatic philosophy for everyday life, Nichiren Buddhism does of course recognise that:

- reframing is easier said than done;
- we are only human and therefore often doubt;
- we are only human and therefore fail sometimes;
- there are nine other life states to grapple with, six of which do not easily create lasting and genuine happiness for oneself and others.

You'll find more on reframing with the Buddha in you in Chapter 12, 'Become the master of your mind'.

Finding your bigger self

To give you a quick and very simplified snapshot of each of the ten worlds and of how they influence the way you interact with the world around you, let's say the person of your dreams sends you a text saying: 'I love you.' This statement, in and of itself, is neutral. It has absolutely no power until it's processed (in a picosecond) through the life state/world that you are in at the time:

1. *Hell*: I bet you don't really, you must have meant to send it to someone else.

2. *Hunger*: I want more! Who else loves me?

3. *Animality*: Come round and rip my clothes off now!

4. *Anger*: I'm not that surprised, but actually I can do much better than you ... ('anger' in a Buddhist context means a false sense of superiority).

5. *Tranquillity*: Great, I can relax now and maybe stop being quite so loveable (the illusion of happiness as a destination).

6. *Rapture*: I am head over heels in love with you too and it's gonna last forever!

All of the above are reactions from our 'smaller self'. These lower six worlds tend to be much more self-centred. The first three, in particular, are a kind of emotional blindness in which we blunder from one suffering to another. In all of these six worlds we are governed by what the American psychologist Julian B. Rotter would call an external 'locus of control' (or reference point); in other words our feelings are largely at the mercy of what other people or situations 'do to us'.

The next three life states are different because they all require effort and come from a bigger, better place. They are signs of an internal locus of control – taking responsibility for how we react to situations:

7. *Learning*: Let's improve our lives through this love.

8. *Realisation*: Let's teach others to do the same.

9. *Bodhisattva*: I now feel more compassionate towards everyone else.

Now, the biggest self of all, or what we call the 'interconnected Buddha self':

10. *Buddhahood*: how can we help create Kosen-Rufu (world peace) together, enjoy this love to the maximum and guide other people to experience something as deeply respectful and wonderful? 'Let's hug the whole world together,' as a treasured friend once said to me.

Re-organise your mental dominoes

As you get to know people (and yourself) and to understand the ten worlds, you can start to predict how they will react to almost any event in their life. You just know that their mental dominoes will fall (very quickly) in the same habitual thought pattern when 'nudged' by a certain situation. The woman who repeatedly attracts angry men, the man who always 'lands on his feet' when changing jobs, the woman who discovers her best talents in the face of adversity, the man who tends to feel like a victim in his relationships.

Buddhists believe that *we* make the dominoes – nobody else – through the causes we make in this and previous lifetimes (karma). In other words, you take complete personal accountability when you begin to chant. And who arranges those dominoes in the unique pattern that makes us who we are? Yep, we do that as well, by 'choosing' the mood or life state we are in and hence how we *subjectively* interpret events and organise experiences in our mind. So, how are you arranging your mental dominoes today?

Take the example of a wife, ten years into married life, moaning about her 'good-for-nothing layabout husband'. Did she complain about this when they first met? Did she heck, in fact she was very attracted to his chilled and relaxed attitude to life, and how it complemented her rather manic non-stop approach. Perhaps her dominant Animality life state, combined with those powerful love hormones, filtered out any possible downsides in his behaviour. What's changed a decade later? He hasn't changed (after all, he can't be bothered ...) but her *perception* has, perception that is driven by her dominant life state – which may now be 'Anger' and therefore a tendency to be very critical.

If her husband was to leave and her fantasy heart-throb Brad Pitt came round for dinner, would she find him 'lazy' for relaxing in front of the fire? Probably not, because her now dominant Hunger state would again influence her perception.

A closer look at the Buddha in all of us

As author Anaïs Nin wrote, 'We do not see the world as it is, but as we are.' As one of my great mindset mentors, Richard Jackson, explains, all events and behaviours are 'neutral', in and of themselves, until we 'choose' our own emotional reactions to them. That's why that text saying 'I love you' is, in itself, neutral. The emotions we attach to that event are always driven by our dominant life state, and in the Buddhist view of the world, this life state is also influenced by our karma – the causes we have made in previous lifetimes that shape the patterns we repeat in this one.

So, let's take a closer look at these ten worlds and see in which ones you most recognise yourself. Each of the first nine has an inherent downside and an equally integral upside:

World	The downside	The upside
Hell	Despair, helplessness, hopelessness, bleakness, frustration, anger, low life force, desire to destroy self and others. 'I lose, you lose' mindset.* Life does not feel precious.	Such an intolerable 'place' that it acts as a spur to action. Also helps develop compassion for others who are suffering.
Hunger	Greed. Insatiable desire for money, power, sex, drugs, status etc ... At the mercy of our cravings and cannot control them. Constantly restless feeling of dissatisfaction, emptiness and 'void'.	Incredible energy to get things done for oneself and others.
Animality	All instinct. Lack of moral sense and reason. Stupidity. No long-term focus. Law of the jungle. Prey on the weak and toady to the strong. Comparing self to others. Deep ignorance of full potential. The core of our S-O-S mindset.	Our instincts are necessary for our survival – as an individual and a species. For example, the danger instinct helps us cross a busy road safely. The sex instinct means life can carry on. The urge to eat keeps us alive. And intuition based on wisdom can lead to great decisions.
Anger	'Anger' has an unusual meaning in Buddhism: valuing only ourselves and holding others in contempt. Needing to feel superior at all times, for example, unable to apologise or negotiate. Monstrously egotistical. Highly critical. Prone to outbursts of temper. Unable to see potential in others.	More self-awareness than lower three worlds. Can become a passion for fairness and justice. A strong driver that fires us to take action and reform society.
Tranquillity	Neutral feeling, neither up nor down, chilled. At peace but fragile, as it's easy to 'fall' from here into the lower four worlds. Lazy, apathetic, careless.	Great place to recharge the batteries! Likely to be more respectful towards others. Peaceful state of life.
Rapture / 'Heaven'	Intense joy, but fragile and fleeting so tends to disappear quickly when external events change. Desire to live in an 'other world' paradise that does not exist.	Fun while it lasts! Celebration of a goal achieved. Head over heels in love feeling. Zest for life, intense joy. (E.g. novelty of driving a new car, or 'honeymoon period' in a new job.)

The next three life states are essentially more positive, so the upside is listed first. Crucially, they don't just happen, they all require effort and are signs of an internal locus of control.

World	The upside	The downside
Learning	High IQ, EQ or PQ (practical intelligence). Learning from people wiser than ourselves. Desire to reflect on our behaviour, improve ourselves and find lasting truths.	Can be selfish, self-absorbed and disengaged from others.
Realisation	Being able to discover things for ourselves and pass them on. Having 'epiphanies' (small or large) about how life works. Creative, artistic, academic, sporting, medical or scientific talent.	Unjustified sense of superiority. Contempt for others. Stubborn. Untrusting, finding it hard to delegate. Can be too arrogant to explore Buddhahood. 'I win, you lose' mindset.*
Bodhisattva	Compassionate altruistic behaviour that empathises with others' suffering and seeks to alleviate it. Unlikely to seek recognition or reward. Maternal love.	Can lead to self-sacrifice, caring for others at expense of self. 'I lose, you win' mindset.*

And finally, the life state that only exhibits positive characteristics and that Buddhists access by chanting Nam-myoho-renge-kyo.

BUDDHAHOOD

All the positive aspects of the above worlds are revealed:

Joy at being alive and grabbing every opportunity to create joy;

Wisdom, courage, compassion, life force;

Understanding how life works;

Freedom from 'karmic shackles'. Highly resourceful state;

Feeling our whole life is 'in the zone' and that our 'self' is an interconnected part of the universal energy;

Titanium-strong determination;

Gratitude. Optimism. Deep awareness of life purpose;

Unconditional reverence for ourselves and others;

Serenity and excitement;

Strong desire to see others fulfil all their potential. 'I win, you win' mindset;*

Feeling a mission to help change the karma (or destiny) of humanity;

A feeling of absolute freedom but absolute fusion as well;

Feeling fully connected to the flow of life.

---

* For more on this and four other fascinating mindsets that can help you have better relationships, see Stephen Covey's book, *The 7 Habits of Highly Effective People*.

For reasons of brevity, I've deliberately skimmed the surface with the above summaries of each life state but for a much fuller explanation see Richard Causton's book *The Buddha in Daily Life* or *The Buddha, Geoff and Me* by Eddy Canfor-Dumas, both available from Rider Books.

Your dominant life state determines what you base your life on. Your unconscious religion, your 'intention', so it is worth choosing what you worship wisely. Everyone, whether they are religious or not, centres their life on something or someone, driven by their dominant life state: a degree, a lover, a career, money ... and what you choose to base your life on will decide your future happiness. These objects of devotion can come and go, though. Lovers can leave, money can evaporate overnight and success in the office can mean failure at home.

Or the lover may not leave, but just fail to follow the script, role and choreography you had (probably subconsciously) written for him/her and therefore fall short of your controlling expectations – they haven't changed enough to 'make me happy'. (Controlling behaviour is rooted, of course, in the S-O-S mentality, which sees happiness as coming from outside yourself and fearing that the source of it will disappear.) Or you accuse your other half of changing too much: 'You're not the person I married!' Of course they've changed. Everything is changing all the time. When gripped by our lower life states, especially Animality, we have low self-awareness – of both our true strengths and deepest weaknesses. It is difficult to 'master our mind' and it is likely that, to paraphrase Einstein, we will carry on doing the same things while hoping in vain for different results.

Incidentally, many relationships start in Rapture state (which you imagine will last forever) but slowly go downhill from there. And as each party slips into the lower worlds, they inevitably begin to draw the worst rather than the best out of each other. That's one reason why marriages fail. Conversely, those who make the effort to reveal their Buddhahood will ultimately enjoy a much stronger relationship, where each person brings the best out of the other – whether or not they decide to remain married.

A deeper understanding of human nature

Did you recognise aspects of yourself, other people and society in these descriptions of the ten worlds? People you work for, live with, love (or once loved)? We all have the potential to experience these ten different worlds. OK, and so what? What are the benefits of understanding this map of the human mind? I think there are several:

1. Increased self-awareness

2. A better understanding of other people

3. Ability to see more of others' potential

4. Increased optimism

5. Reduced complacency

Increased self-awareness means an insight, for example, into the dominant mindset that may be causing you and others to suffer. However, the idea is not to over-analyse these life states (unless you really want to be in 'Learning' state all the time ...), nor is there any point trying to work out why they dominate your life – there's no way of knowing what happened in your previous lifetimes (though speculating can be fun).

The whole point of this model and indeed of Buddhist practice is to focus on the Buddha in me and the Buddha in you in the here and in the now. Then the rest will take care of itself and even your apparently lowest life states will manifest their most positive functions. You may not, for example, get rid of your anger, but you can transform it and point it in the right direction.

At a recent SGI Buddhist meeting I attended, the PA system failed just as a young woman was about to do a solo Greek dance in front of 200 people. Instead of panicking or giving up, she went ahead anyway and it struck me during this moving performance that only a Buddha could dance in silence and still make you feel the music. It was somehow more powerful than if the sound system had worked, and she received a well-deserved standing ovation.

I have coached several people who suffer from believing they are 'too sensitive' (and therefore 'easily hurt') but who then discover that they can use that quality to reveal deep compassion or great creative talent and so come to lead a more authentic life. Or someone who beats themselves up for being shy will realise that other people trust them for being very discreet. All you need to do is reach into this magnificent Buddha state at the core of you. (And then be prepared for the tectonic plates in your destiny to start shifting around a bit!)

The second benefit is that by understanding these different tendencies, we can gain a heightened awareness of what's driving other people and how they too can develop a more resourceful view of the world. And we can more easily see the world through their eyes. Remember, your own interpretation of reality is always subjective, based on your dominant life state(s). Just consider, for example, the passing of time. If you're in Hell state, time goes incredibly slowly and you feel certain that your despair will last forever. In Rapture state, time flashes by. In Realisation, if say, you're composing music or drawing a picture, it can also seem to go very quickly, so absorbed are you in your endeavour. In Tranquillity, you may not know what time it is at all. As I pen this chapter on holiday in Turkey I really am not sure if it is Tuesday or Wednesday – I'm hoping it's the former but have a horrible feeling I'm wrong. Yet of course the clock on the wall is going at its own neutral pace, as quickly and slowly as it always has done and always will, and the earth is still rotating once on its axis every twenty-four hours.

The mysterious case of the mislaid mojo

Perhaps the most exciting benefit of the ten worlds model of the mind is that it enables you to perceive everyone's potential – both positive and negative. To understand this fully, we need to add one more layer to the model shown above, a concept known as the 'mutual possession' of the ten worlds, which was never taught before the Lotus Sutra (and which I've never come across anywhere else either).

Mutual possession simply means that each of these apparently separate ten life states 'contains' all the others, a concept that has some pretty powerful implications for anyone interested in choosing how they feel, or 'reframing'. Let's take a mundane example. You felt angry and frustrated in a traffic jam this morning. You feel upbeat and cheerful two hours later, surrounded by your lovely colleagues at work. So, where exactly has your anger gone? It can't have left your mind or disappeared into the ether, in fact with the right provocation it could come roaring back out of you in an instant. It's just in a *latent state* ('Myo'), whereas during the traffic jam it was in a *manifest* state ('Ho'). Now you feel it, now you don't.

That's why, if a client says to me, 'I've lost my mojo,' I always challenge them and ask: 'Where? Where have you put it? Has it been mislaid?' It may definitely look that way, but it hasn't really 'gone-gone', it's just gone into hiding for a while. Like one of those Russian dolls inside a bigger Russian doll. It's taking a vacation, or perhaps licking its wounds. It's just in a *latent* rather than *manifest* state. Now you see it, now you don't, this Buddha in you and in me. Your mojo (and other qualities, such as confidence) cannot actually be destroyed any more than life force is destroyed when your body dies. Or any more than stars are destroyed when the sun rises. So, if you've never been sure whether you're indecisive or not, now you know the reality: sometimes you are and sometimes you're not ... but the main point is that you'll always find your mojo in your 'Myoho'.

We could do with getting a handle, don't you think, on this latent-manifest thing – one of the key facets of 'Myoho'? It's a very optimistic way to live. How liberating to understand that when someone is apparently consumed by anger or laziness or a desperate Hell state, somewhere *inside* that emotion, not in a separate and distant part of their head (or on a beach in Mauritius), are seeds of hope and happiness, waiting to burst through the mud of despair, able to manifest here and now. Likewise, how fantastic to know that inside those same neighbours having that violent argument is the potential for constructive dialogue. Buddhists believe that when we chant Nam-myoho-renge-kyo, we are simply (though not always easily) bringing this highest of life states to the surface. A kind of 'reframing plus', if you will. Or extra-powerful CBT – 'Cognitive Buddha Therapy'. Or should that be 'Conscious Buddha Transformation'?

Nichiren describes the way that chanting can bring your best innate qualities to the surface: 'Illuminated by the light of the five characters of the Mystic Law [Nam-myoho-renge-kyo], they display the dignified attributes that they inherently possess.'[3]

In short, your innate Buddhahood draws the Buddhahood out of the other nine worlds in your consciousness. To my mind, this distinction between the latent and the manifest is a significant contribution to psychology, explaining why it is that *in every instant* (not in some distant future) we *always* have the potential to think differently; we can, as Nichiren says, bring out the qualities we *inherently possess*, we can be more and do better. And we can do it now. As best-selling author and coach David Taylor frequently says in his brilliant book, *The Naked Leader*: 'Be the best that you *already are*.'

Buddhahood is not a destination

Likewise, enlightenment is absolutely not a place you arrive at, put your feet up and say: 'Right, I am now the finished article and always will be!' Because of the mutual possession of the ten worlds,

Buddhahood still contains all the other nine and therefore if you neglect to maintain your daily practice, the negative aspects of Hell, Rapture, Animality or any of the other nine life states will inevitably resurface in your thinking, emotions and behaviour. So Buddhahood is emphatically not a state where you think you have life sorted and where you kid yourself you've got wisdom and compassion nailed. The moment you feel this kind of complacency kicking in is the moment to expand your life and take on bigger challenges for the sake of others.

Many Nichiren Buddhists will say they can certainly tell the difference between a day when they've done an hour's chanting in the morning and one where they've squeezed in a quick and unfocused fifteen minutes. And as Nichiren warned:

> The great demon of fundamental darkness can even enter the bodies of bodhisattvas who have reached near-perfect enlightenment and prevent them from attaining the Lotus Sutra's blessing of perfect enlightenment.[4]

Believing in everyone's brilliance

Mutual possession also helps you take more responsibility for your sometimes less than brilliant behaviour. Inherent in the philosophy of the ten worlds is the idea that your whole being will be in tune with the particular mood you're in at the time. Have you ever said something to someone that a moment later you realised was harsh or even cruel? Have you then said: 'I didn't mean it'? Well, you must have meant it. Otherwise you couldn't have said it, nor could your eyes have glared, or the vein in your neck bulged, or the volume of your voice risen. You might be in a higher life state now than you were then, but at the time you absolutely did mean it! So take responsibility, say sorry if needs be, then access the Buddha in you and move on.

Over the years I've also heard many Human Resources professionals say that when giving critical feedback, it's important to say that the *behaviour* rather than the person himself falls short. In terms of the ten worlds, though, you can never actually separate the behaviour from the person, at least not if you want them to have some personal accountability. But you can acknowledge that the person was perhaps in a low life state, so although they absolutely did mean to do what they did at the time, they could, given proper (and possibly very candid) direction, reframe their thinking and produce a better behaviour from a higher life state. Apply this principle to your personal relationships and you'll find that forgiveness comes more easily as well.

We are all magnificent works in progress

Buddhism says that each of us is a magnificent work in progress. Complete with our weaknesses, mistakes and failures. In fact, when we give ourselves permission to fail sometimes, rather than risking nothing through fear of failure, life becomes so much more exciting. This philosophy espouses a belief in everyone's innate brilliance, which is one reason why it is so hard to understand and to believe. When we deeply respect others, we get this point and are able to see their potential, even though right now they may be manifesting more of their dark side than their brightness. This makes for more harmonious families at home, more productive departments at work, more forgiving friendships in the pub and better football teams on a Saturday morning. Doesn't that sound like a wonderful way to live?

No such thing as bad feelings

Another benefit of understanding the latent-manifest concept is knowing that every emotion is acceptable, because ultimately every emotion, however evil or destructive, contains latent Buddhahood. So there's no need to feel guilty or bad for feeling what you're feeling – instead you just chant with as much trust as you can muster for that feeling to be transformed, or as Nichiren says, to change 'poison into medicine'. 'It is the heart that is important,' he also stresses, in more than one of his writings.

'Always' and 'never' are almost always never true

Understanding the ten worlds also means you can no longer be 'labelled' by others or put other people in a certain box, a favourite habit of ours in this survival-driven culture, which is at the root of such lazy clichés as:

- 'What's he *really* like under that façade?'
- 'Leopards don't change their spots.'
- 'Then he showed his true colours.'

We are *always* showing our true colours. And our textures, tones, hues and shades of light and grey to boot. If Hell is our dominant life state in a certain moment, then black despair and frustration are true 'colours' for us, at that moment. If we are in Rapture state then a sunshine-yellow joy is our true colour, in that moment.

According to Professor Martin Seligman, former president of the American Psychological Association, one of the charac-teristics of pessimism is the illusion of permanence. So if your daughter criticises you one day, you may choose to feel angry and criticise yourself for being a terrible father. Yet her comment was a single, passing event. In your head though, you can turn it into: 'She's *always* like that. I'll never get on with her.'

Buddhism encourages you to focus on your Buddhahood, whatever is happening in your life right now. To focus on the blossom of the lotus flower ('renge') and to be grateful for the muddy pond in which it grows. I know a Buddhist who stopped drinking five years ago, but he doesn't say: 'My name is John and I'm an alcoholic,' because he feels that label defines his past. He is more likely to think, 'My name is John and I'm a Buddha. I once tried to change my feelings by drinking too much.'

Likewise a recent radio phone-in, lasting nearly an hour,

focused on the question: 'Can drug addicts be good parents?' The media love these simplistic labels but when we lock people up in clichéd boxes such as 'alcoholic' or 'drug addict', we profoundly disrespect their potential. It happens all the time in lovers' tiffs: 'You *never* listen to me properly!' (bet she has, at least once) and 'You're *always* rude to my friends!' (bet he was polite a few times). In short, 'always' and 'never' are almost always never true.

I would suggest that you ban these exaggerations from your arguments. And while you're at it, ban them from your negative self-talk too. Why do I 'always' screw up? How come I 'never' meet my deadlines? And once you've done that, you can also delete expressions like 'he's a complete bastard' from your vocabulary, because he's essentially a Buddha, though he's definitely behaving like a bastard at the moment (in your opinion). In short, no one is ever a 'complete anything'. For more on the very challenging concept of believing in everyone's potential for Buddhahood, see Chapter 6.

'Everywhere', 'every time', 'as usual' and 'there you go again' are not far behind in terms of lazy inaccurate labels. Presumably these judgements were useful in the cave, when survival was everything and seeing things in black and white could prolong your life span. 'Sabre-tooth tiger bad, bison (dinner) good.' We even hear people call themselves 'Idiot!' after playing a poor shot at tennis or on a PlayStation. Another self-slandering label. You're a magnificent work in progress who played one silly shot, that's all.

Changing our hearts to change the world

The concept of the ten worlds has some exciting implications for society, because the world we have created is and always will be a perfect reflection of what is in the depths of our hearts. Let's look at the ten worlds one more time, but this time to see some examples of how our 'collective life state' manifests in the workplace and in wider society:

World	Workplace	Society
Hell	Low morale. Feeling unable to do the job. Bullying culture.	Mental illness, addiction to hard drugs, downward spiral of chaotic lives. Domestic violence.
Hunger	Drive to sell. Desire to earn huge bonuses. Destroying natural environment to make money. Feeling that today's performance is never enough.	Greed in (for example) the banking industry. Focus on material happiness. Alcoholism. Need to 'keep up with the Joneses'. Spending and spending but never feeling satisfied for long.
Animality	Overly hierarchical organisations. Lying and breaking the law to gain competitive advantage. Jealousy of people who succeed more than us. Bitchiness and insecurity. Feeling anxious about 'getting credit' for our ideas and needing to be noticed by people in power.	Feral gang culture where people join 'tribes' to feel safe and protected. Sex without love or respect.
Anger	Bullying. Undermining people. Need to feel superior means we will never get the best from our people.	Authoritarian regimes. Celebrity culture. Media that idolise famous people and then knock them down and enjoy their misfortune.
Tranquillity	Some stability, but … danger of relaxing in the 'comfort zone' and being complacent when business is good. Doing the minimum.	Laziness. People not bothering to communicate with loved ones or to play with their children.
Rapture / 'Heaven'	Celebration of hitting targets. Intense joy at getting promoted. Winning a new piece of business.	'Happy hour' drinking culture. Own country winning the World Cup. New Year's Eve celebrations.
Learning	Improving performance by developing best practice.	Finding ways to improve communities.
Realisation	Creating best practice through innovation.	Great breakthroughs in science or medicine that are copied across the world.
Bodhisattva	Genuine sense of corporate social responsibility.	Raising money for charity. Caring professions.
Buddhahood	Openness, trust, mutual respect, all working for good of self and others. Shared goal of creating value in all situations. Sustainable success.	A dynamic and creative state of peace (not just the absence of war) based on respect for the dignity and individuality of everyone's life. Harmony is valued above conflict when the Buddha in you meets the Buddha in me.

Remember that these ten worlds are not right or wrong or good or evil in and of themselves; Buddhism, as mentioned earlier, is not a moral teaching. These life states do have consequences, though, when blended in with the Law of cause and effect, so it's how we use them that dictates whether we are creating or destroying value, whether we are respecting or slandering the dignity of life. When the lower life states manifest their negative side, this, says Nichiren, is what happens in the world: 'Famine occurs as a result of greed, pestilence as a result of foolishness, and warfare as a result of anger.'[5]

Therefore the world we live in today is a projection of the combined beliefs and emotions of everyone on the planet. Likewise the results of a company are an aggregate of the attitudes and emotions of the people who work for it.

And so it is that your dominant life state doesn't just decide how you *react* to what's happening around you, it actually *shapes* the collective consciousness. Your life state helps compose the mood music of our planet. Yes, you really are that powerful. Once we raise our life states, even the media will stop reporting purely on stories from the lower six and especially the lower three worlds. Because we totally get the media we deserve. And the politicians. In his book *The Happy Depressive*, Alastair Campbell points out that 'much of our media, most of the time, is now slavishly dedicated to making people feel jealous of others, to blame others for their problems, to hate others for their actions and attitudes'.[6]

For news from the world of Buddhahood, you need to look a little harder, for example check out *A Buddhist Podcast* or *The Art of Living* magazine (available from the SGI-UK online shop).

The concept of the ten worlds shows that change is always possible. That there is a truly kaleidoscopic range of empowering thoughts and emotions we can dig out from the reframing powerhouse of Buddhahood.

As Daisaku Ikeda points out in a quote cherished by many practitioners:

A great human revolution in just a single individual will help achieve a change in the destiny of a nation and, further, will enable a change in the destiny of all humankind.[7]

— ◆ —

Mindset mantras for seeing positive potential in every situation

I determine to find the positives, even inside my most negative emotions.

I have the wisdom to understand that all my feelings, even the most destructive, contain something beautiful.

I have the courage to look at myself and decide what I want to change.

I understand that other people in different life states and with different karma will have a different view of the world from my own.

I realise that, at the time, I have meant everything I have ever said and done.

I am a magnificent work in progress.

I begin to see more and more brilliance in everyone.

I ban the words 'always' and 'never' from my criticism of self and others, knowing that they are almost always never true.

Knowing that the world out there reflects our inner heart, I feel optimistic that when people change inside, the world will be a better place.

Journal exercises

1. What situations in your life would you like to reframe or feel differently about?

2. Which of the ten worlds do you think you are in most of the time? Could you bring out more of the positive aspects of these worlds?

3. What hidden talents do you have that could be brought to the surface of your life? What dreams have you given up on?

4. Knowing that you are a Buddha, what labels have you or others put on yourself over the years that you would now like to let go of?

5. What negative labels have you attached to other people? Could you now let go of some of these?

6. Write down five things you love about yourself. (If you are struggling with this list, ask a friend to help!)

7. Write down five things you could learn to love about someone else whom you don't like very much.

8. What are you focusing on most in your life? The muddy pond? Or the lotus flower?

CHAPTER 5

KARMA –
YOUR WHOLE LIFE
IN YOUR HANDS

Now for another principle that is fundamental to Nichiren Buddhism. Since I first started practising I have struggled with the idea that the results (effects) we experience at birth and beyond are the result of 'karma' – previous thoughts, words, deeds and attitudes. I have wriggled and squirmed with the notion that many of those 'causes' were made in previous lifetimes. Lifetimes you cannot remember, any more than you can remember every scene and sound from your dreams last night. And indeed it is impossible to prove with logic or intellect that karma exists or that life is eternal. Or that death is not quite so fatal as we are usually led to believe.

But Buddhists point out that, scientifically speaking, energy (or 'life force') cannot be destroyed, only transformed. They say that karma would explain why children as young as three or four can turn out to be mathematical or musical geniuses, even though their parents are hopeless with numbers or tone deaf. It would explain why some people, when learning a foreign language, feel as if they are actually remembering it or have a perfect accent in that language but are unable to mimic any other accent. This was my own experience of learning French. I'll cover this in more depth later, but for now, just picture my ten-month-old daughter seeing a Bourbon biscuit for the first time ever (after scoffing a very large meal) and nearly leaping out of her pushchair to grab it – categorical proof to my mind that she'd eaten cocoa in a previous life!

As the poet Kahlil Gibran wrote in his wise and beautiful book *The Prophet*: 'Your children are not your children. They are the sons and daughters of Life's longing for itself.'[1] Or as I once heard someone say on the radio: 'You have a child and you think, "It's gonna be a little bit of me and a little bit of my wife" – and then what pops out? A completely different person altogether!'

For any golfers reading this chapter – did you ever hit a putt and wonder why on earth it dived to the right when the borrow of the green was definitely to the left? The answer is because, unseen by you, the underlying lie of the land was towards the right, and karma is a bit like that – invisible but having a profound effect on the 'golf ball' on the surface of your life. Or you could compare it to the undertow in an ocean, the deeper current that can be going in the opposite direction to the surface waves. These analogies may go some way to answering that thorny old question: 'Why do bad things happen to good people?'

Your goodwill account with the universe

OK, you sceptic you, as you've never met my daughter and might have a pathological hatred of Bourbons, think instead of your current life as a visible wave on the ocean and your 'death' as the energy in that wave subsiding. Energy that is never destroyed and is ready to reappear again on the surface when the external conditions are right. Or consider your body as a temporary musical instrument but your life as a tune that goes on forever. We could also compare the 'causes' that we make each moment to little bubbles of energy (some positive, some negative) created in the depths of our lives that are released and which pop up as 'effects' to the surface of daily existence when the external conditions are right. As Robert Ludlum pointed out in one of his white-knuckle (yet strangely philosophical) thrillers, we are born looking for answers and have to make do with analogies.

Biscuits, waves, golf balls, child prodigies, Gibran and Ludlum notwithstanding, did we really 'attract' our parents, the country we are born in and our health at birth? Did you 'choose' to have the singing voice of an angel, die in a plane crash or happen upon the woman/man of your dreams? Did you really 'ask' to get fired by your MD after doing a great job? Did you 'make the cause' to win the lottery after being ungenerous all your life (this lifetime, that is ...)? Did you 'choose' to get 'randomly' attacked in the street after spending years caring for others? Yes and yes and yes. Otherwise, Buddhism says, *it could not have happened*.

To me the idea of karma initially seemed so unfair and brutal – even, in some cases such as 9/11 or child abuse, just plain obscene. After all, how can bad things happen to good people? Why do some bad people seem to get away with their evil actions? And, of course, most coaching and personal development books stop short of teaching karma, for perfectly understandable ethical reasons. When I coach Buddhists I might mention karma; when I coach non-Buddhists, I never would. After all, you wouldn't want to stir up the mud at the bottom of your karmic river (layer 8 of consciousness) unless you had a powerful tool (Buddhahood – layer 9) to handle all the mucky stuff that bubbles to the surface.

How then, is karma 'fair'? How can 'bad things' happen to 'good people'? It's only fair when linked in with the theory of the nine consciousnesses described in Chapter 3. Your life at its first seven layers of consciousness might be full of positive thoughts and deeds, but your eighth consciousness or 'karma' contains all sorts of other tendencies from previous lifetimes – some of them respecting Life's dignity and some of them not. Buddhism, incidentally, makes no judgement about how or when we meet our death.

Karma is a Sanskrit word whose original meaning is 'action'. Karma is a sort of goodwill account with the Universe and with Life itself. It is the deep patterns that repeat over and over in your life, attracting the same results, no matter how often you swap relationships, move house, change jobs or do anything else at the level of your first seven consciousnesses. From this perspective, far from being 'unfair', karma is 100 per cent fair, just like gravity is 100 per cent 'fair'. Even when it doesn't look that way and even when we don't like it very much.

The funny thing is that when it suits us, we do choose to believe in the concepts of karma and cause and effect:

- 'you reap what you sow'
- 'what goes around, comes around'
- 'that was fate'
- 'you make your own luck' (good and bad, by the way).

But these and other sayings like them are mostly throwaway clichés and casual afterthoughts that we can take or leave as the mood or situation suit us. Whereas Nichiren is asking us to put this Mystic Law of cause and effect at the very heart of everything we believe, think, feel, say and do.

Totally responsible, totally free

Intellectually it's a big ask, of course. Trying to work out what cause has led to which effect is as futile as trying to make just one strand move on a plate of spaghetti when you pull it, or attempting to tie up the wind. That's why it's often called the Mystic Law. Did I really make a cause for this situation in my life? Sorry but yes, *or it could not have happened*. This philosophy truly is the height of personal accountability. In the Transactional Analysis psychological framework, it is the ultimate 'adult position'.

I kept chanting about karma and over many years my scepticism very slowly began to recede. I began to see cause and effect as the least unpalatable explanation for personal tragedies, the lesser of three evils – the other two being: 'God made it happen' and 'It was pure chance'.

Though I still struggled to accept the truth of it, I began to see its potential value. That it makes you totally responsible. Yet totally free. That you can never complain about anything or blame anybody for what happens to you. That you can no longer be a victim. That, if you've somehow made the cause to be who and where you are today, then you and only you can make a different cause to shape your life for tomorrow. That, in the context of reincarnation, it's the only explanation of why 'bad things' sometimes happen to 'good people' (and vice versa). That 'what goes around' does come around, but sometimes it takes a long while – maybe not even till a future lifetime. That maybe, just maybe, the cards you've been dealt have actually been shuffled, cut and dealt by you and you alone. As singer-songwriter Howard Jones admits: 'I used to always blame everyone and everything for my predicaments and things that were going wrong. Then I realised that as soon as I took responsibility for it, I had the power to change it. I love that about Buddhism, it's very empowering.'

Nichiren described himself as 'poor, small and ugly' and was quite happy to take responsibility for it:

> One who deprecates those of handsome appearance will be born ugly. One who robs another of food and clothing is sure to fall into the world of hungry spirits. One who mocks a person who observes the precepts and is worthy of respect will be born to an impoverished and lowly family. [...] This is the general law of cause and effect.[2]

I also realised that cause and effect means you can give without anxiety or greed because it all comes back to you from the Universe, when the time and conditions are right. But when we expect a certain response from others, we give our power away. We risk being disappointed when they don't follow the script. That's why, sometimes, the people who we feel owe us everything give us nothing and the people who owe us nothing give us everything. So ... just give without expectation, let go, stop controlling others and trust the Universe.

But the big breakthrough for me was realising (a little late in the day perhaps) that neither Shakyamuni nor Nichiren *invented* cause and effect. They were human beings after all, not Creators of the Universe. They simply noticed that this Law exists – these powers of observation are partly what make them wise Buddhas; they understand how life works. It would have been unfair of them *not* to teach it. It is compassionate to teach karma, even when we don't like it very much.

So, cause and effect just is. It isn't good, it isn't bad, it just is. It's neutral, just like gravity. You don't want to be taking it personally and there's no need to wrap a judgemental god around it. Whether you're in rhythm with it or not and whether you use it with compassion and wisdom are what count. Seen from a helpless Hell state perspective, it is the shackles of your destiny. Seen from Anger state, it could be abused by a dictator to murder people and then say that they deserved to die. But seen and acted on from the perspective of the Buddha in you, cause and effect sets you free and simultaneously gives you total responsibility for your life.

My fellow SGI Buddhist Adam Armstrong sheds more light on this topic: 'I quite often think that we use incorrect language to describe karma. We short-hand things which then get mis-interpreted. From the viewpoint of the four lower worlds (or "life states"), our karma is negative. From the viewpoint of Tranquillity up to Bodhisattva our karma is generally perceived as positive. However, from the viewpoint of Buddhahood, karma is just karma. It is just the inevitable consequence of our past actions, neither good nor bad.' And indeed this is why Nichiren writes: 'For instance, hungry spirits perceive the Ganges River as fire, human beings perceive it as water, and heavenly beings perceive it as amrita [a legendary, ambrosia-like liquid].'[3]

The river remains the same; only the perception of it varies through our moment-by-moment life state. The same is true of our karma. We still made the same causes in the past, but our dominant life state dictates how we view the resulting effect. We could say, 'Chanting transforms *negative perception of* our karma.' And we therefore shouldn't really talk of 'positive and negative' karma. The Buddha in you knows that karma is just karma and, in and of itself, it is completely neutral.

Is morality past its sell-by date?

In recent times the Western media have lamented society's lack of a 'moral compass', a symptom of traditional Christian Church values losing their influence on people's minds. Media commentators attribute everything from anti-social behaviour to riots and under-age sex to this lack of a moral compass. And engaged Buddhists are as concerned as anyone about these social ills. However, Buddhists would argue that destructive and disrespectful behaviour springs from the Fundamental Darkness in people's hearts, rather than from a lack of moral compass. So the Buddhist solution is a bottom-up one founded on the dignity of life, individual human revolutions and a deep understanding of cause and effect, rather than proposing a set of top-down 'right and wrong' rules or more and more layers of legislation, layers that essentially just paint over the rust. Noble and admirable though the Ten Commandments (and similar teachings) may be, and useful though they may have been over the centuries, they have lost much of their power, they no longer work as effectively, they are past their sell-by date. Restoring old-fashioned definitions of a moral compass is not the way forward now. In our heads we might be moral beings, capable of lesser or greater degrees of self-control, but in our hearts we are not. And though commandments cannot transform hearts, Buddhists believe that lives based on Buddhahood can and do.

One of the paradoxes of Nichiren Buddhism is that it has no moral rules and yet in some respects it is the strictest teaching on the planet, as the Law of cause and effect is inescapable.

But because the strictness is inherent in the Mystic Law of life, Buddhism is never black and white in a *moral* sense. The ten worlds, for example, give it subtle shades of grey. It simply cannot be prescriptive about issues such as homosexuality or abortion, because it treats people as individuals and as adults capable of leading their own lives and making their own unique life choices based on deep respect for the dignity of life. No moral mazes or compasses are necessary.

Neither are debates about whether it's nature or nurture that makes someone who they are, because karma explains that it is both – we carry effects from one lifetime to the next and we choose the environment into which we're born. We are born evil. We are born good as well. When we chant, we aim to transform the bad stuff and access more of the good stuff. And we use the wisdom gained from chanting to decide what is right or wrong, without consulting a rule book or scripture. So, for example, a Buddhist woman who has been raped would never be told whether she should keep the baby or have an abortion. Either decision could be for the best, based on her sincere prayer.

As Nichiren says:

> ... we know that the prayers offered by a practitioner of the Lotus Sutra will be answered just as an echo answers a sound, as a shadow follows a form, as the reflection of the moon appears in clear water, as a mirror collects dewdrops, as a magnet attracts iron ...[4]

And because this Mystic Law is neutral, Buddhism does not use words like 'sin' or 'blame' or 'punishment'. We tend to talk more about 'positive' and 'negative' than about 'good' and 'evil'. Because Nichiren Buddhism is a religion that needs no rules or moral commandments, I cannot think of any of Nichiren's teachings contradicting each other. But growing up a Christian, I never knew, for example, whether to 'turn the other cheek' or to take 'an eye for an eye'.

Your destiny is a re-recordable DVD

So, at the risk of giving you one analogy too many, your karma is a bit like a DVD containing 'data' from this and your previous lifetimes, and the passing of time is like a laser beaming over the disc to release words, pictures and music. The good news is that Nichiren was the first Buddhist teacher to argue that it's a *re-recordable* DVD; your life is not pre-determined, your future is not written in the stars as some would have you believe. When people visit an astrologer or have their palm read, they are in effect trying to find out how their 'DVD' will play out in the future – this is a fearful survival-based mindset that seeks reassurance. But Nichiren insists that this script has been written (by you) in the depths of your life and that, with oodles of courage and a big dose of wisdom, you can create a different movie if the one playing out for you is not producing the results you want.

I am good because I am too selfish to be bad

Behind Nichiren's belief about cause and effect is the idea that when we hurt others, we hurt ourselves. When I think somebody is ugly, I'm actually revealing my own ugliness. If I steal from you then sooner or later – via my goodwill account with the Universe – I also steal from me. This is one answer to Richard Dawkins' excellent point, 'If there is no God, why be good?', a question from *The God Delusion* that compares God to a sort of omnipotent and omniscient policeman. As Shakyamuni said: 'If a person commits an act of good or evil, he himself becomes the heir to that action. This is because that action actually never disappears.' So when people ask me, 'How's life treating you?' the real answer is: 'As I have treated life.'

Buddhism does not dispute the idea that we are all naturally self-obsessed, but is equally clear that the bigger and more all-embracing the self we're obsessed with, the better. So the answer to Dawkins' question 'Why be good?' is simple: because I respect my life enough to want good effects to come back to me.

When I first became a self-employed writer and began charging clients for time spent on their jobs, someone once asked me if I was ever tempted to add a few hours on to an invoice, given that the client would never know any different. I replied, 'No, definitely not,' because sooner or later, due to the Mystic Law, I would just be stealing from myself. And why would I want to do that? You could even interpret this as saying: 'I am good because I am too selfish to be bad.'

Karma – you can run but you can't hide

The other important point is that you cannot pick and choose when you do and don't believe in the Mystic Law, any more than you can wake up one day and pretend gravity is not there. Walk out of a fifth-floor window on Friday evening and you'll soon discover it exists just as much as it did on Monday morning (when you very sensibly took the lift). You can try running from your karma, but you can never hide, because you carry it with you; or, as Shakyamuni says, it 'actually never disappears'. Neither can you pick and choose who the Mystic Law does and does not apply to. Buddhists believe that it works on all of us, all of the time. Nobody is exempt. The Law of life never sleeps. It's just the way things are, it's the 'set-up' if you like, and you can't get off the cycle into some imaginary other-worldly paradise. It is futile trying to bargain with it, plead with it or make deals with it. What Nichiren recommends is that you awaken to how life works and experience the joy of putting yourself in rhythm with this Mystic Law, and discover the optimism of finding something valuable in every aspect of your karma.

So, I might not always like karma or cause and effect very much, but I can now accept that they are true. To borrow a quote from Al Gore, the Mystic Law is an 'inconvenient truth' at the times when it means *you* need to change, rather than pointing the finger of blame at your parents or spouse or at politicians or the media or society in general.

Engaging with the gears of the Universe

A Buddha is someone who is awakened to and lives their life in rhythm with this Mystic Law. When you chant, you start to feel the cogs of your life engaging with the gears of the Universe. As faith deepens, you find yourself more often 'in the right place at the right time'. So to Nichiren Buddhists, there is no such thing as coincidence or random events, just effects where we cannot see the connecting cause. When Nichiren survived that attempted decapitation – his would-be executioners sent running by the appearance of a comet shooting across the night sky – he didn't *make* the comet appear, neither was it a miracle, he was 'just' in the right place at the right time, in rhythm with the Universe.

Of course, that does not mean that Buddhists somehow have wonderful things happen to them all the time. On the contrary, when you take on the challenge of changing your karma, in the name of fighting for world peace, all sorts of surprising muck can bubble up to the surface: 'Yuk ... where the hell did that come from!'

In fact, your Buddhahood constantly presents you with surprising opportunities to bring it out of the shadows and into the sunlight. These are often disguised as problems (see Chapter 7). So when it unexpectedly decides that it's time for you to get sacked for no apparent reason (or 'external cause') from that fantastic job, you have a wonderful chance to tune into your highest life state and become happier in a deeper and more sustainable way. A way that may not be built around the ephemeral pleasures or status that your job may have brought you ... Thank you, Spoon!

Every problem is a gift in disguise

From this viewpoint, there are no such things as bad karma or unfair dismissals, there are only beautiful opportunities to discover and fulfil your mission. Your MD's actions in sacking you exist only *on the surface* of reality. Somewhere deep down you already know that she is a gift from the Universe who mirrors the internal causes/sediment/karma that your Buddhahood wants you to change about yourself. She is the spoon stirring up your own sediment from the water of your life. As Ralph Waldo Emerson once said: 'Shallow men believe in luck. Strong men believe in cause and effect.'

Incidentally, bitter feelings of revenge also evaporate under the sun of cause and effect. If you know in your heart that what goes around comes around, there's no need to retaliate against the person who has 'mistreated' you. Neither do you need to seek credit for yourself or look for attention from high-status people; indeed, Buddhism encourages people to rise into action even when nobody else is watching.

The Buddhist approach to problems is to start by thanking the Universe for the events and people you find challenging in your life. Then praise yourself because you are ready to face this challenge! And thank your ex-MD as well, while you're at it, for being the catalyst in the next phase of your Human Revolution! Heck, you can even chant for her absolute happiness (possibly through gritted teeth at first) if you really want to change quickly!

Transforming karma into mission

Over the years various clients in difficult situations have sometimes said things like: 'Why me?' Or 'What did I do to deserve this?' Or 'Why does this keep happening in my life?' This is a very natural but ultimately futile question. I was taught when I trained as a coach that 'Why?' is a negative, backward-looking question. Much healthier, say the coaches, to 'look at the hows of the solution in the present rather than the whys of the problem in the past'.

But it's healthier still, says Buddhism, to look at 'Why me?' as a positive, *forward-looking* question. This happens when you consider your present problem, chant about your future and begin your answer not with a backward-looking 'because I did ...', but with a forward-looking: *'So that I can ...'* Then from your own reservoir of boundless Buddha wisdom will spring insights that complete the answer:

So that I can ... be more compassionate/learn to love my parents/fulfil my full potential at work/find a relationship based on deep respect ... and so on.

This is known in Buddhism as 'transforming karma into mission', harnessing all that emotional angst to strengthen your sense of purpose. 'Mission' does not necessarily mean a destiny to discover new planets, or a noble calling to work with the disadvantaged in Darfur; rather it indicates a strong sense of purpose and a sense of personal responsibility that guide your daily choices and actions, and reveal your unique individual talents. This is surely a more powerful attitude than the old platitude about learning from your mistakes, whose dominant concept is, of course, 'mistakes'. If you are not sure what your own mission is, try asking yourself this question: 'When the wonderful Mystic Law expresses itself through [insert your name here], what does [name] do?'

My fellow SGI member and author Alex Lickerman sheds more light on the benefits of discovering your mission in his excellent book *The Undefeated Mind*:

Ultimately [...] adopting a mission can help sustain us through loss, improve our ability to endure stress, enhance our sense of self-worth, diminish our inclination to give up, make mundane tasks more enjoyable, help us say 'no' more easily, defend us against despair, and imbue the events of our lives with heightened significance.[5]

And I love this extract from a poem called 'Courage' written by my fellow SGI member Patti Dale:

You cannot trade your blotted page
For a clean sheet
You must create
From where you are now
Knee-deep in your own garbage:
In it lie the ingredients
Of your humanity.

It's a great reminder that sometimes you need to get over yourself, yet it's full of hope and encouragement too.

Karma into mission

The concept of transforming karma into mission is beautifully explained in this experience by Goldsmiths College, University of London lecturer David Woodger. David's story tackles the topics of bullying, racism, anger and confrontation. But ultimately it shows how dialogue can create a more humane society.

I was separated at birth from my mum – a first generation Indian Gujarati Hindu – and then was adopted after three months by the Woodger family who raised me in the idyllic Shropshire countryside. My family was supportive and caring but growing up in a white community did not always feel idyllic as I experienced ongoing racist abuse, bullying and violence from my peers. I lived in isolation with no one to share my experience, wishing that I was white like everyone else around me. I wanted to deny who I was and I lived in fear of attack and rejection. This destroyed my self-confidence and my self-esteem. I didn't understand my place or purpose in the world. By day I would wear a smile and try my best to fit into the world and at night I would cry myself to sleep.

One week, I was beaten up by six local boys in a 'Paki bashing' attack, whilst another six watched. The pain and anguish through adolescence turned into an incandescent anger which I directed towards authority, the unequal and unfair system and the injustices of the world. I created, led and organised chaos and disruption through school and university. Though I was never physically violent, I would verbally lash out against the beliefs of anyone who had a different view from me.

In 1983 I trained to be a community worker, which was a perfect profession because it paid me to fight for communities' rights and against injustice. My first job was on an estate in West London working for black and racial minorities. My attitude soon brought me into conflict with my superiors leading me to sue the council for racism and racial harassment. I also sued the trade union for failing to represent me. All this ignited huge conflicts amongst staff and the community. It ended up with security guards escorting me from my desk in the town hall.

I was not satisfied even though I achieved a positive outcome from the court cases and gained financial compensation. I felt cynical, frustrated and exhausted, as I could see no real change in my environment despite my great efforts and deep desire for change.

It was at this point in 1993 that I met Nichiren Daishonin's Buddhism. I was introduced to it by a colleague who impressed me as he was tackling racism in a sustained way and he was white. He explained his approach: 'Whether someone is in a minority or in authority is not the main point, what's needed is an inner transformation. That's what it takes to bring about genuine change in society.'

I did not start practising straight away, even though I was unhappy, because at the time I just accepted the way my life was and that I had to make the best of things. I was never really religious or spiritual – just political. I found the basic philosophy of Nichiren Buddhism very challenging, as I always believed it was the structures and systems that needed changing rather than people's hearts.

But I'll never forget what happened when I first chanted. All the pent-up emotions and feelings that I'd been suppressing since childhood came gushing out. I couldn't hold back my tears. I felt liberated from the anger I had deep inside me towards my birth parents and towards society. As I continued to chant I began to want to be the kind of activist who could sincerely empathise with those who have experienced the same suffering I went through.

From now on I decided as a starting point to work on my own internal change and then, based on this, create change in my work and family. I knew that however much justification I had for blaming others, ultimately this wasn't going to resolve my previous experiences or give me the courage to make real changes to my current situation. In fact blame made me unhappy and took away my power to take action.

My approach to tackling various issues in the black community began to change. Whereas before I would hurl anger at the perpetrators of racial discrimination, after I began chanting I learned to be more tolerant and opted for patient, tenacious dialogue instead of confrontation. This change bore fruit.

The same community leaders and organisations that I had been fighting against were now partners with me in working to better society. We gained the government's support in setting up projects and workshops in the black community and most importantly encouraged public sector white professionals to reflect on their services to black and racial minority communities.

I have learned from this experience that I am ultimately responsible for changing my sadness and anger. No one else could take away the unhappiness for me and I couldn't keep blaming other people or my environment for how I felt.

I now advise organisations on how to tackle institutional racism and racial conflict. I work as a full-time lecturer at Goldsmiths College, University of London, teaching, amongst other subjects, solutions to institutional racism. I have written and published articles on the subject and been invited to speak at various academic conferences both nationally and abroad.

For many years now my relationship with my mum and dad has been open, honest and meaningful. I was able to embrace my dad and value him for doing his best to be a caring and loving father. As I grew more secure and at ease with my identity, they in turn were able to support me and appreciate the experiences that I had faced.

I have used my past to create a positive and strong self-identity. It has taken tremendous courage to face issues and to take responsibility for them. I feel proud and grateful for the journey I have made so far and excited about the challenges ahead. This is the Buddhist principle of 'transforming karma into mission'. My belief and vision is that we establish a more humane society of genuine racial equality based on respecting the dignity of all life and transcending our differences.

So, to summarise, here are the benefits of believing in karma and in the Law of cause and effect:

1. Death is not as fatal as it first appears;

2. You are neither the puppet of a superpower nor the victim of haphazard chance;

3. You are totally free and totally responsible for your life;

4. You begin to see every 'problem' as a 'gift in disguise';

5. You see 'why me?' as a positive, forward-looking question that gives your life a mission and sense of purpose;

6. You create your own future and your own goodwill account with the Universe;

7. If enough of us live with this belief in cause and effect we can change the world.

Mindset mantras for being the architect of your future

Knowing that karma is unfathomable with thoughts alone, I do not waste energy wondering why bad things have happened to me.

I take full personal responsibility for my whole life, including my goodwill account with the Universe.

I have made, shuffled, cut and dealt the karmic pack of cards that have created my life as it is today.

I can make, shuffle, cut and deal the pack of cards that will create my future.

I am always recording my own destiny DVD, based on my dominant life state.

I now release the illusion that complaining about life and blaming other people is a useful way to spend my energy.

I rejoice in the knowledge that I am totally responsible and totally free.

I put myself in rhythm with the Law of the Universe and in this way I begin to change my karma.

Every time I have a problem, I find myself 'Thanking the Spoon'.

I begin to see that all problems are a gift in disguise, a chance to discover and fulfil my deepest potential and mission.

I start all challenges from the point of victory.

Journal exercises

1. What patterns seem to repeat themselves in your life, despite your best efforts to change them?

2. What aspects of your karma can you feel grateful for?

3. In what areas of your life can you release feelings of guilt, victimhood and blame?

4. What problems can you feel grateful for? What are the gifts hidden inside them?

5. Knowing that you are totally responsible and totally free, what can you feel more optimistic about?

6. What brilliant life can you see unfolding for you in the future?

7. How could you benefit others with what you have learned from your suffering?

CHAPTER 6

EVERYONE'S
A BUDDHA

Yes, that includes you, your best mate, your lover, your beautiful kids, your gorgeous grandma and your favourite teacher from school. But you knew that already, right? The thing is, it also includes the colleague who bitches about you, the friend who betrayed you, the lover who stopped loving you, the driver who cut you up at a roundabout, the father who judged you, the boss who sacked you and that snotty little kid down the road who you feel like strangling sometimes! Although this may be hard to believe, Nichiren was adamant that everyone has Buddha-potential, explaining that fire can be produced by a stone taken from the bottom of a river, and that a candle can light up a place that has been dark for billions of years.

Of course, the qualities of Buddhahood (wisdom, courage, joy, life force and compassion) are more *manifest* in some people than others, but the big and bold claim of the Lotus Sutra was that *everyone* has Buddhahood somewhere deep inside, in a *latent* state waiting to be tapped. And as a fellow coach once said to me: 'If you cannot see another's greatness, you are looking at your own limitations.'

In the thirteenth-century Japan into which Nichiren was born, this spirit of equality had long since disappeared, with priests acting as intermediaries between ordinary people and the 'divine'. There is no better example of this than the belief, vehemently opposed by Nichiren, but taught in pre-Lotus Sutra teachings, that women were unable to attain enlightenment and deserved no better treatment than animals.

However, he writes: 'Our mothers are human women; they do not belong to the realm of animals, nor have they the bodies of reptiles.' He expresses his appreciation of mothers by describing pregnancy as:

> ... a period of nine months during which your mother [...] undergoes suffering that is close to death. And the pains she endures at the time of birth are almost too great to imagine, the panting breath, the sweaty steam rising from her forehead ...[1]

In the same letter he points out that the only way to repay the debt one owes one's mother is to follow the Lotus Sutra because all the other sutras 'speak disparagingly of women'.

Not a 'pick and mix' religion

The challenge is that the teaching of everyone having Buddhahood, like the principle of cause and effect, is all or nothing. It's either true or it isn't, this Buddha in me, this Buddha in you. Nichiren Buddhism is not one of those religions where you can 'pick and mix' the bits you agree with (tempting as that may sometimes be), because they're all ultimately inseparable, they're intertwined and, I believe, watertight.

Let's get back to the main point I want to emphasise: everyone's a Buddha. Everyone's life can be more magnificent right here, right now, in the midst of daily reality. This was a revolutionary teaching in feudalistic thirteenth-century Japan and still ruffles a few feathers now. I'm a Buddha, you're a Buddha ... and so what? Well, to me this is a message of great hope. It means that you and everyone else can become indestructibly happy, that we have enormous untapped potential, that we are capable of progress even in the most difficult of circumstances, often in ways that we never imagined.

Again, so what? Don't all the modern personal development books say the same thing? Yes, they do. But 750 years ago, Nichiren took it a step further. If everyone's a Buddha, it means that you *and everyone else* are worthy of respect, so it's more inclusive than a self-help philosophy. It's also more democratic than any political system ever will be. If everyone's a Buddha, it means that we can overcome the differences that separate us; it means, in short, that the destiny of the human race is completely and totally in our hearts and our hands. The fundamental spirit of Buddhism is that all people are equal. A person is not great simply because of his or her social standing, fame, academic background or position.

As Nichiren explains in a letter to one of his followers, Abutso-bo:

> ... no treasure tower exists other than the figures of the men and women who embrace the Lotus Sutra. [...] Abutso-bo is therefore the treasure tower itself, and the treasure tower is Abutso-bo himself. No other knowledge is purposeful.[2]

Nichiren is referring to an allegory used by Shakyamuni who, when preaching the Lotus Sutra, compared our Buddhahood to a magnificent and gigantic tower adorned with seven kinds of treasure. As we might come to expect with Nichiren, there are no holds barred when he states his beliefs – 'no other knowledge is purposeful' is a typically pragmatic (and simultaneously dogmatic) view that says awareness of our incredible potential is the most important knowledge of all.

Nobody is totally evil

Our heavily ingrained tendency is to divide the world starkly into goodies and baddies. Films do it, cliché-ridden newspapers (especially) do it, books do it. It starts young, because kids' cartoons and video games do it too. And of course this plays perfectly to our S-O-S, because when we were living in caves it no doubt made a lot of sense to quickly identify others as either friend or foe, with no grey areas. It might, after all, have made the difference between life and death! But millions of years later, could it now be time to move on, update our neural pathways and get over our smaller selves?

As I write this chapter, the UK tabloid newspapers are describing the acts of a mass murderer as 'pure evil'. But Nichiren is adamant that a person cannot be 'pure evil', because of the mutual possession of the ten worlds described earlier. Remember that Anger state, for example, contains Buddhahood within it. Was this man damaged? Yes. Dangerous? Yes. Deluded? Yes. Mentally ill? Certainly. Pure evil? No, even though it must feel almost impossible for the families of his victims to come to terms with what he did.

As we have seen, Nichiren also mentions that it only takes a single candle to light up a place that has been dark for billions of years – so from this perspective there is no such thing as a purely evil person, just people who haven't yet discovered their inner candle and how to ignite it.

All of us are capable of evil and of good. A 'cruel murderer' can come home and show compassion to his children, a 'kind nurse' can come home from work and be aggressive to her family. As Nichiren says: 'Even a heartless villain loves his wife and children. He too has a portion of the bodhisattva world within him.'[3]

It therefore follows that nobody is totally evil. Neither is anybody totally good – you're guaranteed disappointment if you choose to worship someone else and then expect them permanently to demonstrate the higher aspects of human behaviour.

You yourself are a true Buddha

It's only our S-O-S, our untrusting obsession with certainty, that wants to put people in these boxes and keep them there, to label someone as a complete hero, a complete zero or a total villain. And of course we often buy newspapers whose editors choose which stories to publish based on these black and white clichés and stereotypes. I think Nichiren would say that this is nonsense; seductive and understandable nonsense maybe, but nonsense all the same.

It's also the kind of nonsense that makes arguments between friends last longer than they need to, that asserts colleagues can never change, that can even cause decades-long rifts in families. All because we've permanently labelled someone as a liar or a bigot or a coward or a whatever, thereby slamming a door on the common sense from which forgiveness can bloom. We even do it in business and, although psychometric tests have value in terms of identifying strengths and weaknesses, people can too easily label themselves as an 'Introvert' or a 'Plant' or a 'passive-aggressive' or whatever moniker the computer churns out. Yes I found it interesting to discover that on the Myers-Briggs profile I am an ENFP (Extraversion, Intuition, Feeling, Perception), but ultimately I feel that such labels are better at describing your past than your potential. You are not the role you have played in order to survive so far; you are not your psychometric profile, you are not the product of your childhood, you are not your job description, you are a Buddha, you are who you choose to become.

Many readers may be familiar with this extract from Marianne Williamson's beautiful book *A Return to Love*. It was read at Nelson Mandela's inauguration as President and is analogous to how Buddhists often feel about their latent Buddhahood:

Our deepest fear is not that we are inadequate.
Our deepest fear is that we are powerful beyond measure.
It is our light, not our darkness, that most frightens us.

We ask ourselves, who am I to be brilliant, gorgeous, talented and fabulous? Actually, who are you not to be?[4]

And as the Lotus Sutra itself says:

> You have been able to accept, uphold, read, recite and ponder this sutra and to preach it for others. The good fortune you gain thereby is immeasurable and boundless. It cannot be burned by fire or washed away by water. Your benefits are such that a thousand Buddhas speaking all together could never finish describing them. Now you have been able to destroy all devils and thieves, to annihilate the army of birth and death, and all others who bore you enmity or malice have likewise been wiped out. Good man, a hundred, a thousand Buddhas will employ their transcendental powers to join in guarding and protecting you. Among the heavenly and human beings of all the worlds, there will be no one like you.[5]

Why do we struggle so much to embrace and accept the Buddha in our hearts? Why do we refuse to love ourselves and treasure the very core of our lives? Often it's because we're worried about what other people may think. In our survival mentality, we want to blend in safely with the crowd, even if that means a miserable lowest common denominator existence. We may be concerned that our confidence will be seen as arrogance and we have been taught that there is a fine line between the two. We don't want to 'play God' in case the 'real God' strikes us down.

The difference between arrogance and confidence

But arrogance and confidence come from completely different places. Confident people want other people to reveal their talent and will not feel threatened by it, whereas arrogant people need others to continuously feel inferior so that they can protect their own low self-esteem (fragile ego) and hide their own deep anxiety, their S-O-S. Arrogant people need everyone else to agree with their point of view and for the world to revolve around them, whereas confident people can embrace differences and put themselves in other people's universes. Guess who is ultimately happier and more influential – the arrogant person or the confident one? Despite the superficial similarities, the contrast in attitudes could hardly be more profound.

The Buddhist scholar T'ien'tai, oft quoted by Nichiren, sheds light on the matter when he writes about someone dominated by Anger state, which is the fundamental mindset that drives arrogance:

> The person in the Realm of Anger has an irresistible urge to win out over everyone else. Like the hawk flying high in the sky in search of prey, he looks down upon others and respects only himself. He makes a superficial show of benevolence, righteousness, propriety, wisdom and faith, and he may even display a primitive form of moral integrity, but inside he is a monstrous egotist.[6]

Religious fundamentalism, terrorism and wars started in the name of one particular god have their roots precisely in this kind of monstrous egotism.

I think this whole topic of arrogance versus confidence also works powerfully in the context of Stephen Covey's famous 'I win, you win' model of successful relationships, much beloved of personal development fans and business leaders. It strikes me that when we both lack self-esteem, I lose and you lose. When you are arrogant, I lose and you win. When I am arrogant, I win and you lose. And when we are both confident, I win and you win (or we choose to walk away from each other – Covey's 'no deal' option).

When you genuinely believe in your own Buddhahood, you're not trying to be superior, because you're as sure of others' brilliance as you are of your own. Many personal development books emphasise individual self-esteem, personal brilliance and so on. But Buddha-confidence means realising that everyone else is essentially as amazing you; why on earth wouldn't they be? That's why Buddhists strive to cultivate a feeling of profound reverence and awe for our own *and others'* lives. That's why this book is called *The Buddha in Me, the Buddha in You*.

What stops us, then? It might sometimes be a subconscious belief that 'such and such' a person cannot possibly have Buddhahood. If this is your thought, then Anger is probably your dominant life state. Or we occasionally project and protect our own prejudices: 'She'd be OK if she was more patient, or more intelligent, or if she agreed with my point of view.' Or, 'I'd respect him if he was slimmer/less intense/more dynamic,' or whatever fits our own mental map of how we think other people 'should' be, based on our own individual values. These 'shoulds' are the shackles we place on other people – and ultimately on ourselves, when others inevitably fall short of our self-centred expectations. This is an arrogant yet far too commonplace attitude and it will never make us happy. And underneath arrogance we very often find deep vulnerability. And many of the most painful lessons in life are either about learning to be more confident, or more humble, and sometimes both. The late Shin Yatomi of SGI-USA wrote: 'Buddhas accept their innate goodness without arrogance and recognise their innate evil without despair.'

Why we struggle to love ourselves

Our Christian conditioning does very little to encourage self-love. Some biblical commentators say that self-love is assumed within the phrase 'Love your neighbour as yourself.' But what if you don't love yourself at all – how can you possibly have a great relationship with your neighbour?

As a seven-year-old at Catholic Sunday School, I vividly recall the teacher asking us whom we should love. The children trotted out the expected answers: God, Mummy, Daddy, my sister and so on ... Then someone piped up: 'Me, I love me!' The teacher frowned slightly and said: 'Oh, erm, now then, I'm not so sure about that.'

Self-love in Buddhism, I should stress, is not about believing you are perfect or never need to change – on the contrary, when you put Buddhahood at the centre of your life, you launch your revolution from the inside and this can be painful at times as your inner gremlins (or negativity) fight your highest life state for control of your current mindset and your future results.

As we touched upon in the Introduction, anything that blocks you from seeing your own and others' full potential is known in Buddhism as your 'Fundamental Darkness', or 'FD' for short. Stuff like laziness, despair, agonising indecision, being over-critical, low self-esteem and relentless pessimism. We'll take a closer look at FD in the next chapter.

Another reason we may not want to believe in our Buddhahood is that we don't want to raise our expectations of life or other people's expectations of us. We are quite happy, thank you very much, in the cotton wool of our S-O-S comfort zone. Revering and revealing the Buddha in ourselves entails a responsibility to relieve others of suffering, a responsibility that may sometimes feel daunting, that tests the depths of our faith and the limits of our compassion; but that is, ultimately, a source of the most profound joy.

How can I awaken the Buddha in others?

Every day, when Nichiren Buddhists recite extracts from Shakyamuni's Lotus Sutra, the very last words are: 'At all times I think to myself, how can I cause living beings to gain entry into the unsurpassed way and quickly acquire the body of a Buddha?'

Let's look at this more closely. First, this desire to connect everyone to their own Buddhahood is a constant thought – 'at all times' – rather than a spiritual experience you might engage in once a week. It takes effort to chant, especially on a cold winter's morning, say, or if you've just rolled out of bed with a hangover, or if you're battling tooth and nail with a tough bit of your FD ... or if all three of these things are happening at once! Second, it talks about compassion for 'all living beings' – not just the ones you personally like or admire. Third, it's very significant that this sentence is a question. Not an order, a commandment, or a conclusion. But a question. And an open question at that, rather than a closed 'yes or no' question. A question that begins with 'How?', which means we can unlock the answers from within us. And fourth is that little word 'quickly'. Yes, there is a sense of urgency here too. Of every moment as well as every life being precious. Fifth, it's the last thing recited in the morning and evening prayers, so it's the thought that tops and tails the daily life of a Nichiren Buddhist. This book is my own answer to that question.

So, all of it is up to us. We make a choice every day: do I reveal my innate stupidity, greed and anger (the three main ingredients of FD)? Or do I battle to reveal my wisdom, joy, energy, courage and compassion? The first approach makes society a dark, depressing, angry place. The second, which takes huge effort and repeated determination, makes the world more peaceful, inspiring and creative. Which one will you choose? Might it be time to take a closer look at the Buddha in you?

— ◆ —

Mindset mantras for realising you are a Buddha

I accept that I have both light and darkness
in my heart.

I choose now to turn up the volume on the good stuff.

I myself am wonderful and worthy of the
deepest respect.

And so is everyone else.

I am brilliant, gorgeous, talented and fabulous.

And so is everyone else.

I treasure and revere the very core of my life.

And everyone else's lives.

A Great Buddha is reading this book, is brushing their
teeth, is going to the shops, is ... (list whatever you are
doing today).

And other Great Buddhas are doing their stuff
around me as well.

I choose to tap into my wisdom, confidence, joy,
life force, courage and compassion.

I am a Buddha, I am a Buddha, I am a Buddha.

Journal exercises

1. Are there people in your life whom you have labelled as 'bad' or even 'totally evil'? Could you learn to look at them differently?

2. Make a list of people you have refused to forgive or against whom you are holding a grudge. Then remember to 'Thank the Spoon'.

3. List the areas of your life where you feel confident and brilliant. Then congratulate yourself.

4. Are there any situations in your life where you tend to be arrogant and disrespectful towards others? How could true confidence change these situations?

5. How can you awaken other people's best qualities?

CHAPTER 7

YOU HAVE A PROBLEM? CONGRATULATIONS!

Twenty-two years ago when I first went to a senior Buddhist leader (the late, great John Delnevo) to ask for help, I said to him in no uncertain terms: 'I have a big problem,' and he replied with a broad smile and a slightly irritating twinkle in his eye, 'Congratulations.' I thought he must have misheard me so I repeated that I really was struggling with something (I can't remember what but it would've felt massive at the time – money/job/girlfriend/parents).

Again he said, 'That's great news, well done you.' Humph, why was he taking the mickey? Did this man have no respect or compassion at all? Didn't he realise that this so-called amazing Buddhist practice was failing me miserably and that he should feel as sorry for me as I did for myself?

It turned out that he was very big on both compassion and wisdom and it was me who was failing to understand Buddhism. Seeing my perplexed (and possibly irritated) face, he patiently made several points:

1. Happiness is not the absence of problems.

2. Problems are a fact of life.

3. The problem is never the problem, it's the life state from

which you approach the problem that's the problem (how you process the problem and react to it are what count).

4. The lotus flower only grows in a muddy pond: your challenge is a sign that your life is asking to grow – you can choose whether to say Yes or No.

5. You've made the cause for this situation (otherwise it couldn't happen), so therefore you (and only you) have the power to change it.

6. Any problem is a chance to change for the better (it might be heavily disguised, but it's a gift all the same).

7. When you change for the better, the world around you does too, as surely as a shadow follows a body; that's how, one by one, step by step, we create world peace.

I quite quickly felt better. Perhaps there was after all a little more to celebrate than initially met the eye! Hence his congratulations. But don't the self-help courses cover all of the above? Isn't this just resourceful thinking? Well no, not as far as I can see. Life coaches definitely touch on point number 6 in the list above; in fact the whole concept of 'reframing' – or seeing a 'bad' event from a more positive perspective – is a very powerful tool. And I love the coaching technique that teaches you to 'focus on the hows of the solution, not the whys of the problem' in order to put your mind in a 'resourceful state'. But mostly coaches only include a nod towards one or two of the other points above.

The most positive approach to problems

Let's imagine two characters, John and Jane, caught up in an on-going dialogue about the challenges of daily life. The most common non-Buddhist reaction that I hear when John is facing a problem in his life is Jane saying (without a smile or twinkle in her eye): 'Oh well, these things are sent to try us, aren't they?' (Jane has no useful advice on what John can do, by the way, though she may offer bags of consolation.)

Buddhism says that 'these things' are not 'sent' by anyone other than ourselves: like it or not, we've attracted every situation we experience through the workings of the Mystic Law of cause and effect. And thanks to our Buddhahood we can, if we so choose, use them to push ourselves beyond our current limits.

Variations in the John and Jane conversation include:

- 'Oh well, it's all part of life's rich pageant.'
- 'You just have to get on with it.'
- 'We all have a cross to bear.'
- 'It could be worse.'

Well-meaning though the words are, might it be time for us to stop lazily plucking such phrases from our mental library of clichés?

Suffer what there is to suffer, enjoy what there is to enjoy

Here is one of Nichiren's most famous quotes about problems and personally I find it oodles more useful than the 'sent to try us' platitude: 'Suffer what there is to suffer, enjoy what there is to enjoy. Regard both suffering and joy as facts of life and continue chanting Nam-myoho-renge-kyo, no matter what happens.'[1]

I have known Buddhists who base their whole lives just on these thirty-two words, re-reading them whenever the going gets rough. Or when it gets smooth. Or anything in between. Or for no reason at all. But how many of us get this advice completely back to front? Instead of suffering what there is to suffer and enjoying what there is to enjoy, why do we instead choose to suffer what there is to enjoy (for example, by thinking about work problems when we're meant to be playing with our kids)? And how often do we thoroughly enjoy what there is to suffer (I'll just wallow a bit longer in my misery, thank you very much)? And, ignoring the fact that both suffering and joy are 'facts of life', how many of us expect life to be non-stop enjoyment (indulging in mindless optimism)? Or indeed non-stop suffering (ridiculous pessimism)? I for one plead guilty to all of the above. We need to get over ourselves, don't we?

Very often our suffering comes not so much from the situation itself but rather from a misplaced belief that 'this shouldn't be happening to me'. Often we are suffering not because life is difficult but because we expect it to be easy. And 'expecting life to be easy' is a more and more prevalent attitude in a society where almost every new product or service is marketed on a promise of increased ease and convenience. In his book *The Inner Philosopher*, a dialogue written with Daisaku Ikeda, Lou Marinoff, Professor of Philosophy at The City College of New York and founding president of the American Philosophical Practitioners Association, said: '... our greatest enemies are our own deluded mind-states ... Many Westerners have been lulled by affluence and indulgence into expecting lives free of all difficulty.'[2]

As Daisaku Ikeda points out:

> True happiness is not the absence of suffering; you cannot have day after day of clear skies. True happiness lies in building a self that stands dignified and indomitable like a great palace – on all days, even when it is raining, snowing or stormy.[3]

And Nichiren says: 'Even sages are sometimes sad.' So, true happiness is not the absence of problems any more than true health is the absence of illness, or true peace is the absence of war. It's only our S-O-S that would have us believe problems are always bad news; probably because when we lived in caves, they were!

The wise rejoice and the foolish retreat

Here's another famous quote from Nichiren which sheds further light on the Buddhist attitude to problems, maintaining that truly happy people see difficulties as welcome fuel for developing their humanity and for contributing to society:

> There is definitely something extraordinary in the ebb and flow of the tide, the rising and setting of the moon, and the way in which summer, autumn, winter and spring give way to each other. Something uncommon also occurs when an ordinary person attains Buddhahood. At such a time, the three obstacles and four devils will invariably appear, and *the wise will rejoice while the foolish will retreat*.[4]

'Obstacles and devils', by the way, are Buddhist metaphors for the problems that can surface from the depths of your life when you start chanting. When faced with obstacles, happiness means knowing in your heart that, as Nichiren taught, 'the wise rejoice and the foolish retreat'.

OK, hands up, I admit that rejoicing is not always my first reaction when I'm suffering. Yes, just like anyone else, we Buddhists (here in the UK anyway) normally start tackling a problem by putting ourselves through a bit of grumbling/ avoidance strategies/bad moods/blaming (delete as appropriate). But this habit gets shorter and shallower the longer you've been chanting and the deeper your faith becomes.

Apologies if all this sounds a bit glib or flippant, because that is not the intention; I'm aware that as you read these pages, you or a loved one may be going through a seriously tough time. You may have been battling with the same difficult issue for years, and recently failed to beat it. Again. And you may feel helpless and emotionally exhausted. You may have tried loads of other techniques, so why would Nichiren Buddhism be any more effective? Or you may have lost someone close to you, or the job/house/man/woman of your dreams. Perhaps you're feeling lost, lonely, confused, desperate or even suicidal. You may be a practising Buddhist and be feeling some of these emotions as you battle with your karma – I for one have experienced versions of most of these situations in my thirty years of practice ...

Bouncing back from rock bottom

Although I've never quite felt suicidal I do remember one bright, sunny day driving down the M5 motorway thinking that if my nearside front tyre had a blow-out and I hit the next bridge at eighty mph, oblivion would be OK. Embracing that warm black void would be easier than facing another moment alive, such was the depth of the depression I felt. The illusion that death can put an end to suffering is very seductive (but, in the context of the eternity of life, is a complete myth). But such is the power of our FD.

Buddhists find that when they chant they realise that suffering is an opportunity to see that, ultimately, it is less painful to change than it is to stay the same. As author Anaïs Nin so eloquently wrote: 'And the day came when the risk it took to remain tight in a bud was more painful than the risk it took to blossom.'

That day normally comes when you hit rock bottom, so let's talk about it – because if we can crack that one, anything else will be easier. Six years ago, I decided to chant about the fact that (since time began) I've always tended to wake up in a grumpy mood. I can't pretend that I started chanting with a deep deter-mination to wake up feeling chirpy, after all I was generally quite cheerful by ten o'clock. It was more a casual decision born of curiosity and no little guilt that my bad mood too often had a negative impact on my family during breakfast and on other road users during the school run.

I would love to report that the chanting had an immediate impact and that within a week I was leaping out of bed full of the joys of spring, gambolling down to breakfast like a newborn lamb. After all, that's usually how the story goes in books like this. I would love to be able to tell you that by nine o'clock every day I had brightened the lives of my family, my neighbours, my childminder and my clients, not to mention the postman, the newsagent and the cat. I would love to, but, dear reader, none of it would be true.

The chanting did have an immediate impact, but it didn't quite follow the script my 'smaller self' had set. This is because Nam-myoho-renge-kyo goes deeper than the conscious or sub-conscious mind and because it exists to expand your life and relieve others' suffering rather than to keep you in your old thinking patterns or a small self-centred life. In short, Buddhists will say that the practice works, but we don't always like the result, at least not to begin with.

The first immediate impact of chanting to wake up feeling cheerful was that I began feeling miserable until midday rather than just ten o'clock. A week later and I was feeling blue all afternoon. By the end of the month I felt depressed all evening as well. In fact, after six weeks' chanting to have more cheerful mornings, such were my all-day feelings of despair (Hell state) that all I looked forward to was sleeping at night, because that was the only time I felt nothing – luckily I have never suffered from insomnia. This was when an accidental collision with the motorway bridge looked tempting.

But of course eight hours of sleep seemed to pass in no time, whereas the days seemed to go as slowly as a double-decker bus ploughing uphill through wet tar, and there was no reason or evidence to believe the depression would ever lift.

Did I feel like 'rejoicing' rather than 'retreating', as Nichiren suggests? Did I heck. Did I feel angry, lethargic, panicky, fragile, tearful, irritable and bleak? Nearly all the time. Did I wonder why the hell I'd started chanting about my morning mood? Just a little bit (whilst also knowing there was no turning back ...). Was I critical, distant from others and blaming them for my suffering? Absolutely. Did I feel that Buddhism was working?

Er, no, not really, certainly not after fifteen months had gone by with only one or two occasional glimmers of progress. Did I carry on chanting? Only just – the mental anguish and pain was almost enough to stop me. The epitome of Hell state.

Saying yes to the Buddha in you

It felt, as I chanted, as if my very soul was grinding on its axis. But a Buddhist friend of mine called Robert, who had been through a similar experience, said:

> This rock bottom point is the crucial moment, this moment when you realise that your life is asking to grow and that you can either say 'No' and give up or say 'Yes' and carry on. When you're a snivelling mess on the floor, and you think your FD has beaten you, this is the moment when, Nichiren says, 'poison turns to medicine'. When the negative forces have got you on your knees, they are, paradoxically, exhausted and this is the very moment to strike back. The moment when you can find total determination within your utter hopeless-ness. When one more minute of Nam-myoho-renge-kyo can defeat your FD. When gasps of despair dissolve like dew in the morning sun. You just need to say a resounding and definitive 'Yes' to the Buddha in you.

Of course being a stubborn git, I said 'No' – to begin with anyway. And so I remained stuck for a few more weeks in a surviving rather than striving mindset. As Nichiren points out: 'Foolish men are likely to forget the promises they have made when the crucial moment comes.'[5]

(By the way, I'm sure 'foolish men' includes women as well, though in my experience the fairer sex are somewhat more reliable at the crucial moment.) And I'm not sure we always 'forget' our promise (to reveal Buddhahood), but we often modify it. Or, over time, we ever so slowly soften our promises.

I was very tempted to see my GP and get some Prozac (I know Buddhists who have done so and it was definitely right for them) but in my prayer this never felt like the best way forward. Incidentally, there was no major exterior trigger for this depression.

Finally, I dragged myself to a senior SGI leader for guidance (i.e. a chat with someone who could see my Buddhahood when I no longer could). I wanted him to realise that this so-called amazing Buddhist practice was failing me miserably and that he needed to feel as sorry for me as I felt for myself. This is what he said after listening intently to me:

1. You are arrogant (this is a major cause of depression).

2. You have separated yourself from other people (a side-effect of being arrogant).

3. You are over-critical (a side-effect of being arrogant).

4. You are disrespecting life.

5. Change your family's karma of suffering from mental illness.

6. Get over yourself.

There was much more to the conversation and I have paraphrased his incredible insights but I still feel deeply grateful for his compassionate candour and the ability he had to see my Buddhahood before I dared to. He also saw my FD, those illusions we have about how life works. Illusions that protect us from the fear of changing ourselves and from taking responsibility for changing the world in which we live. Yet as illusions crumble, good stuff naturally flows into our lives. I should add that he warned me the ride ahead would definitely be bumpy and gave me his phone number so I could call if I needed support. My closest friends, fellow Buddhists and family were likewise a huge source of strength, especially when I found the courage to be vulnerable enough to share my feelings with them.

Become a brilliant beacon

I also came across these encouraging words of Daisaku Ikeda:

> Become a brilliant beacon, shining with joy and happiness and live your life with confidence and courage. If you shine with a radiant light, there can be no darkness in your life.[6]

When you realise that this is true, you stop desperately hoping for a light at the end of the tunnel, because it finally dawns on you that you, yourself, are that light. And you are that light *in the tunnel*, not on some distant horizon. And you are a light that can illuminate other people's lives when they feel desperate.

Slowly, very slowly, I developed an attitude of 'I will do whatever it takes to become the person I need to become.' And a reflex of saying to my FD gremlins: 'Come on then, if you think you're hard enough!' Little by little, almost in reverse to how the depression had started eighteen months before, I began to have the odd bright afternoon, hopeful morning or cheerful evening. Eventually I managed one whole day of the week feeling happy. Gradually one day became two and three and four. Now, five years later, I very rarely get a 'blue day' at all.

Could I have got through this depression without Buddhism? I will never know as it is impossible to turn the clock back. Perhaps counselling or coaching or Prozac could have had a positive effect, quite possibly more quickly than chanting. But I believe that *in my particular case at that time*, in terms of depth and 'sustainable performance' (as the business folks say), Nam-myoho-renge-kyo was a more powerful medicine.

When you chant, when you do your human revolution, you

strip away illusions and negative emotions, layer after layer – like an onion – until you fuse with and become the love and light at the core of you and find within you the courage to share it with others.

I will never know what 'cause' I had created that led to me feeling that desperate – as I said before it's like pulling at one strand of spaghetti on the plate of your eternal karma. I guess that somewhere along the line I deeply disrespected life itself and my goodwill account with the Universe needed to get put back in the black.

Kintsukoroi – more beautiful for having been broken

But viewed from the perspective of the present and future and the Buddha in me, I feel now that I went through that eight-een-month morass of despair because *nothing less powerful* could have made me understand the dignity of life and the depths of suffering to which people can sink. I am a wiser, less arrogant, more compassionate person because of the experience. I now really appreciate that life is precious. I am a better life coach. I am more open to others and I am better at sharing stuff (especially with other men) rather than soldiering on alone. It was the second toughest experience of my life and I shall treasure it forever. It was fast-track human revolution, even though every minute seemed agonisingly slow at the time. In the words of mythology professor and author Joseph Campbell: 'The cave you fear to enter holds the treasure you seek.' If I ever go through depression again, I don't think I will view it as an illness to be cured but as a crucible or furnace in which to forge a stronger and wiser me. I sometimes call it my 'Kintsukuroi experience', 'Kintsukoroi' being the Japanese art of repairing pottery with gold or silver lacquer and understanding that the piece is more beautiful for having been broken.

Sometimes, when I'm suffering, I still ask that backward-looking question: 'Why me? What cause did I make for this to happen?' But now, instead of futile speculation about what the answer from a past life might be, I look to the future. And the answer to the 'Why' question begins: *'So that I can ...'* become wiser/more compassionate/more respectful/more resilient (or whatever).

The main conclusion I have reached is this: if all suffering is in fact an opportunity to transform an illusion, then to call your problems 'suffering' is in itself an illusion. So, as the wise John Delnevo said: 'You have a problem? Congratulations!'

—— ✧ ——

Mindset mantras for seeing problems as a source of growth

When obstacles appear I rejoice instead of retreating.

I accept that at a karmic level I have attracted everything that happens to me, both positive and negative.

I will go through whatever it takes to become the person I need to become.

I understand that all 'suffering' is an opportunity to transform my illusions.

I say YES to the Buddha in me.

I am a brilliant beacon. When I shine with a radiant light there can be no darkness in my life.

I gradually realise that it is less painful to change than it is to stay the same.

I find the courage to blossom instead of staying in a tightly closed bud.

I find the wisdom and courage to release my illusions and allow myself to change.

No matter what, I know that my Buddhahood is ultimately stronger than my Fundamental Darkness.

Journal exercises

1. Are there areas of your life where you are enjoying what there is to suffer?

2. Are there areas of your life where you are suffering what there is to enjoy?

3. What promises have you made to yourself but then broken or softened along the way?

4. What can you learn from the times in your life when your FD has beaten you?

5. What could you do differently the next time you face a huge challenge?

CHAPTER 8

BEYOND THE SURVIVAL MENTALITY

Let's have a closer look at this notion that we over-use our survival instincts and become stuck in our S-O-S, our Survival Obsessed Self. Obviously there's nothing wrong with survival *per se*, and of course there are poverty-stricken places on this challenging planet of ours where surviving another day really is the only goal. And we wouldn't be here if our genes hadn't proved their mettle in the egg'n'sperm race/natural selection obstacle course. And you wouldn't be sitting there reading this book. And as someone who, five years ago, was just a whisker away from a fatal encounter with a 249 bus in Tooting, south London (the rush of air past my nostrils started me thinking just how precious life is), I'm not averse to having decent reflexes when I already have one unwise foot in the gutter.

It's just that I think it's time for us human beings to move on a bit, grow up (spiritually, that is) and realise that there's more to life than following the ingrained habits anchored in our survival mentality. In short, it's time to get over our smaller selves.

Does my bum look big in this?

The survival-focused brain is essentially self-obsessed, constantly monitoring itself and asking, 'Am I OK? Am I safe? Do I have enough? Do they like me? Do I look good? Do I belong? Can

I drink enough to keep up with him? Will I get the credit for this? Does my bum look big in this?' In the words of seventeenth-century English philosopher Thomas Hobbes, we are still subconsciously wired to believe that life is likely to be 'nasty, brutish, and short', a philosophy that many managers bring to the jungle of corporate life ...

I was once coaching an executive called Katie who said that at the start of her sales career, after leaving university aged twenty-two, she felt she had been pushed out of a plane but had carefully steered her parachute onto the thin ledge of a mountain to land her first corporate job. Over the years she had made this 'thin end of the ledge' wider and wider, until she felt more and more secure. When she got a directorship and her first huge bonus she 'used the money to blast a hole in the rock and then made a deep, safe cave'. Meanwhile, building a big team and expanding her role was like 'putting up a strong fence to keep out prey'. So, all that sounds good, I remember saying, what's the problem, then? 'Well, I still live in fear,' she said, 'that the whole damn thing could come crumbling down. That's why I always want more money and the next promotion – it's not greed, it's just wanting to feel safe. And, by the way, I'm terrified of dying young.' She has since quit her high-flying corporate job and is setting up her own wedding planning business, a dream she had abandoned many years before.

Incidentally, the 'will there be enough?' mindset is knowingly exploited by salesmen across the world and is known as the 'scarcity sell' – I still remember an estate agent saying, when I was looking to buy my first ever house: 'This one will be gone by the weekend, sir.' (I nearly fell for that one until my very wise wife set me straight.) And for the same reason, airline websites often say 'last seat available at this price'.

Below is a list of the kinds of behaviour we succumb to when we're subconsciously gripped by our S-O-S. Feel free to tick any that apply to you. When I just want to survive I:

1. am obsessed with keeping up with the Joneses (in case the material stuff 'runs out' and threatens my survival).

2. have 'eyes bigger than my stomach' and end up throwing good food away.

3. feel the need to be right all the time.

4. try to control how other people think and behave – that way I reduce the risk of things going wrong.

5. am envious of people who are richer and more famous than me.

6. feel the need to score brownie points with the 'leader of the tribe' (a boss in the office maybe?)

7. take the credit for other people's ideas.

8. am arrogant towards others so that they feel inferior and I feel I have more power.

9. 'name-drop' the names of famous or 'powerful' people I have met.

10. carry a knife and get my sense of security from a gang that bases its identity on a postcode.

11. get incandescently angry with Spurs fans (I support Arsenal) because of course they come from a postcode three whole miles away in North London.

12. make friends with Spurs fans because when we are both on tour supporting England there is a common enemy (Germany/Holland/Argentina/Italy) threatening the

'national pride' (Anger state) that we borrow as a thick
veneer to cover our subconscious obsession with survival.

A slow suicide of the spirit

Of the above types of action, we often say, 'Oh well, that's just
human nature' – isn't that a wonderful excuse for our less than
brilliant behaviour? Yes, it is human nature, but *only one aspect* of
it, the survival aspect – Animality in the context of the ten worlds.
The thing about all these behaviours is that in and of themselves
they're not especially destructive. None of these on its own can
land as fatal a blow as a sabre-toothed tiger. And therein lies their
very sneakiness and danger. These are all actions that, repeated
over time, can slowly corrode our optimism, steadily undermine
our potential and invisibly stifle our heart. Their grip is insidious
and, like cholesterol or cancer, the destruction can at first go
unnoticed. Nothing is sadder than seeing people experience this
slow suicide of the spirit, this gradual narrowing of the mind that
sucks away all light and joy. As nineteenth-century American
poet Henry David Thoreau famously said: 'The mass of men lead
lives of quiet desperation.'

Of course such destruction was never part of the plan. On
the contrary, behaviours based on the survival mentality have a
thoroughly positive intention – to protect your life/self-esteem/
race/country/football team. But because they are limited within
your smaller self they're highly vulnerable to the gremlin of your
Fundamental Darkness. They can be like an allergic reaction in
which the body over-defends itself against a perceived threat.
In the end, the defence is more dangerous than the threat and can
even, in extreme circumstances such as anaphylactic shock, kill
the body it's trying to protect. Speaking in early 2015 at London's
Science Museum, theoretical physicist Stephen Hawking seemed
to echo this idea: 'The human failing I would most like to correct
is aggression. It may have had survival advantage in caveman
days, to get more food, territory or a partner with whom to

reproduce, but now it threatens to destroy us all.' Exactly!

S-O-S behaviours will never create a strong and profound happiness for yourself or other people. They are based on coping rather than challenging. On achieving and ring-fencing our own little pocket of contentment, rather than sharing happiness with those around us. They are, to use the NLP jargon, 'away from' motivations – in other words, impulses that send us flying from things we don't like. Since death is usually Numero Uno on our List Of Things To Avoid, we can perhaps forgive ourselves for letting this survival mentality become so dominant – after all, it's been hardwired in our brains during 14 million years of primate evolution.

And yet there is another way: cultivating a state of life where we experience such joy that even at the end of our lives we can say: 'That was wonderful! Where shall I go next?'

Reaching beyond your small self

The challenge is that, because we're hardwired to survive, we tend only to change our attitudes when in danger, or in order to avoid something happening that we don't like. But if as individuals we remain blindly anchored in our survival mentality, then, collectively, we will only see beyond our superficial differences (such as differences of nationality, social class, religion, football teams) if, say, we are threatened by another species entirely. For example, we suddenly find ourselves facing extermination by aliens from the Planet Zorg who come from A Different Galactic Postcode: the threat of their attack would probably unite us. But just in case this sort of extra-terrestrial invasion fails to materialise any day soon, might it now be time to get over our smaller selves? To start seeing the Buddha in me and the Buddha in you? The alternative is to carry on wasting money and young lives on violent, senseless wars. As always, it's up to us.

Coming a close second to warmongering is our obsession with material wealth, motivated as it is by the worry of having nothing, of our survival being threatened – driven ultimately perhaps by our understandable but unnecessary fear of death. This obsession with consumption is something that Earth will not sustain forever. We are living in a destructive culture of entitlement on a planet screaming out for a new era of enlightenment. An era founded on a belief in the dignity and nobility of all Life – the only type of abundance that really matters.

So, once we can overcome our fear of death, by realising that Life really is eternal, we can begin to use our survival instinct wisely and only when it adds value to our existence. Instead of subconsciously placing it at the centre of our lives, we can use it in the right place at the right time to the right degree – by avoiding stepping out in front of London buses, for example. And though you can never actually *know* that life is eternal (as I've said, it's a big ask, especially in the West), try imagining and acting as if it's true – it's one of the most empowering and liberating beliefs you'll ever adopt!

Therefore (and illogical as it may seem at first sight) the best way for the human race to survive, rather than destroy itself or the planet, is for each individual and each nation to get over their default survival mentality.

How to challenge rather than just cope

In the following advice, from SGI-UK's Kazuo Fujii, the 'coping' behaviour that he so eloquently evokes is firmly rooted in the survival mentality:

> There are two ways of approaching life. The first is coping and the second is challenging to change a situation. The situation is the same but the results are different. Coping is linked to the past and our past knowledge and experiences. It is a conservative attitude, limited, restricted, passive, defensive, dependent. There is no vision and no hope. This is not Buddhism. Buddhism is about change. Changing ourselves,

society and humanity for good. The way to change is determination based on wisdom. Change is a projection towards
the future. It is positive, creative, independent, attacking and
seeking. It is an attitude of great hope and vision. Coping is
the past projecting to the present. Changing is the present
projecting to the future. We can choose. The difference
between ordinary and great lives is up to us.[1]

I have read and re-read this guidance umpteen times since 1993
because it seems to encapsulate the essential difference between
a small-minded victim mentality and the broadminded winning
attitude developed and taught by Nichiren. When I coach a new
client, one of my first priorities is to discern whether they are in
a coping or challenging mindset, because experience shows that
this can make all the difference to the results that they achieve.

There are really only two ways of looking at life: you can be
backward-looking, negative and pessimistic, or you can be forward-looking, positive and optimistic. We can flounder, or we
can flourish. Life for everyone is a constant struggle between
light and darkness, so the first decision you have to make is
whether you make this struggle a joyful combat or a painful
ordeal, whether you accept and enjoy it or refuse and endure it.
Too many people suffer not because a situation is difficult but
because they think it should be easy. And the second decision is
whether you battle on your own (which can be difficult) or with
support from others (a good idea).

So, what does a 'challenging' mindset look and feel like –
again feel free to tick any of these if they apply to you.

On the days when I do manage to embrace my bigger awakened
self and challenge instead of just coping and surviving, I:

1. am strong enough to know that it's OK to feel vulnerable.

2. trust the Universe to give me just what I need, just when I
need it, rather than trying to 'force' things to happen.

3. understand that life is eternal, so there is no need to worry and no need to hurry.

4. am as happy about other people's success as I am about my own.

5. have the courage to be myself.

6. have the compassion to understand others.

7. am able to graciously accept defeat in an argument and feel secure enough to change my point of view.

8. *systematically* and *instinctively* look for the best in everyone else, all of the time.

9. realise that we all share the same life force.

10. engage with others rather than staying locked in my protective shell.

11. give myself 100 out of 100 in the self-esteem stakes.

12. enjoy every moment, but also look forward to my next lifetime rather than dreading the end of this one.

Of course, this is not a code of conduct or a list of behaviours to copy. As we've seen, Nichiren Buddhism doesn't do commandments. The above is just a personal list of how my bigger self affects me and your own list might be very different because we are all unique.

Inner revolutions will change the destiny of humanity

This may all sound very nice and lovely but of course the question you may be asking is: how on earth do I embrace this bigger awakened self? Nichiren's answer is very simple: by revealing your own latent Buddhahood through chanting Nam-myoho-renge-kyo – then over time these more positive thought patterns, emotions and behaviours will naturally emerge. In short, Buddhists believe that chanting helps you let go of your illusions and surrender to your bigger self. That's how you begin to lose your ego and connect with the Buddha in you. Whereas when we are trapped in our narrow and arrogant survival mentality we see ourselves as separate from others and from the cosmic life force and therefore tend to focus on 'away from' goals.

When more people commit to carrying out their own human revolution, what will be the effect on communities and on the planet as a whole? Might it be truly amazing? Might loads of good stuff start happening? Doesn't that sound like a great way to live? How will you live your life today? Challenging or just coping? Winning or just getting by? Shining or just doing OK? Sharing your happiness or ring-fencing your own little pocket of contentment?

Right, that's the survival rant over, though you won't be surprised to learn that the theme will pop up again in future chapters.

But first, here is a beautiful and moving experience shared by my fellow SGI Buddhist Caroline Spokes, who spent twenty-three years battling with alcoholism, prescription drug addiction, self-harm and anorexia. At the age of thirteen she began to see psychiatrists and counsellors, making enough progress to function as a thriving 'high achiever' at school, university and work. She then went through a pattern of being admitted to private treatment centres and discharging herself against medical advice. She takes up her tale:

In 2003, at the age of twenty-five, I was introduced to Nichiren Daishonin's Buddhism through a friend I met in a recovery group for my illness. I was intrigued as to how he maintained his 'sparkle' and inner glow. I attended a local SGI meeting and initially started chanting purely to prove that it wouldn't work for me! I continued to struggle and often life seemed to be getting worse but some positive proof did occur, enough to keep me going. However, in 2006 my anorexia worsened drastically and by 2007 I had been admitted to an NHS eating disorders in-patient clinic, where I was to spend extended spells over the following years. I hated it. The rules, the food, the lack of freedom, the control. I judged and resented the treatment, staff, and patients. Despite this, I received support from Buddhists who continued to rally round, visiting me and offering crucial guidance. After yet another crisis, I continued to chant with the last bit of energy in me. Always hearing what my Buddhahood needed to hear to keep me going. As long as I wasn't giving up, I was winning, I now realise.

Gradually I learned my most fundamental need was to chant for self-respect and self-belief and gratitude, gratitude, gratitude – as I resented so much! This led to me finally realising that I had to take full responsibility for my life. Only when I chanted was I able to act and react differently, which in turn led to the nurses, patients and family responding to me differently. I have now transformed my relationship with my family!

In order to change my addictions I have had to believe I am a Buddha and chant Nam-myoho-renge-kyo with my whole heart instead of just using my head. My life has expanded. I have also been encouraged by these words of Daisaku Ikeda:

> Though you may perhaps lose trust in others, or feel defiled and broken, please remember that no one can destroy who you are. No matter how badly you have been hurt, you remain as pure as fresh snow. Having gone through what you have, there is pain and suffering in others' hearts that only you can notice. Having suffered what you have, there is true love and affection that only

you can find. There are definitely people out there who need you. If you give up on yourself, it is only you who will lose. Please have courage. Please tell yourself that you are not going to let this ordeal defeat you. Those who have suffered the most, those who have experienced the greatest sadness, have a right to become the happiest of all. What would the purpose of our Buddhist practice be, if the most miserable could not become happy? The tears you shed cleanse your life and make it shine. To live with this conviction and keep moving ever forward is the spirit of Buddhism. It is also the essence of life.[2]

My story has not ended. I live in a constant battle to transform my karma! Even today I fight with my anger, self-doubt and shame that can drown me. But this is my mission, and I hope by dedicating myself to Buddhist practice in this personal but potentially so powerful way, I can help others with similar experiences, thus making my fight and journey worthwhile.

Caroline passed away soon after sharing this experience with me. Her funeral (or celebration of her life) was the most moving and joyful I have ever attended. It was more like a wedding. Aware that her weakened body could give up at any time, she had meticulously planned her own send-off. She wanted everyone, including the men, to wear nail varnish and in case they forgot (I did...) there was a nail bar at the party that followed the ceremony. She had also hand-made dozens of colourful little cards with inspirational self-help quotes for us all to take home. I still have one on my altar. She had written a poem for the order of service, simply called 'My Buddha, Your Buddha' and it ended with these beautiful words: 'Bask in the greatness of your potential by honouring the Buddha nature within you. Unlock it, dance with it, sing with it, love with it, die with it. We are always here, I am always here, we are always together, you are never alone.'

Mindset mantras for finding your big, brave, Buddha self

I choose to connect every day with my bigger self,
the Buddha in me.

I am strong enough to know that it's OK to feel
vulnerable.

I take risks without needing to know exactly what will
happen next.

I understand that I am enough and there is enough.

I deeply trust the Universe to give me just what I need,
just when I need it.

I understand that life is eternal, so there is no need to
worry and no need to hurry.

I am as happy about other people's success as I am about
my own.

I have the courage to be myself.

I have the compassion to understand others.

I *systematically and instinctively* look for the good stuff in
everyone else, all of the time.

I engage with others rather than staying locked in my
protective shell.

I have the courage to challenge, not just cope.

Journal exercises

1. In what situations do you find your 'S-O-S' tendencies coming to the fore? What could you do differently next time?

2. In what areas of your life could you do more challenging instead of just coping?

3. Are there people whom you are jealous of? Could you learn from and feel happy for their success or find it within you to congratulate them?

4. In what ways could your life be different if you adopted the attitudes outlined in the 'mindset mantras' above?

CHAPTER 9

CULTIVATE THE TREASURES OF THE HEART

In one of his most famous writings, Nichiren said:

> More valuable than treasures in a storehouse are the treasures of the body, and the treasures of the heart are the most valuable of all. From the time you read this letter on, strive to accumulate the treasures of the heart![1]

This quote is from a letter that Nichiren wrote to one of his most determined and loyal disciples, Shijo Kingo. A samurai and skilled physician, Kingo was well known for his fiery temper and for being partial to drinking a little too much saké. He was also persecuted by his lord for his religious beliefs (in today's terms that's equivalent to being bullied by your boss) and at the time of receiving this letter, many of his lands had been confiscated (a bit like getting a written warning and having your wages slashed) … Shijo Kingo famously accompanied Nichiren to the attempted execution on Tatsunokuchi beach in 1271, prepared to die by his teacher's side.

What matters most

The above quote about the 'three kinds of treasure' defines what Buddhists believe is most important in life (or 'values', to use the life-coaching term), and as any half-decent coach will tell you, much of your happiness hinges on discovering and honouring these values. That's why Nichiren's guidance here is so relevant to modern life: by revealing what he sees as the three different 'kinds of treasure', he suggests a yardstick against which to measure what we value most. In ascending order of importance these are:

1. Treasures of the storehouse – material wealth, possessions, tangible stuff.

2. Treasures of the body – health (obviously perhaps) but this also means your skills and reputation, including fame.

3. Treasures of the heart – all the 'Buddha-You-bigger-self' qualities we've been talking about so far – courage, wisdom, compassion, gratitude, joy etc …

This ranking can be seen as a thirteenth-century forerunner of Maslow's influential hierarchy of needs [see diagram], with the 'storehouse' fitting in at levels 1 and 2, the 'body' echoing level 4 and the 'heart' chiming with the self-actualisation peak of Maslow's famous pyramid. It's worth noting, though, that the 'treasures of the heart' cover much more than is suggested by Maslow's finishing point because, amongst other differences, they encompass 'actualisation' for others, not just for yourself. In Buddhism it's possible to have treasures of the heart without owning any material wealth at all; there is not the same idea of scaling a pyramid – happiness in Buddhism is not about reaching a destination.

So let's look more closely at each of the three treasures: interestingly, and surprisingly to people who expect Buddhists

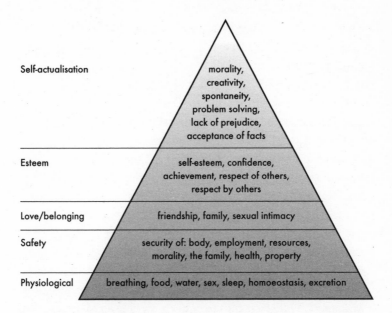

to be hermits living ascetic lives in caves, Nichiren absolutely recognised the value of material well-being (treasures of the storehouse) and the practice does encourage people to improve their physical circumstances. Over the years I've met scores of Nichiren Buddhists who've chanted with great determination for promotion at work, more money, a lovelier house or better car. Indeed, one area where Nichiren's teachings differed radically from the established beliefs of his time was his insistence that you do not need to lose your desires to attain enlightenment.

No Nirvana

The pre-Nichiren schools of Buddhism (the ones more commonly known in the West) had claimed that it was our desires that produced suffering and therefore if you had no desires you could no longer suffer – QED. Makes sense at first glance, doesn't it? And like all Buddhist teachings, this undoubtedly had value for a time. Until you realise that the desire to have no desires is a desire in itself ... And that following this route can leave you feeling numb and empty. And that to suppress your desires is to risk becoming a lardy, lumpy blob of nothing.

Of course, the dictatorial government of Nichiren's time was quite happy for people to know their place and keep their ambitions in check, all on a 'jam tomorrow' promise that when you died there would be salvation in a 'Pure Land' or nirvana (heaven) – a place whose existence Nichiren vigorously denied (see Chapter 10). Where his Buddhism is so radically different is that rather than encouraging us to selfishly follow all our desires or, at the other extreme, selflessly suppress them, or indeed veer between the two poles, he talks about *transforming* them, often using the analogy of turning 'poison into medicine'.

I once knew a Nichiren Buddhist who sincerely chanted for a woman who had hurt him to suffer a terrible accident and die, so angry did he feel about what she 'had done to him'. Because there are no moral rules in this practice, he was not advised to suppress this desire or feel ashamed of it. Because Buddhism is non-judgemental, any starting point is acceptable; practitioners trust the power of Nam-myoho-renge-kyo to drive their lives in a positive value-creating direction. His chanting slowly but surely harnessed the passion in his anger and transformed it into more positive and creative thoughts about the woman in question. He slowly began to feel respect, gratitude and even compassion towards her, realising that what she had 'done to him' was a reflection of the sediment in his own life. Thank you, Spoon.

Desires are a vital driving force

So, do Buddhists just chant a bit and magically get exactly what they want? A better job, a sexier partner, improved health, an accident befalling an enemy? No, of course not – which might, of course, sound like a cop-out and evidence that prayer doesn't work. It does work, but only on our bigger selves. Our smaller self doesn't always know what is best for us, however powerfully it claims to. By activating the bigger Buddha self, Buddhists believe they discover what really matters most in the happiness stakes.

Nichiren recognised that desires are our driving force and the fuel for our seeking spirit. Desires are a springboard to enlightenment, not an obstacle. I still find it amazing that 750 years ago, he realised that neither suppressing nor blindly following your desires is healthy in terms of your mental health, a revelation that psychology only embraced in relatively recent times.

As Nichiren wrote: 'Chanting Nam-myoho-renge-kyo during the physical union of man and woman is indeed what is called "earthly desires are enlightenment," and "the sufferings of birth and death are nirvana."'[2]

More about sex later, first let's talk about money. In and of itself, of course, money is neither good nor evil. Just like gravity and the internet, it's neutral. It's what you do with it and because of it that makes the difference and, as with everything else, that will depend on what life state you're in.

Why money won't make you happy

Chances are that when you bought this book, nestled on nearby shelves (or web pages) were all sorts of tomes guaranteeing you wealth beyond your wildest dreams. Authors promising to make you rich. Books focusing on the 'treasures of the storehouse' and so reflecting the high value that society tends to place on accumulating cash. As I've said, Nichiren Buddhism does not discourage wealth. I would hazard a guess that practitioners such as Roberto Baggio, Boy George, Orlando Bloom, Maxi Jazz (and many less famous Nichiren Buddhists) all have more than a bob or two in the bank. And there's no doubt that money can give you more options, more security and more freedom. For instance, when you want to change your mood – a constant preoccupation of the human condition – spending money is clearly a quick and easy way to a temporary high. The aforementioned stars are also pretty well off in the 'treasures of the body' (skills and fame) department – and again Nichiren did not discourage this. But he does put money, status and fame lower down the hierarchy.

The distinction he makes is that we build a fragile kind of happiness when we make money or fame, rather than Buddhahood, our 'object of worship'. When we measure our happiness only in hectares and horsepower. When we have the illusion that winning the lottery or adulation will definitely make us happy. When we forget that there are miserable people in mansions, from Birmingham to Boston to Brisbane and beyond. And 750 years ago, Nichiren pointed out that you can't take it with you:

> Though you may move among the most exalted company of court nobles, your hair done up elegantly like clouds and your sleeves fluttering like eddies of snow, such pleasures, when you stop to consider them, are no more than a dream within a dream. You must come to rest at last under the carpet of weeds at the foot of the hill, and all your jewelled daisies and brocade hangings will mean nothing to you on the road to the afterlife.[3]

It doesn't interest me what you do for a living

The emphasis placed by Nichiren on treasures of the heart – above status or wealth – is echoed in these extracts from a beautiful (and angry) poem called *The Invitation* by Oriah Mountain Dreamer:

> It doesn't interest me what you do for a living. I want to know what you ache for, and if you dare to dream of meeting your heart's longing. [...]
>
> It doesn't interest me to know where you live or how much money you have. I want to know if you can get up, after the

night of grief and despair, weary and bruised to the bone, and do what needs to be done to feed the children. [...]

I want to know if you can be alone with yourself and if you truly like the company you keep in the empty moments.[4]

The author had just returned from a party where the sole topics of conversation had revolved around the 'treasures of the storehouse' – money, status and possessions. So, next time someone asks: 'How are you?', don't just tell them what you've got, or what has happened or even what you've been doing – share with them also the soundtrack of your mind. (Note: if you are a man, you may find this quite hard at first.)

I have known wealthy people who live in a state of permanent anxiety that they could lose it all and are constantly trying to reinforce their 'cave' on that 'thin end of the ledge' as my coaching client Katie called it. Others who would swap all their millions just for a good night's sleep. There are many big lottery winners who wish they'd never won such a huge fortune. And men (mostly) who have cashed in their deeper values for a swanky business card, executive jet and five-star hotels. And then come home one night to discover that their wife and kids have upped and left, because they no longer recognise the loving husband and father that the family once adored. Stephen Covey memorably describes this scenario as a man reaching the top of the ladder only to realise that it's 'leaning against the wrong wall'.

In my own experience, I still feel a twinge of regret that I spent three years in a global job as a director of a multinational, feeling more and more attached to my status (car, business card, posh hotels ...) while losing connections with friends, family and fellow Buddhists. In short, I was too busy wanting to look important to keep sight of what really was important. Luckily a change at the top saw the company let me go and this brought me crashing down to a place where I rediscovered the treasures of the heart. One minute I was on a private jet flying to a board meeting in the South of France and a few months later I was spending my way through my employer's severance package, scratching around for bits of freelance work and watching too much daytime TV. Perhaps the upside of the current global recession will see humanity re-evaluate what matters most, focusing on the treasures of the heart, not just the storehouse. In the words of ecological economist Tim Jackson: 'We spend money we don't have on things we don't need to make impressions that don't last on people we don't care about.'

To pursue money at the expense of other kinds of treasure can therefore lead ultimately to the destruction of yourself and of those around you, not to mention the environment. Or just dissatisfaction, emptiness and a nagging restlessness: isn't there more to life than this? If you make your happiness depend on any external factor (such as money or food), you will ultimately be disappointed. If you escape into hedonistic pleasures every time you have a problem, you will perpetuate your suffering. If you choose to stay in a miserable marriage because you can't bear to lose the house that you share together, you're putting the storehouse above the heart and will ultimately be unhappy. As someone so eloquently wrote: 'People were created to be loved, things were created to be used. The reason why the world is in chaos is because things are being loved and people are being used.'[5]

Comfort eating is another method we use to change the way we feel; my wife calls this kind of fake therapy 'putting in, putting in' – rather than drawing out the treasures we have in our hearts. In the Viagra generation we strive to make ourselves happier by making pleasures last longer; in fact we pursue longer and longer pleasures instead of deeper happiness. We could all do our bit to reduce global warming by learning to draw on our inner resources instead when we want to change the way we feel. As author and activist Kalle Lasn says: 'Our present system is ecologically unsustainable and psychologically corrosive. It screws our planet, and it screws our mind.'[6]

Now I've got the life I wanted, do I want the life I've got?

But it's easy to see why pursuing wealth is a seductive option. After all, the more cash you have, the greater your chances of survival. We can buy faster cars, build higher walls around ourselves, ring-fence our happiness and gain admiration from those who have less than us. In the end, though, valuing only wealth will impoverish our spirit. That's why people often reach an impasse once they've achieved all their status and material goals. It's a case of: 'Now I've got the life I wanted, do I want the life I've got?'

And of course poverty can also enrich us. I've weathered my third recession since leaving university and have (in hindsight at least) needed the experience every time it has come my way – without fail it has been valuable. On each occasion, I have found more or better work by making my conviction in my Buddhahood deeper than the recession. I'm not pretending I'd immediately leap for joy if my biggest corporate client were to dump me tomorrow, but I'd be much more likely now than I used to be to welcome the experience as a gift rather than begrudge it. And, of course, compared to the material poverty of people in places like Darfur, my occasional cash-flow issues are on a completely different scale.

What you become is more important than what you have

Nichiren also makes a really useful distinction between conspicuous and inconspicuous benefits. Or as I prefer to call them, tangible and intangible rewards. The tangible stuff is that better car, house, job, holiday, whatever – the 'treasures of the storehouse'. But the main benefit is not the visible benefit, *it's the person you've become to achieve it*. What illusion or limiting belief you've overcome. What you've understood, realised or learned. To borrow from Plato, what 'virtues' you've developed. Or, to use the words of Martin Seligman, what 'signature strengths' you have acquired. Buddhists believe that this is the really important and intangible stuff – the 'treasures of the heart'. Perhaps you've become more supportive, more confident and more grateful. More responsible, more determined or more patient. More respectful or more spontaneous. Perhaps you're laughing or smiling more. Worrying less. Being more *you* and with a deeper understanding of *us* too.

Amassing 'treasures of the heart' means developing the mental and spiritual capacities to have genuine fulfilment, a bright spirit, self-control, conviction, a sense of justice, courage, empathy and compassion. All of these qualities will improve your relationships and, as recent happiness studies show, such as Professor Ryan Howell's research at San Francisco State University, it is happy relationships and experiences rather than money that bring us true fulfilment. Think about the goals you set for yourself. Are any of them focused on treasures of the heart?

I once asked actress and SGI member Cathryn de Prume if Hollywood was a tough and competitive place where you had to be ruthless to reach the top (this was my assumption from the outside looking in). But her answer surprised me: 'The real movers and shakers who I've met, such as heads of studios, acclaimed directors, many A-list actors – do you know what I've noticed? They are kind. They are warm, they have courage and compassion. They have a high life state. And that's why they do well in Hollywood.' Incidentally, the people she mentioned were not necessarily Buddhists, but they clearly were enlightened human beings with an abundance of treasures of the heart. Explaining the value of her own daily chanting, she added: 'Thanks to my Buddhist practice, I can develop myself. It's a daily effort, like brushing your teeth, and I do it every day because otherwise the plaque comes back! Chanting creates a higher life state. And when you have a high life state, you make better causes for your own and others' happiness.'

A revolution from the inside out

Developing stronger and stronger treasures of the heart is the process that Nichiren Buddhism calls human revolution and, unlike politics (in which we usually place our greatest hopes of change), it is a profound transformation from the inside out rather than the outside in. It brings a deep sense of well-being, feelings of peace but also of excitement, a sense of individual purpose but also of shared humanity.

All these qualities, the ones that most people agree they would like to see more of in society, are what Nichiren terms the 'treasures of the heart'. These examples that we are all able to identify yet seem to find so hard to reveal, stuck as we are in our S-O-S attachments to money, status and fame. That's why the 'If' poem by Rudyard Kipling has made such a huge impact on people over the years – because it focuses on character not status, on the intangible rather than measurable qualities required to become 'a man'. As he famously wrote: 'If you can meet with Triumph and Disaster, and treat those two impostors just the same ...'

Treasures of the heart cannot be destroyed

I think Kipling would agree with the Buddhist view that unlike the treasures of the storehouse and body, the treasures of the heart cannot be destroyed, taken away, burgled or burned. They cannot go bankrupt or walk out the door. Sure, they can temporarily go into hiding but they're always there ('now you see them, now you don't') ready to manifest on the surface. And of course they cannot be valued in monetary terms. And, says Buddhism, you do take them with you into your next lifetime.

Too often we tend only to seek the treasures of the heart when we have hit a major problem in which we have lost treasures of the body and the storehouse. We seem to kid ourselves that we can only develop spiritual qualities without worldly distractions – influenced perhaps by ancient tales of Brahmans carrying out ascetic practices or of monks, nuns and hermits suppressing their earthly desires.

The treasures of the heart are also inherently democratic because, unlike, for example, athletic or intellectual prowess, we're all equally capable of developing them. Even if I chanted Nam-myoho-renge-kyo till I was blue in the face, I know for a fact that I will never play for Arsenal – even when my knees didn't go 'snap crackle and pop' I was bloody awful at football. But I feel that the more I chant, the more I can develop the wisdom, courage and compassion that are so highly valued in Nichiren Buddhism. And that this, more than anything else, will make the soundtrack of my mind – and those around me – more joyful. And how do you put a price on that?

Singer-songwriter Meri Everitt can help us answer that question in this experience that she shared with me, where she recounts how her Buddhist practice has helped her overcome the trauma of rape, express her creative talent and rebuild her relationship with her mother.

When I first started to chant I suddenly noticed the colour of the trees and how beautiful they were. Even at twenty-four years of age I had already forgotten. When I met the practice I had struggled with bouts of depression lasting up to around three weeks at a time. I was very lost in terms of my career, having worked abroad after graduating from university. I didn't know where I wanted to live or what I wanted to do and my love life was very rocky too. I hadn't come to terms with the sexual abuse in my past or the problems I had with my family. I was working in a job I hated and felt very little hope for the future, which manifested in me drinking most nights after work.

When I started chanting the first guidance I received was to chant for the happiness of a boyfriend after I had found him in bed with someone else. This wasn't by any means natural but I did it anyway. I ended up making friends with the girl I had found him with and getting back with the guy for another three years, who at one point chanted to be able to tell me he loved me in a way that would really touch my heart. And it did! He admitted that he had been chanting for that in secret. (He was not chanting when we met.)

I also chanted for justice some years after I had been raped as a teenager, because I felt I needed to move my life forward and had not done so at the time as I mistakenly thought it had been my fault. Chanting really increases my self-esteem every day. I ended up contacting a DJ whose music I was introduced to by the guy who raped me. Then we made a record together! I didn't have any prior experience of creating dance music so it was a very unexpected first official release. It was played on UK national radio. This is how to transform negatives into positives and how to turn something painful into a treasure of the heart.

The most wonderful benefit from my Buddhist practice is finding love and respect for my mother. It's taken twelve years but it's the greatest joy for me. Better than money or health. I never understood her and I resented her past anger. Now I realise that much of what I love about being me, I owe to her. Despite having some counselling for family issues after I had begun chanting, I still found the relationship with my mother so difficult. I didn't feel understood when I was diagnosed with fibromyalgia or depression and many of our conversations would end in arguments and tears. It felt impossible to get on with her. Something clicked fairly recently after I had some experience of abuse in a relationship. I was supported by Women's Aid (a UK charity) to take part in the Freedom Programme, which taught me more about abuse and manipulation. I started to see my mother's life from a different perspective. Most importantly, I realised that her anger wasn't my fault.

She has become more understanding of my various illnesses and we have a mutually supportive and much more loving relationship now. There was one point where she asked me for advice recently. I really felt something had changed then and felt trusted, which was wonderful.

After I received my Gohonzon I really had no idea what direction I wanted to take with my life. I chanted to see my heart's desires clearly and remembered I was a musician – until this point I had put music on the back burner to the point where I really had no time for it and did not recognise myself as a songwriter in any way, despite playing guitar and writing songs since I was sixteen. Becoming a musician has not been an easy journey as the norms of life I wanted to live by did not involve this. My personal norms and needs had not been based on accumulating treasures of the heart but my true heart's desire uncovered by my chanting was to pursue a life where I treasure my heart.

My fibromyalgia has consistently stopped me doing anything other than music. I'm still working so hard to have faith after ten years that I can succeed, despite the fact that every year there has been a substantial breakthrough. For example, last year my band, Flying Kangaroo Alliance, released a song on vinyl through an independent record label who asked for absolutely nothing in return. I often write when I feel low and normally writing brings me back into positivity. Creating something, anything, from a dark place is a powerful way to transform negativity. My music is aimed at those who feel alone at times, or those who feel sad or angry. I want people to feel there is someone who understands because I think that's the most important thing anyone can feel when they are in a dark place. This is a manifestation of my wish to help other people treasure their own hearts, regardless of what mood they are in!

The treasures of the heart are the most important of all. I'm not always so rich in treasures of the storehouse or the body, having been poor often and having had various health problems, but I am so very very rich in the treasures of the heart: precious memories, good friends and there is always someone there for me when I feel bad, however random the connection might feel. To be honest I am always protected anyway in terms of the treasures of the 'storehouse' and 'body', with the amazing good fortune I have accumulated through chanting. I have attracted phenomenal healthcare professionals and important concrete benefits. For example I currently live in a three-bedroomed house for free.

When I'm faced with problems, I no longer think 'why me?' (not for too long anyway and certainly not non-stop for three weeks like I used to!). Instead I think – what can I do with this suffering to transform it into something positive? How can I inspire others with this? I WILL overcome this and show others that they too can transform their problems and unhappiness! I also have this inner knowledge that when something really horrible is happening, there will be a breakthrough and the nastier the run-up to something, the more successful it will be and the happier I will feel.

Ultimately, the more I cherish myself, the more my environment treasures me. This is not an easy road when a person has suffered many unjust experiences, but I can guarantee that it is an exceptionally worthwhile effort. Daisaku Ikeda states: 'Hardships make us strong. Problems give birth to wisdom. Sorrows cultivate compassion. Those who have suffered the most will become the happiest.'[7]

The heart always wins in the end

The leaders I really admire in society (whether they're Buddhists or not) are the ones who've understood that it's the heart that moves other people to action, that gets stuff changed, that makes the world a better place. People like black civil rights activist Rosa Parks, Northern Irish Nobel Peace Prize winner Betty Williams or anti-poverty campaigner Bob Geldof. It is their passion, compassion, courage and determination that have inspired people to follow them and to generate a momentum for social reform. When it comes to inspirational leadership, it is the heart rather than intellectual argument that always wins the day. And a mighty heart is forged only in the heat of battle with your own Fundamental Darkness. How, after all, can you fight for another's happiness if you are not battling with your own demons?

Incidentally, if you're wondering what happened to good old Shijo Kingo, he managed to rebuild his relationship with his boss Lord Ema after curing him of a grave illness. As a result he got his lands back. And then some. But I'd guess that what was more impressive was the man he became and the character he developed above and beyond all those fine acres, and the fact that 750 years later he is a hugely inspirational figure to millions of Nichiren Buddhists around the globe.

— ❖ —

Mindset mantras for cultivating the treasures of the heart

I understand that all my desires can be a springboard to enlightenment.

I treasure the energy within my desires, even the ones that seem destructive.

I am beginning to see that the treasures of the heart are the most important of all.

I feel grateful that the treasures of the heart can never be destroyed.

I am already revealing many such treasures in my daily life and there are many more still to discover.

I decide to start a revolution from the inside.

The person I am becoming is more important than the things I own.

I have a strong seeking spirit and want to become absolutely happy.

Journal exercises

1. What are you currently most focused on? Treasures of the body? The storehouse? The heart?

2. What are the upsides and downsides of this approach?

3. Do you ever feel you are trying to 'ring-fence' your parcel of happiness, keeping the rest of the world at arm's length?

4. When do you find yourself spending money on 'stuff' rather than facing your own demons?

5. What might happen if you stopped and looked your FD straight in the eye instead?

6. Take a look back at the greatest achievements in your life. What qualities (or 'treasures of the heart') did you need to draw on and develop to achieve these goals?

7. What treasures or qualities would you still like to develop? What stretch goals could you set yourself that would require you to bring such treasures to the surface of your life?

CHAPTER 10

LIVING IN THE MOMENT – HAPPINESS HERE AND NOW

When Nichiren began to spread his teachings, the dominant school of Buddhism in Japan was the Pure Land sect, which advocated asking a Buddha called Amida for salvation so you would reach heaven (the 'Pure Land' believed to be 'in the West') after you died. After studying all of Shakyamuni's teachings, and all the Buddhist schools of his time, Nichiren came to a radically different conclusion, which the ruling authorities found inconvenient because it went against their 'jam tomorrow' promise of happiness in nirvana:

> First of all, as to the question of where exactly hell and the Buddha exist, one sutra states that hell exists underground, and another sutra says that the Buddha is in the west. Closer examination, however, reveals that both exist in our five-foot body.[1]

Perhaps not everyone was actually quite so petite in thirteenth-century Japan, but you get the picture and even if you're a seven-foot colossus, the principle remains the same – Buddhism says that heaven and hell are not places outside us, they both exist in our hearts or minds, which, Nichiren maintained, create the culture we live in:

There are not two lands, pure or impure in themselves. The difference lies solely in the good or evil of our minds. It is the same with a Buddha and an ordinary being. While deluded, one is called an ordinary being, but when enlightened one is called a Buddha. This is similar to a tarnished mirror that will shine like a jewel when polished.[2]

Incidentally, when Nichiren uses the word 'pure', he's not referring to moral propriety, but rather to a mind unclouded by illusions. And if you're wondering why a mirror would need regular polishing (through daily prayer), it's because in those days mirrors were made of brass not glass.

Comfort and consolation are not enough

So in his usual revolutionary way, Nichiren challenged the notion of heaven and hell as physical places that we go to when we die, putting them instead firmly in the hearts of human beings in the here and now, and in the environment we have created around us. Again, this 'no nirvana' notion would have been unpopular with the imperial rulers of the time, who favoured a teaching that threatened the disobedient with eternal damnation while rewarding the compliant with paradise – but only after they died. Not a huge surprise perhaps.

And remember, when life felt really awful in that era, you were supposed to console yourself with the thought that when all the pain was over you'd get your place in nirvana. After all, consolation and comfort are the son and daughter of our over-used S-O-S mentality. By contrast, Nichiren's message is empowering and optimistic: ours is a world of suffering and there is *everything* we can do about it.

Belief in some other-world paradise did of course come with the promise of everlasting life. I'm amazed how seductive this promise can seem, this offer of eternal life. Your life is *already* eternal – always has been, always will be … It's like that old story about the management consultant who nicks your watch off you then charges you a hefty fee to tell you the time!

Why did Nichiren preach so passionately against a belief in heaven as being a separate place to be reached at a later date? The answer is because he felt such deep compassion for people in the here and now. For the suffering of his fellow people in a nation afflicted by plague, floods, drought, famine and Mongol invasion. In his view, all of this suffering was itself hell, an 'impure land' perfectly reflecting clouded minds and distorted views.

Improving the fabric of society

It followed therefore, from the teaching that our minds create our environment, that if people could overcome their illusions, then the bad stuff would gradually stop happening around them and a 'Pure Land' – a dynamic peaceful nation – would be created. This was Nichiren's ultimate goal, his deepest wish and his life's mission – to fundamentally improve the fabric of society by raising the life state of the people in it. A mission that has been picked up and reignited by the three successive Presidents of the SGI: Tsunesaburo Makiguchi (1871–1944), Josei Toda (1900–1958) and Daisaku Ikeda (b.1928).

And so, I hear you ask, what relevance can this possibly have to me here and now? Quite a lot, I would argue. For even though many of us no longer believe in the nirvana portrayed by some schools of Buddhism or the heaven described in the Bible, we still have a profound subconscious belief that happiness can only be experienced in another place at a different time and with different people – rather than here and now, with the family, friends, enemies, colleagues, neighbours and strangers who are already in our lives.

The powerful myth of 'I'll be happy when …'

Very often I hear clients say things like, 'I can't wait till …' or 'I'll be happy when …', or 'it will all be OK as soon as …' (tick any that apply to you):

1. I stop work;

2. the kids leave home;

3. I'm on that beach in Turkey;

4. I'm in the pub;

5. I get a new office/job/boss/girlfriend/boyfriend;

6. my husband starts working harder;

7. we move to our retirement home in Spain;

8. I've got my feet up in front of the TV;

9. I've had my breasts enlarged/reduced;

10. I'm driving my new Jag.

But if we're busy looking forward to all of the above, we are failing to live in the moment – emotionally and spiritually, at least. It's all too easy to disconnect from our kids on Saturday afternoon if we're constantly looking forward to watching TV in the evening; and we'll probably have a miserable time at work if we're always thinking about retirement. Similarly, how many of us have experienced days when we're dying for the weekend to come, only to spend Saturday and Sunday dreading the arrival of Monday morning?

Nichiren Buddhism does not dispute that all the things in the above list – or whatever floats your boat – can bring a temporary rush of pleasure or even rapture; that each may be a well-deserved reward ('treasure of the storehouse') for risks taken and noble efforts made. But they're all examples of relative, conditional happiness, often based on Hunger state – rather than absolute unconditional happiness (treasures of the heart) based on Buddhahood.

Mirroring and aggravating this 'I'll be happy when ...' mindset is a multi-billion-dollar global advertising and marketing industry, in which each product or service tries to convince us that we can't possibly be happy here and now, because – wait for it – we haven't bought one of these yet! In other words, every purchase that a shopaholic convinces themselves they need is rooted in that subconscious 'heaven mindset'.

Happiness here and now

And you'll often find that the new car or the villa in Spain or the new boss or the bigger/smaller breasts are not quite as fantastic as you imagined they would be. After all, you still carry your karmic goodwill account with you, interacting with the Law of cause and effect wherever you are and attracting challenges into your life.

Yet such is the mirage we create in our clouded minds, fantasies that have their roots buried deep in the heaven myth – the terrible notion that happiness cannot be found in the here and now. Might it be time to realise that a nirvana or heaven in the sky is nothing more than a seductive figment of our powerful survival-driven imaginations?

The heaven myth might also explain our tendency to procrastinate in this sort of circular fashion:

- I'll spend more time with my kids when work calms down.
- I'll treat my wife better when my mum's not ill.
- I'll look after my mum more when my kids need me less.

There will always be problems and challenges that stop us taking action, unless we have a big enough life state to see them for the gifts that they are. As SGI Buddhist Jan Hillgruber said: 'Reality is created. It is the result of action. If we do not have the courage or imagination to choose and then create our own reality, someone else will do it for us. The future is a vacuum that fills itself with reality when it becomes the present.'

Do it now, not tomorrow

In a letter to a woman called Niike, Nichiren vividly describes the dangers of procrastination in a famous story about the Kankucho bird:

> Deep in the Snow Mountains lives a bird called the cold-suffering [Kankucho] bird that, tortured by the numbing cold, cries that it will build a nest in the morning. Yet when day breaks, it sleeps away the hours in the warm light of the morning sun without building its nest. So it continues to cry vainly throughout its life. The same is true of human beings.[3]

And Shakyamuni himself pointed out that theoretical knowledge has little value: 'If you know but do not do, you do not know.' Action, therefore, is the gap between the known and unknown.

From my own experiences I have learned that wisdom without action produces only regrets (and incidentally, action without wisdom can do much the same).

I once coached a client whose career was stagnating and who was desperate to leave her secure but soulless job with a big corporation and set up her own business. She conceded she had behaved like the Kankucho bird, never quite finding the courage to take the leap into freelance life, other than making some half-hearted 'toe in the water' efforts. As our conversation progressed she suddenly went very quiet. I felt she was having an epiphany and was looking for the words to express it, so I also stayed silent and waited for her insight to bubble to the surface. Then she said: 'I've just realised that I'm scared of starting my own business because I believe for some reason that I have to be perfect all the time and people will soon realise that I'm not. That's why I'm stuck and am going round in circles.' Such is the paralysis created by perfectionism.

God – the Mystic Law with a beard on?

The notion that there is no heaven or hell follows from the Buddhist principle that there is no God or Creator. In Nichiren's view there is only me and you and the Mystic Law. My guess is that, quite early on, human beings perceived the Mystic Law of cause and effect or the 'universal life force' or the 'law of attraction'; however, they couldn't quite get their heads around something so abstract or understand how something so powerful could be impersonal, and they therefore mapped human characteristics onto it. (Male characteristics, to be precise, even though the Law is genderless.) From this perspective, it could be argued that it was man who made God, rather than the other way round.

By the way, it is not my intention here to disrespect people who believe in an omnipotent God as Creator. There are definitely people who manifest the incredible wisdom, courage and compassion of Jesus in their lives, practising their faith sincerely and wholeheartedly. Indeed it could be argued that the Christian who does so can create more value in the world than a half-hearted Nichiren Buddhist. I still retain many of the aspirations I had as a Catholic – to be more forgiving, to be more loving, and I can still sometimes feel a warm bond with Jesus or feel very moved by beautiful hymns. It's just that I personally believe Buddhism provides me with the tools and philosophical framework to achieve these goals more effectively.

And although many people are drawn to Buddhism precisely because it has no concept of God, the Eastern and Western belief systems are perhaps more similar than they first appear. For if you take the personality and morality out of sin (actions that bring punishment) and out of virtue (actions that bring reward), you get something close to the Buddhist notion of an impersonal law of cause and effect. So in a sense God is the 'Mystic Law with a beard on'.

Because belief in Buddha as a god to be worshipped was so ingrained in thirteenth-century Japan, Nichiren frequently wrote letters to dispel this notion – here's another of his famous quotes:

> You must never think that any of the eighty thousand sacred teachings of Shakyamuni Buddha's lifetime [...] are outside yourself. Your practice of the Buddhist teachings will not relieve you of the sufferings of birth and death in the least unless you perceive the true nature of your life. If you seek enlightenment outside yourself, then your performing even ten thousand practices and ten thousand good deeds will be in vain. It is like the case of a poor man who spends night and day counting his neighbour's wealth but gains not even half a coin.[4]

That's right, you have the answers inside you – as any half-decent life coach will also remind you. You yourself are a Buddha. As Nichiren says: 'If you seek enlightenment outside yourself, [it] will be in vain.' Yet we do precisely that all the time, don't we? Many of us no longer believe in God, but just as retirement/TV /new shoes/holidaying in Spain are forms of surrogate heavens, so we often look for surrogate god figures in our lives: that one person who will 'make' us happy, such as a new lover, boss, business partner or friend, for example. And if we see the divine as being only outside ourselves, we are likely to be over-seeking of approval from others. To think the divine exists only outside us is as absurd as believing that it lies only within us.

The divine is within you and you are within the divine

So what relevance can this teaching possibly have to us here and now? Quite a lot, I would argue. For even though many of us no longer believe in the various personalities attributed to God (loving, wrathful, creative, judgemental), teachings about this sort of Supreme Being have left many of us with a profound subconscious belief that can cause great suffering. The legacy is our tendency to believe in an external locus of control – in somebody or something outside ourselves that can be blamed if things go wrong and thanked if things go right. Our lover, boss, business partner or friend, for example. Or Fate, or the stars, or Friday the thirteenth or black cats crossing our path.

The concept is deeply embedded in our language. For example, most days we can read stories in the media about actors/singers/footballers battling booze/drugs/a gambling addiction. From a Buddhist perspective, this perceived state of combat is not true. The actor/singer/footballer is battling with the Hell or Hunger state *inside him* that makes drinking, injecting or gambling seem like the best way to change how he is feeling. Admittedly that's far too long for a tabloid headline, but from a Buddhist point of view it's a more accurate diagnosis. In short, the 'divine' (or 'Buddhahood') is within us, but we are also within the divine (as entities of the Mystic Law).

We are essentially brilliant, not inherently sinful

Nichiren, in advising against looking outside ourselves for enlightenment, is clearly arguing for an internal locus of control, thereby urging us to accept complete personal accountability and responsibility for our circumstances. Buddhism is sometimes misrepresented as being a purely introspective navel-gazing belief system, but this is to ignore the mindset it promotes, which acknowledges that we are all essentially inseparable from the universal life force, rather than advocating a mindset based on our small self or ego.

Crucially, Nichiren Buddhists believe that people are essentially wonderful, but that we are rough or encrusted diamonds that need polishing so that we can become incredible human beings. The Buddhist focus is on brilliance rather than sin. On the surface the practice of faith can look similar, but the difference in perspective/starting point could not be more profound. As Daisaku Ikeda says:

> Prayer is the courage to persevere. It is the struggle to overcome our own weakness and lack of confidence in ourselves. It is the act of impressing in the very depths of our being the conviction that we can change the situation without fail. Prayer is the way to destroy all fear, the way to banish sorrow, the way to light a torch of hope. It is the revolution that rewrites the scenario of our destiny. Believe in yourself! Devaluing yourself is contrary to Buddhism, because it denigrates the Buddha state of being within you. Prayer is the effort to align the gears of our life with the movement of the universe. Prayer is the key that opens door after door to the full potential in each individual.[5]

Prayer is about deciding, not begging

Prayer in Buddhism is about deciding and determining rather than asking or begging. Furthermore, as Ikeda says, it never ends with the mere act of prayer:

> Prayer by itself isn't enough. Just as an arrow flying toward its target contains the full power and strength of the archer who shot it, our prayer contains all of our efforts and actions. Prayer without action is just wishful thinking, and action without prayer will be unproductive.[6]

Because Buddhists believe that we are all potentially Buddhas, the main choice is whether we decide to reveal our brilliance or not. We all have the golden opportunity to accept the invitation

Life has given us, to choose whether or not to honour our own and other people's highest potential.

So, to summarise:

1. Heaven does not exist as a place, only as a concept to stop you from living in the moment.

2. Your life is eternal, whether you believe in a theistic superpower or not.

3. The concept of 'God' can be seen as an anthropomorphic interpretation of the Mystic Law of Life.

4. Even if you don't believe in God or heaven, you may still subconsciously attribute your happiness to an external locus of control (including shopping or a new lover) or you may postpone it to another time and place.

5. We are all essentially brilliant rather than essentially sinful.

6. Prayer is about deciding and taking action, not wishing and waiting.

The best of both worlds?

But as philosopher Jules Evans points out on his blog (www. philosophyforlife.org), pluralism, moral relativism and neo-liberalism can leave us feeling 'atomised, disconnected, and lacking a sense of the common good'. That's why the most admirable aspect of theistic religions is that belief in God brings an awareness of a greater power at work in the Universe, which accords with the Buddhist view that we are part of the Mystic Law. But the downside of theistic doctrines can be a resulting lack of self-empowerment and self-esteem, combined with rules that stifle individual expression (e.g. teachings that forbid homosexuality).

Similarly, the upside of personal development teachings is that we recognise our own brilliance; whereas the downside can be self-centredness, a sense of 'entitlement' and ignorance of the universal life force. It seems to me that Buddhism provides the upsides of both theistic and personal development teachings, but with neither of their downsides. And in the long term, in my view, it may prove to be the more relevant teaching and the tool that takes humanity to its next level of spiritual evolution.

Is it profound? Complete? Practical? Inclusive?

When considering other philosophies and ways of life, I always ask myself these four questions:

1. Is it profound – does it reach deep inside the heart?

2. Is it complete – does it answer all the difficult questions about life?

3. Is it practical – can we use it every day? Does it work?

4. Is it inclusive – can anyone do it?

Buddhism ticks these boxes for me, but if I ever found another philosophy that did the job more powerfully, I would practise it. Here is some useful advice to discourage blind faith:

> Do not believe in anything simply because you have heard it. Do not believe simply because it has been handed down for many generations. Do not believe in anything simply because it is spoken of and rumoured by many. Do not believe in anything simply because it is written in Holy Scriptures. Do not believe in anything merely on the authority of teachers, elders or wise men.

Who said this? Why, Shakyamuni, of course! In other words, Buddhism is empirical, it is designed to be tested.

Mindset mantras for living in the moment

Happiness is here and now, not if and when.

I am always fully present 'in the moment'.

I realise that my life energy is eternal.

I value my life enough to take action today as well as tomorrow.

Every day I find the courage to persevere.

I choose to honour my highest potential.

Journal exercises

1. Think of examples of when you've felt 'I'll be happy when ...' such and such has happened. Could you live more in the moment and less at the mercy of future events?

2. Think about the books, websites and magazines you read and the news programmes you watch or listen to. How much do they help you turn up the volume on the good stuff in your heart?

3. In what areas of your life are you procrastinating like a Kankucho bird? What needs to change for you to take action now?

4. What more could you achieve in your life if you spent more energy deciding and taking action and less time wishing and waiting?

5. Look at your current belief system and ask yourself: Is it profound – does it reach deep inside the heart? Is it complete – does it answer all the difficult questions about life? Is it practical – can you use it every day? In short, does it work?

CHAPTER 11

DETERMINATION THROUGH THE UPS AND DOWNS

Chapter 7 may have made a huge and lasting impact in the depths of your life, but just in case it didn't, let's revisit the whole business of suffering. But this time we're going to explore it from the perspective of determination. Or, as my nineteen-year-old daughter calls it, 'stickability'. Let's find out how Buddhism can guide us through the magnificent undulations of daily life ...

Determination is an oft-recurring theme in Buddhism. In fact a famous definition of a 'Buddha' is 'one who perseveres'. Nichiren Daishonin was twice exiled by the government of his day, spending three years living in a dilapidated shrine in a desolate graveyard on the remote island of Sado. Discarded corpses surrounded his dwelling and he was not expected to survive the harsh winter conditions. The whole area was knee-deep in snow, yet in these conditions he produced some of his most important writings, relying on the kindness of strangers who risked their lives to bring him food, drink and writing ink.

While Nichiren survived the attempted decapitation, as well as some other equally unsuccessful attempts on his life, the persecution did not stop at him. Many of his followers were oppressed, some were executed, and many others stopped practising his teachings. Far from complaining about all these challenges, Nichiren saw them as proof that his teachings were correct, fulfilling the prophecy in the Lotus Sutra that its votary would be attacked; so he refused to bow or bend to the authorities. Obstacles, he realised, come with the territory when you stand up for the happiness of all humanity. As he famously wrote in a letter to a close disciple: 'And still I am not discouraged.'

Keep right on to the end of the road

After Nichiren's death in 1282 his teachings hung by the most fragile of threads until freedom of religion reached post-war Japan in 1945. And even now, in modern-day Japan, members of Soka Gakkai (the largest Nichiren movement in the country and the world) face a degree of opposition, mainly from the tabloid press.

Nichiren urged his followers to develop deep determination, 'as if you are trying to strike fire from damp sticks or extract water from hard ground'. And in his famous 'Letter to Niike' he talks about literally keeping right on to the end of the road in order to reach the [then] capital city of Kyoto: 'For example, the journey from Kamakura to Kyoto takes twelve days. If you travel for eleven but stop with only one day remaining, how can you admire the moon over the capital?'[1]

(You may be relieved to know, by the way, that the journey now takes less than two hours, but you get the point ...)

Interestingly, when Nichiren Buddhists talk about what they want to achieve in their lives (for example at the start of a new year) they tend to use the word 'determinations' rather than 'goals'. And because we do not believe that the divine exists outside us, prayer in Buddhism is not about asking, begging or bargaining with a deity. It is not about yearning. It is about deciding and determining. Again and again. Over and over.

If you are still not achieving what you want in a certain area of your life, despite huge efforts, then resolve to change at an even deeper level than before, at a karmic level, digging into that wonderful Buddha-core of you. (Harsh as it may sound, in all likelihood you would already have a result if you had changed at that very deepest level.) So if you are struggling to achieve a goal, ask yourself, 'How badly do I really want it? How much do I really believe I deserve it? And how much action have I consistently taken to make it happen?' When I am working with clients to check or boost their motivation levels I often say: 'Tell me about a time when you cared enough to keep going, despite seemingly impossible obstacles.'

Drug addicts have incredible determination

As with everything else in Buddhism, the key is to understand in your heart that every moment and every life is precious. Then you can point your determination (along with your imagination, anger and compassion ...) in the right direction. Everyone, without exception, has this 'stickability' inside them.

For example, drug addicts have a huge will to succeed when they need to score, going to incredible lengths and using great imagination to get the fix they crave. But once they channel their determination in a direction that is more respectful of themselves and others, they can lead valuable and inspirational lives. They can change their consciousness from the inside out, rather than the outside in (via a syringe).

Personal development books are full of wonderful examples of determined people. Thomas Edison's 10,000 attempts to create a light bulb, Nelson Mandela's '28 years in prison preparing to be President', James Dyson's 5,127 failures before his bagless vacuum cleaner worked, John Motson writing to every provincial newspaper in the UK to get his first job as a sports reporter. And I was recently inspired to hear a speech by former Team GB rower Steve Williams OBE, winner of two Olympic gold medals, who quoted the last words of his coach Jürgen Gröbler before the Athens 2004 coxless four final: 'It will get so dark and hurt so much that you will cry out for your mother and your father, but you will win on the last stroke.' (And they did, by 0.08 of a second.) And my daughter remarked, after recently 'hitting the wall' in a seven-mile run: 'It's surprising how much you can still find in the tank when you think you are running on empty.'

Why determination is different in Buddhism

So, can Buddhism add anything useful to the topic of determination? I would argue that it can – in five ways:

1. It acknowledges the power and cleverness of your illusions (or Fundamental Darkness), the fact that there will always be some negative thinking in your mind. Nichiren Buddhism is intensely pragmatic: there are no false promises of a 'la-la land' where challenges do not exist. and no obligation to try to think positively all the time.

2. Because we are each connected to the universal Mystic Law, chanting consistently with sufficient determination will, sooner or later, produce a change in your external circumstances that reflects your inner success in changing your karma.

3. Determination and perseverance can be joyful experiences rather than painful ordeals (we choose our attitude).

4. It acknowledges the power of prayer. The challenge is, for an hour or so per day, to let go of our limited rational minds, which want to work out solutions based on previous conditioning, and instead trust that the three principles above (especially number 2) are true. This is known as the 'strategy of the Lotus Sutra', or touching your ninth consciousness.

5. When each individual becomes more determined to reveal their Buddhahood, the world will inevitably change for the

better. A Nichiren Buddhist facing a personal problem therefore believes their situation is part of a *collective mission* to change the karma of humanity at its very core – and this can be a powerful driving force when the going gets tough. It also creates a movement where people have a big enough shared goal to overcome their individual differences and support each other through difficulties.

To me, the fifth difference is the most significant contribution that Buddhism brings to determination. This sort of practice requires a wider, deeper will to succeed and a bigger heart in which the small ego has no place. It is a sometimes agonising prayer that seeks to change the destiny of the planet and it can attract FD at its most vicious and determined as surely as the moon is reflected on the water.

The choice every Nichiren Buddhist has is this: shall I be courageous and determined, myself? Can I be brave enough, if needed, to swim against the tide? Or will I follow meekly and at a safe distance in the slipstream of the brave? The second option, being fundamentally self-centred, is easier and more comfortable. But Buddhists believe only the first leads to absolute happiness. Nichiren said: 'It is better to live a single day with honour than to live to 120 and die in disgrace.' His words anticipate those of Ramothibi Tiro, a follower of Nelson Mandela who was killed at the age of twenty-eight and who said: 'It is better to die for an idea that will live than to live for an idea that will die.'

SGI Buddhist and Hollywood actor James DuMont has spent over thirty years building a successful career, appearing in box office hits such as *The West Wing*, *Ocean's Thirteen*, *Jurassic World*, *Seabiscuit* and *Catch Me If You Can* alongside actors such as Jared Leto, Tom Hanks and Jessica Lange. What I love about his CV is that he has slowly, surely and steadily carved out his niche through repeated efforts and a stubborn resilience in the face of rejection. In fact, to land his 100 movie and TV credits, he has had to do more than 3,000 auditions! And this reminds him of a famous Buddhist quote: 'From the indigo, an even deeper blue.' This means that, if one dyes something repeatedly in indigo, it becomes even bluer than the indigo leaf itself. In an interview with James for my blog (www.thankingthespoon.com), he told me:

> This practice gives you the strength, power and hope to fundamentally transform your own human journey while on this earth. As an actor/artist I can have a deep and profound effect on the planet, if I just dig deep into my own humanity and then bring this to light by unearthing human behaviour in all its beauty, pain, joy and sorrow. That is my mission while I am here. I audition more than 300 times a year, and in a good year I will only succeed with ten of those 300 attempts to share myself and my skills. I can't imagine having to deal with that without this practice. It gives me a sword to wield through all these setbacks and come away from them feeling happiness, joy and hope. I hope my life and human revolution will encourage people to stand up and fight even harder.
>
> I cannot stress enough the resilience this Buddhism gives you and how necessary this is for my life and career. Also, sometimes you may 'step in some dog shit' in life and it takes a while to get rid of the smell from your shoes or even from your mind. You smell it, others do or even if they don't, you think they do. You have to shed that mindset and make greater causes in order to counter the temporary nature of 'having shit on your shoes'. I share that analogy a great deal to encourage actors going through seriously dry spells of work.

Your Fundamental Darkness (FD) is powerful and versatile

How then does FD attempt to defeat a determined spirit? In a myriad of ways, for example by:

1. pretending you're useless but everyone else is amazing;

2. pretending you're amazing but everyone else is useless;

3. activating your innate laziness;

4. distracting you;

5. pretending you don't deserve to be happy;

6. sapping your courage;

7. playing bleak soundtracks in your head;

8. draining your energy;

9. making you ill;

10. turning you into a victim (or worse, an angry victim – see next chapter for more on this little devil).

And then, just when you think you've got its number, your FD can suddenly change tack by:

11. showering you with oodles of relative happiness;

12. wrapping you in arms of consolation;

13. manacling your positive imagination.

And change again by:

14. getting you to bitch, moan and whine;

15. getting you to try and control other people;

16. hiding the wise stuff in your head;

17. hiding the good memories in your head;

18. hiding your gratitude;

19. hiding your sense of responsibility;

20. making you think you will never win over your weaknesses.

Illusions seem like the whole unchanging truth

And each of these feelings will seem to you – at the time – like the *whole and unchanging truth*. Like the only conceivable reality when it is happening. Amazingly versatile is your FD, a highly flexible and resourceful enemy. A master illusionist. Sly, seductive, almost impossible to spot sometimes, let alone defeat. Adept at fighting rearguard actions. Oh yes, and a very smooth talker too. Its sole purpose being to destroy your faith in your greater self.

Come on then if you think you're hard enough

Thanks to my Buddhist practice I'm training myself to say, as soon as any symptoms of FD manifest: 'Come on then if you think you're hard enough.' Or 'Hello darkness, my old friend, what are you trying to stop me doing? Do you want me not to make that sales call? Play with my kids? Look after my health? Support someone who is really struggling?' And then I just do it anyway. Because there's one thing that FD cannot handle and that's you taking action to transform it. Thoughts alone are never enough. You have to take action. That's why I love the title of Susan Jeffers' book, *Feel the Fear and Do it Anyway*. Moreover, because – as discussed previously – the lotus flower of enlightenment grows only amidst the challenges of daily life, it is important to accept our FD as part of us, indeed as the cause for our chanting Nam-myoho-renge-kyo and therefore of our enlightenment. When chanting, it's best to watch any negative feelings you have without judging or rejecting them. Accept them as part of you. Then you will, over time, gradually learn to treasure all suffering as fuel for your human revolution.

Because we bring into our lives what we focus on, focusing for too long on a problem is rarely the best way forward. Focusing on and attaching our happiness to a single solution can also be a bad idea because we don't know what the solution is yet, and by doing so we can rule out new, creative options. Focusing on our positive potential is all that remains. That's why the 'Gohonzon' – the scroll to which Nichiren Buddhists chant – is defined as the 'object of devotion for observing your Buddha mind'. It is not the object of devotion for observing your poor health karma nor is it the object of devotion for observing your 'here we go again' pattern of failed relationships!

Understand that you will understand

It is perfectly normal to want to give up in the midst of a long struggle, before the problem is resolved, the goal achieved, the mission accomplished. Faith means knowing that we will win, but *staying open-minded about the 'how'*. That's the bit we often find difficult – not knowing exactly *how* a problem will resolve itself. Our smaller self or ego needs to know the detail in advance. It's only our over-used Survival-Obsessed-Selves, our untrusting obsession with certainty that needs to know exactly what the solution will look like. Wouldn't it be great to understand – whilst in the midst of the battle – that you will understand. This too is becoming a mantra for me: 'I understand that I will understand.' This is faith.

And Nichiren's words – poetic yet rooted in everyday life – provide huge encouragement:

> Just as flowers open up and bear fruit, just as the moon appears and invariably grows full, just as a lamp becomes brighter when oil is added, and just as plants and trees

flourish with rain, so will human beings never fail to prosper when they make good causes.[2]

As easy as ABC CDE?

If victory is about me and you and society winning over our own weaknesses, then every failure we experience is actually an opportunity to check our:

- Ability – do I have the skills and knowledge?
- (Self-)Belief – do I believe I can do it and do I believe I deserve it?
- Clarity – am I sure this is what I want?
- Courage – am I brave enough to take a risk and defeat my fears?
- Desire – how badly do I really want it? (Go on, be honest with yourself: do you absolutely yearn to achieve that goal? With every breath and sinew of your being?)
- Empathy – do I have the people skills to get the support I will need from others?

With most of my clients, I find that a blockage in one or two of these areas is slowing their progress or stopping them taking action at all.

Once we have acquired those six qualities, what can possibly stop us? Lack of luck? No, because, as explained by the theory of karma, we make our own luck. Lack of resources? No, because determined people will always find the resources. All that can stop us are our illusions about how life works, our lack of determination, our lack of faith, our inability to see our own and others' brilliance. Our FD, in other words. As W. Timothy Gallwey, author of *The Inner Game of Tennis*, proposes: 'Performance equals potential minus interference.'[3] 'Interference' is another word for 'FD'. And as Professor Lou Marinoff explains: 'I am acquainted with many people who are unhealthy because they are unhappy, are unhappy because they are unfulfilled, and are unfulfilled because they themselves have obstructed their fulfilment.'[4]

According to traditional Eastern wisdom, this is what often happens when we set ourselves big goals:

1. You decide to achieve something.

2. You have a setback.

3. You re-determine once more.

4. You fall flat on your face.

5. You decide yet again to go for it.

6. You get another knock-back.

7. You re-determine to win.

The secret of success? 'Always finish on an odd number.' This formula typifies the joyful Buddhist's attitude towards challenges and is much healthier than the 'here we go again' weariness that our FD will prefer us to feel. As we saw in Chapter 6, 'the wise rejoice and the foolish retreat' when faced with obstacles. There are times when I feel that all I have left is my determination. And in the end, that is always enough.

A close Buddhist friend of mine, whom I will call Bill, once shared with me one of the toughest battles he has fought with this practice – the surprising struggle he had to bond with his first child, a daughter who is now eleven. When she was five weeks old, he wrote down what he was feeling:

> It is five weeks since you were born. I've always felt broody and paternal, yet when I hold you, nothing moves, nothing clicks, it's like 'so what?' I feel no recognition, no warmth, no joy, no

hope with you. You could be anyone I do not know. Loving you should be the most natural thing in the world, but it is not happening and it is not something I can fake. I feel pretty bloody useless.

It's just such a massive shock. Like any expectant parent I worried about things going wrong, but this was the last problem I ever imagined. I've read the right books, I've been to the NCT [National Childbirth Trust] classes, I've even loved looking after babies who were not my own.

There seems to be no explanation. I've heard plenty in the media about mums not bonding with children, but never Dads. True, I wasn't allowed to be at the birth because you came by Caesarean, but I was the first person to hold you very soon after.

And you didn't give your mum a hard time being born. You aren't keeping us up all night. You're not the 'wrong' gender. You're not disabled. You're none of the things that new parents sometimes struggle with. In fact every other relative and friend loves you so much, and says you are perfect and beautiful. That makes all this even harder. And of course I need to be saying all the right 'loving Dad' things when these other people are connecting with you. Maybe it'll be easier when you start smiling, but what if it doesn't get easier? I don't even feel I can tell your mum what I'm going through as she has enough on her plate becoming a mother for the first time. I feel desperate, angry and inadequate. I cry a lot when I chant about this, it is sooooo tough.

So, this must be a karmic rather than a psychological cause, I suppose it's a deep, deep slander from a previous lifetime. My cause. I will win this battle, my child, for you and for me as I have won every other battle with Nam-myoho-renge-kyo. This pain will have a purpose. A value. A use. Even a beauty. Maybe when the love kicks in, it will be so much stronger for the struggle.

And ever so slowly over the next twelve months, this is exactly what happened, as Bill's chanting gradually transformed the relationship, turning 'poison into medicine'. And so he wrote for a second time in his diary on his daughter's first birthday:

> I am starting slowly now to feel some warmth, to feel we are deeply connected, to feel love and delight in us. I have also realised that our karma – the destiny we create for ourselves every moment of every lifetime – can throw absolutely anything at us, often when we least expect it. But that determined prayer can handle all of it and more.

Joyful responsibility is better than irresponsible joy

Looking back from a vantage point nearly twelve years down the line, Bill agrees with the idea that this experience helped him realise, at the very deepest level, that every life and every moment is precious:

> I am certain that had I buried the suffering or turned to alcohol (for example) rather than facing it fast and head-on, I would now have a very damaged (and damaging) relationship with my daughter, whose vivacity, joy and determination are an inspiration to me and everyone around her. The roots of our relationship are strong and deep and vigorous. And we laugh a lot, and there is a delightful lightness about our time together. I knew I had transformed this karma when my son arrived two years after my daughter, because his very first cry pierced right to the core of me and it felt like I was holding in my arms someone I had known forever.

Discard the shallow and seek the profound

During those twelve months Bill tells me that there were many long moments of despair, rage, frustration and doubt. Worst of all is doubt. As Nichiren points out: 'Shakyamuni taught that the shallow is easy to embrace, but the profound is difficult. To discard the shallow and seek the profound is the way of a person of courage.'[5]

When we 'seek the profound' we deepen our faith, strengthen our determination, raise our self-esteem and feel a deeper connection with other people. Sure enough, our FD then fights its rearguard action by raising doubts in our minds. This is normal. As SGI-USA leader Linda Johnson says:

> All life at every moment inherently contains two opposing forces or functions. A bright, enlightened, confident, powerful side and a delusional, negative, dark side. These are the two powers in life. No human being is missing either one. This is the nature of life. It will never change. There is no enlightenment in Buddhism that is not the by-product of facing adversity head-on, walking through it and transforming it into something of greatness.[6]

What I have realised from reading and re-reading this quote many times over the years is this: the biggest threat to our own individual happiness and to world peace is not suffering or challenges or problems. The biggest danger is that we underestimate the power of either our Fundamental Darkness or our Buddhahood, our negative or our positive potential, our ability either to destroy or to create value.

Having heard many experiences like Bill's, I feel now that the purpose of determination and of winning in our lives as Buddhists is to encourage others who are struggling. If we win today in our lives, if we defeat our darkness, our lesser self and our illusions, then people on the verge of victory will have a final breakthrough, people who are fighting will keep going, people who have given up will find the strength to start again and people who have never fought will discover the spark of hope. This is what can happen when the Buddha in you meets the Buddha in me.

Mindset mantras for developing resilience

Because every moment is precious, I develop deep determination.

I always finish on an odd number.

I find joy in developing stickability.

I replace vague yearnings with an exciting vision.

I acknowledge that my FD is powerful but I know that my Buddhahood is stronger.

Although I might be suffering now, I understand that I will understand.

I know I will win in the end and remain open-minded about how it will happen.

When I transform my karma on the inside, my life changes on the outside.

Journal exercises

1. Can you be courageous and determined, yourself? Or will you follow at a distance in the slipstream of the brave?

2. Think of a time in your life when you accessed your deep determination in order to achieve a goal. What did you learn about yourself from the experience?

3. What goals are you so passionate about in life that you are prepared to go through great darkness to achieve them?

4. From the 20-point list in this chapter, what aspects of FD do you recognise in yourself?

5. What is your FD trying to stop you doing? Could you just 'do it now' and defeat your FD?

CHAPTER 12

BECOME THE MASTER OF YOUR MIND

Nichiren Daishonin said: 'One should become the master of his mind rather than let his mind master him.' There are many ways to interpret this quote, including the idea that we can choose how we want to perceive a situation, rather than being tossed around by the ebb and flow of our minds. In popular psychology, this ability is often called 'reframing'. As Auschwitz survivor Viktor Frankl famously wrote in his book *Man's Search for Meaning*: 'Everything can be taken from a man but one thing: the last of the human freedoms – to choose one's attitude in any given set of circumstances, to choose one's own way.'[1] Frankl's situation was horrific: everything (seemingly) had been taken from him – family, friends, dignity, food, clothing and freedom. And yet he found from somewhere this inner strength to master his mind when so many around him were losing theirs.

Another example of choosing our response to situations was given by the judge who sentenced singer/DJ Boy George to community service cleaning the streets of New York, and who said to him: 'It's up to you whether you see this experience as a lesson in humility or in humiliation.'

Another example much closer to home as I write is the economic recession we recently experienced here in the UK and in many other parts of the world. In and of itself the recession was a neutral event. Some of the media will try and persuade you it's universally awful, not neutral, because fear sells newspapers and plays straight into our S-O-S mentality. Yet there are people who have succeeded. People who have had the courage to stand on a roundabout wearing a sandwich board saying 'Give me a job!' Or who have grown in their lives because of the economic challenges, reassessed priorities and developed more treasures of the heart. Who have illuminated this seemingly awful (but in and of itself neutral) situation with the light of great wisdom. Ultimately, the battle is to make your conviction or confidence deeper than the recession. Or your perception of the recession. And then to take action. Then you will attract work into your life.

Hence when Nichiren speaks of 'becoming the master of your mind' his words go beyond reframing, beyond just choosing how we react to situations; instead, he asks us to be aware that our mind attracts everything that happens in our life at a karmic level. Our 'bad karma' in itself is not the problem. The problem is our attachment to that karma – both the bad karma itself and the beliefs and behaviours that feed it – and how we subconsciously cling to our illusions; our need, for example, to play the angry victim, the misunderstood partner, the spoilt child, the drama queen or whatever other role has brought us some emotional gain in the past and helped us cope or survive so far.

By contrast, our bigger Buddha self is the source of profound conviction and confidence. It transforms confusion into clarity. We can feel, to use Ikeda's words, 'expansive and perfectly serene' about any challenge we are facing, through our determined chanting ... and then the environment will reflect our life state. In the words of my Buddhist friend and successful businessman Roy Leighton: 'There is no recession in my head.'

SGI's second President Josei Toda, who experienced severe and repeated challenges in his own business life, without doubt developed this ability to master his mind, describing Buddhahood in this way:

It is like lying on your back in a wide open space looking up at the sky with arms and legs outstretched. All that you wish for immediately appears. No matter how much you may give away, there is always more. It is never exhausted. Try and see if you can attain this state of life.[2]

Where was Toda when he experienced this state? On holiday? In a beautiful park in Tokyo? At the top of a mountain watching the sun edge below the horizon? None of the above. He was actually in solitary confinement in prison for disagreeing with the militarist authorities. He had simply been chanting a lot, using prayer beads that he had fashioned in his cell from cardboard milk bottle tops.

Stop painting over the rust

Shakyamuni once said:

Everything is based on mind, is led by mind, is fashioned by mind. If you speak and act with a polluted mind, suffering will follow you, as the wheels of the oxcart follow the footsteps of the ox. Everything is based on mind, is led by mind, is fashioned by mind. If you speak and act with a pure mind, happiness will follow you, as a shadow clings to a form.

Sound counsel, eloquently spoken. And as strict as we have come to expect from Buddhism. Yet our first instinct is nearly always to tinker with the oxcart rather than to steer the ox more wisely. We tend to cope with the symptoms rather than attacking and transforming the root cause. We prefer to swap jobs, move house or change partners, seeking happiness outside ourselves, instead of transforming our inner consciousness. We opt to paint over the rust rather than scrub away the underlying karmic corrosion, stuck as we are in our survival mentality. This approach will very often deliver relative – and temporary – success and satisfaction, but over time the same old pattern of results will always repeat itself unless we tackle the destiny we have carved for ourselves, the deep-seated patterns that help determine the future course of our lives.

All that you become begins in your mind

Nichiren Daishonin also said: 'From the single element of mind spring all the various lands and environmental conditions.' As he, Shakyamuni and Ikeda suggest, Buddhism claims that *all* the situations in your life are a manifestation of what is happening in your mind – your conscious, subconscious and karma. And the society we have created is a result of our collective mind. Everything, including what happens to you (from a karmic perspective) – all of your 'be, do and have' – begins in your mind, which is why Buddhism says it makes so much sense to master your mind if you want to change the results you are getting.

'Mind' in this context also includes 'heart', or, if you prefer, the emotional, artistic, creative side of your brain. Nichiren Buddhists believe that chanting Nam-myoho-renge-kyo is a powerful tool for truly observing your mind; indeed 'increased self-awareness' is often reported as one of the biggest benefits of the practice, although of course it can be tough at first when you see your own yucky stuff reflected back at you!

Our strength of mind is always tested most rigorously when we face a big problem in our life. Recapping some of the points made so far in these pages, I would summarise 'The Buddha Mind for dealing with challenges' as follows:

1. I created this situation, therefore I can create the solution.

2. Because life is precious, every 'problem' is a gift in disguise.

3. Therefore when faced with obstacles, the wise rejoice and the foolish retreat.

4. Any problem is my life asking to grow, say YES (instead of grumbling inside).

5. Here's a great chance (yes, another one) to get over my smaller self.

6. The lotus flower only grows in a muddy pond. I focus on the flower, not the mud.

7. How can I use this to fulfil my life purpose?

8. I will face whatever it takes to fulfil my personal mission in life.

9. This low life state (angry, grumpy, blue, resentful, frustrated ...) absolutely does contain latent Buddhahood.

10. What is the 'problem' trying to stop me doing? Then Just Do It! Now. Darkness disappears when the sun of action shines.

11. Suffering and problems are a fact of life, for me, you, saints, sages and everyone else.

12. I make my desire for others' happiness bigger, deeper and more sincere.

And if none of the above seem to be working, remember to finish on an odd number:

13. 'And still I am not discouraged.'

To be strong is to master your mind

Buddhists believe that to master your mind is to *instinctively and increasingly* realise that all of the above is true. To constantly develop the *strength* to choose how you feel, make great decisions and develop a bigger all-embracing state of life *whatever is happening to you*. And at the deeper ninth-consciousness level, when you master your mind, you also start to influence what you attract into your life. As Seneca, the Stoic Roman philosopher, once said: 'It is not because life is difficult that we lack courage, but because we lack courage that life is difficult.'

At first glance this assertion can seem absurd or harsh – or both. I remember having to re-read it several times just to get my head around it. It turns received wisdom completely on its head; it seems to reverse action and consequence. It places responsibility for our happiness closer to home than we are usually comfortable with; and it's that inconvenient truth again of the Mystic Law of cause and effect. Following Seneca's train of thought, here are some other examples of our lives reflecting what is in our minds, rather than our moods being dictated by what is happening to us:

- It is not because I am lonely that I lack confidence, it is because I lack confidence that I am lonely;
- It is not because I am unloved that I am angry, it is because I am angry that I am unloved;
- It is not because I am sick that I feel sorry for myself, it is because of my self-pity that I am ill;
- It is not because I am unemployed that I am frustrated, it is because I am frustrated that I am unemployed.

When first hearing this kind of thinking from a Buddhist leader, I remember feeling quite indignant: 'What do you mean I'm single because I'm angry? How can that be right, I wasn't angry until I was chucked and surely I wouldn't feel this way if I had a partner!' It just felt too glib.

But this leader went on to remind me that once you transform the frustration in the depths of your life, you will find a job that perfectly mirrors your higher life state. It all comes back to the 'latent-manifest' concept we discussed earlier, because your life at this moment is a visible manifestation of the invisible workings of your mind. So if you're ever wondering 'Why does such and such keep happening to me?', the answer is that the Universe responds to what is in the core of your heart, not in your head; so somewhere in your heart you must be attracting it into your life.

In the above examples, lack of confidence together with anger and frustration are all deeply buried (or 'latent' or 'invisible') karmic tendencies that seem to appear from nowhere but are actually bubbling to the surface from the depths of our lives. So although you may not be frustrated *on the surface* until something 'bad' happens, in your heart you must be harbouring deep frustration, otherwise the event you find frustrating could not have happened to you in the first place. I don't always like it, but I believe that it's true and when I catch myself blaming my environment, a strict little voice on my shoulder will sometimes whisper in my ear: 'Wrong way round, David ...' As playwright George Bernard Shaw said: 'We don't stop playing because we grow old; we grow old because we stop playing.'

Strict words such as this guidance from Daisaku Ikeda have also helped me dissolve my excuses for unhappiness; there really is no 'wriggle room' in this advice:

> Fearing hardships and bemoaning and resenting our environment is to live with the belief that the Law is outside our own life. So is losing confidence in our ability to overcome our circumstances and turning to others in the hope that they will save us, or blaming others for our problems, or giving in to hopelessness and resignation.[3]

In a nutshell: 'Don't moan. Don't lose confidence. Never blame other people. Don't give up. Never retreat.' The thing is, when I'm gripped by my FD, this is exactly what I do. All of it. Every bit of it. To the letter. With great skill and commitment, I might add.

Stop shouting at the shadow

Buddhists see this strictness as great news, because when we re-record the 'karmic DVD' of our destiny, we are attacking our sufferings at their source rather than just dealing with the symptoms; we develop confidence, we transform anger and frustration (or any other negative emotion). In short, through chanting Nam-myoho-renge-kyo, we change ourselves, rather than 'shouting at the shadow' – the shadow being a metaphor for someone or something that we blame for making us unhappy. We are scrubbing off the karmic rust, rather than painting over it. We turn up the volume on the good stuff in our heads. Over time – and sometimes it feels painfully slow – the environment reciprocates, reflecting our Buddhahood rather than our lower life states.

Personally, I think that the Universe only fully rewards complete and utter conviction. For when we doubt, it knows we are not completely ready to receive benefit. Anxiety and doubt block benefit. Faith attracts benefit. The power to change is within us. Thank you, Spoon.

We are nothing without courage

Nichiren explains:

> A mind now clouded by the illusions of the innate darkness of life is like a tarnished mirror, but when polished, it is sure to become like a clear mirror, reflecting the essential nature of phenomena and the true aspect of reality. Arouse deep faith, and diligently polish your mirror day and night. How should you polish it? Only by chanting Nam-myoho-renge-kyo.[4]

Buddhists believe that, as faith deepens and develops, based on a deeply-held feeling that life is precious, we slowly reveal our highest qualities, attracting benefit into our lives:

- It is because I am wise that I make great decisions and attract good fortune.
- It is because I treasure life, that life treasures me.
- It is because I trust my heart, that the risks I take are rewarded.
- It is because I develop compassion, that I am supported and loved.
- It is because I respect myself, that others respect me.

And of course courageous action is an essential part of the mix, as Nichiren bluntly points out to one of his disciples:

> A sword is useless in the hands of a coward. The mighty sword of the Lotus Sutra must be wielded by one courageous in faith. Then one will be as strong as a demon armed with an iron staff.[5]

Re-reading this passage many times since I began chanting in 1985, I have gradually come to understand that courage is utterly essential. That when we are paralysed by fear we are nothing. And that when we are brave, we are everything. It is then that we take action. Courage is truly the *sine qua non* of Buddhist practice. But too often we humans prefer instead just to survive and feel safe. Some people (bullies, for example) seek to feel safe by frightening others more than – deep down – they are frightened themselves.

Winning over your weaknesses

We all experience defeat at some point in our lives, but the only true defeat is when you give up on yourself in the midst of difficulty. Likewise true success in life means winning in your battle with yourself. As Daisaku Ikeda writes: 'Those who persist in the pursuit of their dreams, no matter what the hurdles, are winners in life, for they have won over their weaknesses.'[6]

In other words, the only thing that can defeat me is my life state (rather than what happens to me). Mastering our mind means chipping away at our illusions about how life works, it means discarding our attachment to some of the tried and trusted habits that we think will bring us happiness. Habits such as:

- Getting angry too often, too quickly or too destructively
- Being jealous of others
- Holding grudges
- Comparing ourselves to others
- Being unable to apologise

Recognise any of these? If so, they're just part of having that very human ingredient called Fundamental Darkness.

Point your anger in the right direction

Of all the emotions that people struggle with, anger is perhaps the most challenging and the one most often discussed in coaching sessions and on personal development courses. We get angry with ourselves – about what we did and didn't do. We get angry at others – what they have or haven't said or done. We get angry with (tick any that apply to you ...) politicians, bosses, neighbours, colleagues, drivers, referees, cyclists, husbands, wives, children, siblings, friends, customers, call-centre agents and traffic wardens. We even get angry at *inanimate objects* such as traffic lights, flat-pack furniture and doors. Worse still, we get angry about things that haven't even happened yet, just so we can be ready to rant or punch if and when they do. We even rehearse upcoming arguments in our heads! Sometimes we stay angry with one person or situation for a very long time, carefully nurturing our resentment. Or we bury our anger inside until it manifests as depression. At other times, our anger can erupt into violence – verbal or physical. On a national and international scale, anger manifests as war.

Meanwhile, a situation that one person may feel incandescent about might not even register with another. In some cases there is a definite external trigger for our anger, whilst at other times we can feel irritated for no apparent reason. Our anger also spans a whole spectrum, from mild irritation through flashes of temper to eruptions of volcanic proportions. Occasionally, without knowing why (no doubt the causes are buried deep in my karma), I have felt inside me a rage that would tear down mountains.

Road rage might be your particular speciality and if you find yourself becoming excessively irate when stuck in traffic, let's hope you're equally grateful and energised when driving down a beautiful open country road with nothing blocking your way. You're not? Me neither. Personally, I am quicker to get angry than to get grateful, which is one reason why I chant every day.

But just how big a deal is it when someone is (in your opinion) driving too slowly in front of you and holding you up? I mean, really? On a scale of one to ten? Logically we know that, on a scale of importance, it's usually nearer one than ten, but of course we're not logical beings. If we're in a low life state, it can feel like nearer eleven as the expletives fly, the horn sounds and one or more fingers go up. Not much logic in any of those reactions, is there? But of course we're emotional beings, aren't we?

Say goodbye to your angry victim

Of all the emotions we feel on the anger spectrum, the rage of the angry victim is one of the most damaging and difficult to change. My fellow SGI member Patti Dale writes: 'Victims do hurt other people. Because they break the first law. They hurt themselves.'

The angry-victim role is a manifestation of FD, and keeps the victim stuck in the past, sabotaging positive affirmations and feeling sorry for him- or herself. The angry victim blames other people for difficulties, and does not forget nor forgive. No recompense or apology is ever enough because, deep down, the angry victim wants to stay that way forever; there is some sort of emotional comfort to be gained from it.

Here's a suggestion. Tell your angry victim to leave now; he or she has served a purpose and is not needed any more. Once the victim has gone, you can make room in your heart for something strong and beautiful that will serve you and others better. Become a sculptor of your future, not a victim of your past. (Incidentally, the only thing worse than one angry victim in a household or workplace is two angry victims blaming each other for their unhappiness!)

Having said all that, going through an angry-victim phase, especially following trauma, can be a crucial and necessary part of a healing process. As singer-songwriter Meri Everitt says, expressing her feelings about rape:

> Most of my songs start from 'angry victim', but when people hear them they witness angry victim becoming determined woman! Writing songs is a safe way to express anger. And getting the anger out and transforming it into a passion to fight for women's rights, that's human revolution.

Discover the value in anger

Nichiren colourfully describes how anger can alter our appearance:

> Once in India, there was a jealous woman who hated her husband so much that she smashed everything in the house. Her excessive rage completely altered her appearance; her eyes blazed like the sun and moon, and her mouth seemed to belch fire. She looked exactly like a blue or red demon.[7]

I wonder what the husband had done to incur her wrath? And whether every wife would have unleashed such destructive (though colourful) fury?

Whatever kind of anger you experience, from mild irritation to belching fire, it is worth remembering that, as always in Buddhism, you are totally responsible for how you feel and act. For example, if someone hits you and you strike back, the first blow is the external trigger for the second, but it is not the ultimate, inner cause. You can claim that you retaliated because he hit you, but in fact you hit him *because you are you*. Because, we might add, of your own sediment in your own glass of water. This scenario is a reminder that not everyone reacts in the same way to provocation. Anger, it often seems, is the first reaction of the stupid when it should be the last resort of the wise.

So, what are we to do with this incredibly powerful emotion? People have developed a myriad of ways to handle anger. We hide it, release it, control it or manage it; we suppress it, express it, cope with it or channel it. Sometimes we explode with it and very often we wish (in vain) that we didn't have it at all; in short, we will do almost anything except face our anger full on, with all its terrible ugliness, and transform it into something of beauty.

And as with any other emotion, anger in and of itself is neither good nor bad. It all depends on what you do with this powerful energy. Is your anger protecting your small ego? Your reputation? Your low self-esteem? Or is your anger standing up for the dignity of life? Do you get angry at others because you don't want to apologise for your own mistakes, such is your need to be right all the time? Or are you using your anger to benefit others as well as yourself? Is your anger aimed purely at winning an argument? Or are you fighting on a wider scale for justice? Is your anger protecting your own vulnerability? Or is it battling against inequality? Are you using your anger to magnify a problem? Or to find a solution? Is your anger keeping you stuck in the past? Or are you channelling it to improve your future?

Is your anger destructive or creative? And does your anger help someone else connect with their Buddhahood? If so, it is anger well placed.

We are all muddy potatoes

Josei Toda used a powerful metaphor to describe the friction in some angry relationships:

> Potatoes are rough and dirty when harvested, but when they are placed in a basin of running water together and rolled against each other, the skin peels away, leaving the potatoes shiny and ready for cooking. The only way for us to hone and polish our character is through our interactions with others.[8]

Interaction sometimes means friction. But only friction knocks off the mud. Thank you, mud. Thank you, water. Thank you, friction. And thank you most of all to all my fellow muddy potatoes.

Very often, and rather surprisingly perhaps, the emotion that seems to surge forth when anger subsides is compassion, one of the key qualities we can develop through chanting Nam-myoho-renge-kyo. Where ego-driven anger separates us by focusing on what makes us different, compassion focuses on our shared humanity. There is a saying that 'only hurt people hurt' and compassion enables us to keenly perceive and empathise with the pain of the person we may find it most difficult to be with. We all have Berlin Walls of prejudice in our hearts and it takes courage, humility and strength to tear them down.

One of the things I found most irritating (ironically) when I first read Nichiren's writings was just how angry he sometimes seemed – this did not fit in with my preconceived ideas of a serene and meditative Buddhist guru. Nichiren got angry with the authorities of Japan. With corrupt priests. With other Buddhist schools. Anger was in many ways the fuel that fired his determination to spread the revolutionary and compassionate teachings of the Lotus Sutra amongst the ordinary folk of Japan, aiming to show all people how to become truly happy in this lifetime. Unsurprisingly, the government reacted angrily, as Nichiren says:

> ... I risked my reputation and life to remonstrate with the authorities. But just as a high wind creates great waves, [...] so my admonitions called forth increasing animosity. The regent's supreme council met to discuss whether to behead me or banish me from Kamakura, and whether to confiscate the estates of or execute my disciples and lay supporters, or to imprison or exile them to distant places. Hearing this, I rejoiced, saying that I had long expected it to come to this.[9]

He rejoiced (rather than retreating) because he knew he and his followers were fulfilling Shakyamuni's prophecy that the votary of the Lotus Sutra would meet with persecution (including decapitation and exile) and this knowledge helped him to master his mind. His sense of purpose or mission, partly fuelled by anger, was so powerful that he could endure any hardship:

> ... I was taken to a small hut that stood in a field called Tsukahara. [...] One room with four posts, it stood on some land where corpses were abandoned, [...] the boards of the roof did not meet, and the walls were full of holes. The snow fell and piled up, never melting away. I spent my days there, sitting in a straw coat or lying on a fur skin. At night it hailed and snowed, and there were continual flashes of lightning. Even in the daytime the sun hardly shone. It was a wretched place to live.[10]

But his reaction to this was: 'Nothing is more joyful to me than to ... suffer persecutions because I propagate Myoho Renge Kyo.' And it is noticeable that in all of Nichiren's writings, not once do we find him feeling sorry for himself. There is no self-pity, no angry lamenting of his situation, no 'poor me' feelings of victimhood.

Aristotle, the fourth-century-BC philosopher, famously claimed: 'Anybody can become angry, that is easy; but to be angry with the right person, and to the right degree, and at the right time, and for the right purpose, and in the right way, that is not easy.' He is right, it is not easy. But followers of Nichiren believe it is easier when you connect with your Buddhahood.

Complaining destroys your good fortune

Here's a list of people that I've heard being blamed for someone's unhappiness:

- My partner
- My bank manager
- My wife
- My mum
- The cat
- My dad
- The dog
- My children
- My boss
- My football team

And here's a list of things that we often blame:

- The weather
- The car
- The house
- The media
- The traffic
- The government
- 'The system'
- 'Society'

When we find ourselves blaming 'the system' or 'society' it might be time to remember that we ourselves are part of both. Unless you channel complaints into taking positive action, they will just suck away your good fortune by denying your own and other people's Buddhahood. It is, as Nichiren says, 'conduct utterly unbecoming of a worthy man'. When you complain and blame, you slander yourself by giving away all your power to the thing or person you are blaming. Complain about Life and Life will complain about you. When you use the power inside you to change your heart for the better, the outside world must, through the Mystic Law of cause and effect, respond in kind. Complaint doesn't necessarily mean whingeing out loud. It is very insidious – it can be rumbling away in the back of your mind for years, a soundtrack that you don't even notice after a while, because begrudging your life has become a habit, as automatic as breathing. But if you believe you are a Buddha, you can choose instead a soundtrack of joy and gratitude.

Transforming jealousy

The 'green-eyed monster' is another common challenge for those seeking to master their minds. But when we are jealous of others, we are disrespectful of both our own lives and the other person's. We are begrudging their right to happiness while simultaneously disparaging ourselves by refusing to believe we are also capable of fulfilment. Furthermore, we are ignoring our own uniqueness.

Jealousy is also rooted in being overly concerned about what other people think of you and comparing yourself unfavourably to them, a condition that the big brands exploit to sell us more stuff. Indeed, in some countries there is an unhealthy obsession with not 'losing face' – another symptom of our over-used survival mentality. If you're constantly thinking, 'I wonder what they think of me?', it might be time to get over yourself. Can you imagine walking into a room full of people where everyone is focusing on what everyone else thinks of them? Would anyone have a meaningful conversation with anyone? Would any *connections* be made? Most other people will not be judging how you look and walk, they're too busy wondering what you think of *them*. Our small ego even worries about what other people think of our children, concerned as we are that their behaviour might 'reflect badly' on us.

Over the years, I have coached many managers whose self-esteem goes up and down like a yo-yo, depending on what the CEO ('king of the jungle') thinks of them this week. Comparing ourselves to others no doubt made a lot of sense back in the cave, when survival depended on being servile or on being the biggest /strongest/fastest etc ... but might it now be time for us to get over ourselves?

Be yourself, everyone else is already taken

The best advice I've had on this issue from Buddhist leaders is to 'compare yourself to your own positive potential rather than to other people' (except if that person is an inspirational mentor whom you can learn from – see next chapter). If you waste loads of energy comparing yourself to others, you are just giving your own power away and rejecting yourself. And you risk becoming a fragile mish-mash of all the people you have wanted to be while you've been running away from the authentic you. So treasure your own brilliance rather than comparing your inside to your perception of other people's outside.

I have realised recently that whatever topic my different (and lovely) clients want to be coached on (e.g. relationships, career choices, work-life balance, assertiveness, leadership skills etc ...) the one thing they all really want to feel is that their lives are *authentic*. They often realise, usually after one or two sessions, that the real reason they're unhappy – for example in a job or relationship or town – is because they find it hard to express their true feelings. When that happens, life quickly begins to feel empty or meaningless. Or the discomfort may manifest as restlessness (what am I here for?) or anxiety (will I ever make anything of myself?) or as a sudden loss of 'mojo'.

We learn to hide our true feelings from an early age. We do it with the best of intentions: usually to fit in, to feel safe, to gain approval or to avoid conflict – it's that powerful S-O-S mindset again. Gradually it can become a habit, as it often seems easier to back down or roll over when more powerful people decide they want you to play a certain role, or to use you to fulfil their own goals.

Recently I came across this great quote by author Robert McCammon from his book, *Boy's Life*:

> We all start out knowing magic. We are born with whirlwinds, forest fires, and comets inside us. But then we get the magic educated right out of our souls. We get it churched out, spanked out, washed out, and combed out. We get put on the straight and narrow and told to be responsible. And you know why we were told that? Because the people doing the telling were afraid of our wildness and youth, and because our magic made them ashamed, and sad of what they'd allowed to wither in themselves.[11]

Wow, how powerful is that? But more importantly, how can Buddhism help with this search for authenticity? Nichiren famously explained that the cherry, the plum, the peach and the damson possess their own innate value – without having to change into a different fruit. We can interpret this as meaning that a cherry can never become a peach and moreover, it does not need to. And if it did, it wouldn't be happy. It is much better to live our precious and irreplaceable lives by being true to ourselves. For we cannot become someone else, no matter how hard we may try to.

In other words, cherish yourself and strive to be the shiniest and shapeliest cherry you can be, rather than wishing you had been born a peach (or having facelifts and other cosmetic surgery until you look like a prune). To me, this sums up what Nichiren meant when he spoke of 'attaining Buddhahood in one's present form'. And I love this famous quote from Oscar Wilde: 'Be yourself; everyone else is already taken.'

So, when you chant Nam-myoho-renge-kyo, it is vital to do so without constantly judging your feelings. Buddhism is not a philosophy based on morality or on a dualistic view of good and evil. That's why all feelings are an acceptable starting point in front of the Gohonzon. Just as importantly, other people come to see your sincerity and authenticity and they will trust you, even if they disagree with your views or lifestyle. So, instead of constant self-judgement, chant instead with a mindset of: 'I give myself permission to express my feelings, for all of them contain Buddhahood.'

I tried this not so long ago during a week of depression. At first, as per my karmic tendency, I put pressure on myself: 'Why the hell are you going through this again? You've written all about depression on your blog – re-read it and stop begrudging your life!' But as it turned out, this episode had a new lesson to teach me. After a couple of days, during which I chanted for two or three hours each day, instead of judging my low mood or resisting it or fighting it or even wanting it to go away, I began to accept the sadness, then slowly began to treasure it and then finally came to see how it could help me fulfil my mission. I realised that a Buddha is someone who accepts their innate goodness without becoming arrogant and accepts their innate evil without despair. I realised there was no value in judging myself or pressurising myself to change.

Silence the pessimists

When we are struggling, the idea of feeling hopeful seems almost impossible, but in just such situations I am reminded of a quote much loved by followers of Nichiren, who wrote:

Those who believe in the Lotus Sutra are as if in winter, but winter always turns to spring. Never, from ancient times on, has anyone heard or seen of winter turning back to autumn. Nor have we ever heard of a believer in the Lotus Sutra who turned into an ordinary person.[12]

His implication is that Buddhism is a teaching of profound optimism. But it is perhaps a symptom of the age we live in that the word 'hope' is often used negatively or at best as some kind of weak and watery consolation:

- 'We live in hope.'
- 'More in hope than expectation.'
- And not forgetting that old favourite: 'You haven't got a hope in hell.'

So we can actually become quite miserable thinking about hope! This is what happens when our FD gets its claws into something bright and beautiful, and twists it.

Here are some pessimistic beliefs I have heard over the years:

- 'Israel and Palestine will never stop fighting, will they?' No, never, that's the way it is.
- 'That's just mothers and daughters for you ...' Yep, no mothers have ever got on with their daughters, have they? And never will.
- 'There will never be peace in Ireland.' Correct, hell will freeze over first.
- 'The Berlin Wall will never come down.'

So, even if we ourselves might never say such things, I believe that every time we passively accept and agree with these statements made, say, around a dinner table, with everyone nodding in agreement, we are letting our Fundamental Darkness win. Remember that FD has a habit of sneaking in the back door, clothing itself in affable bonhomie and catching us unawares.

Just by agreeing with these negative beliefs, we are actually saying 'winter never ends' or, even more ridiculous, 'spring turns to autumn'. We are slandering our Buddhahood and the highest life state of other people. It is worth remembering that seemingly impossible progress *has* been made, such as the fall of the Berlin Wall, the end of apartheid in South Africa and the outbreak of peace in Ireland.

As we've seen, from an S-O-S point of view, it makes some sense to be pessimistic – expecting the worst would tend to prolong our life spans when we lived in caves. But these days pessimism feels more like the culturally acceptable attitude of people who are scared of success, don't understand their own personal power or don't believe they deserve to be happy. I have noticed, during my work as a leadership trainer, that pessimists – though rarely disappoint*ed* – are invariably disappoint*ing*, which means they don't contribute enough to the team. Close cousins of the 'cynic', they drain others' energy and are focused on survival and damage limitation rather than on fulfilling their own and their team's potential.

Hope changes everything

The profound optimism of Buddhism is wonderfully illustrated in the film *A Mighty Heart*, starring Angelina Jolie. In this movie, the Hollywood star plays the role of SGI Buddhist Mariane Pearl, who faced the deepest despair when in 2002 her journalist husband Danny was kidnapped and then beheaded by Islamic fundamentalists in Pakistan.

At the time Mariane was heavily pregnant with their only child and poignantly describes how, after news arrived of Danny's decapitation, she resolves nevertheless to move forward with hope:

As the hopes for Danny's release grew fainter, our son continued to grow inside me. Of all the journeys I had taken, none had prepared me for the one across this blurry frontier between life and death, hope and despair. All I knew was that one of the two men in my life was not born and the other might be dead. And when it was confirmed that Danny would not come home, I flew to my brother in Paris with my husband's little legacy kicking in what felt like the very centre of my soul. I thought about a Buddhist saying I'd once heard, about how even a cave plunged in darkness for millions of years can be illuminated by a single candle. This thought gave me hope: I wasn't powerless, I told myself. All I had to do was nurture my faith – my own flame – and inspire our son to do the same. Throughout the flight, I prayed. I prayed for the new life inside me. I prayed that Adam's light would shine brighter than the darkness that had claimed his father's life.[13]

Buddhist practice helps us develop a deeply resilient and optimistic approach to life, as Daisaku Ikeda explains:

Hope transforms pessimism into optimism. Hope is invincible. Hope changes everything. It changes winter into summer, darkness into dawn, descent into ascent, barrenness into creativity, agony into joy. Hope is the sun. It is light. It is passion. It is the fundamental force for life's blossoming. Hope is a decision you make.[14]

'Hope is a decision you make.' How true. Yet we tend only to feel hopeful reactively, in response to good things happening – a job interview, a compliment, a good weather forecast and so on. By chanting Nam-myoho-renge-kyo we can become proactive about hope, tapping a deep reservoir of optimism in our hearts, igniting our inner Buddha and spurring us on to keep fighting when obstacles appear in our lives. Of course this is not easy. Twenty innocent children and six adults die at the hands of a gunman at Sandy Hook. Women are gang-raped and murdered in India. A lone gunman murders thirty-eight people on a beach in Tunisia. We can decide to feel desperate about this. Or we can choose to fight back with the transformative power of hope, until everyone feels in their hearts the dignity, nobility and sanctity of their own and other people's lives. So, as Mariane says, 'May we all shine brighter than the darkness' that sometimes engulfs us.

Cultivate the gratitude attitude

Buddhists believe that gratitude is also a powerful force for transformation in our lives and is therefore a central theme running through Buddhist writings. Indeed, Nichiren's letters to his followers, before embarking on doctrinal discussions or personal encouragement, invariably start with a sincere thank-you such as this one:

> ... I have received your gifts of a horseload of salt, a sack of soybeans, a bag of seaweed, and a bamboo container of sake. I have not seen you since you returned home from the province of Kozuke, and I have been wondering how you are. I can hardly find words to say how much I appreciate your sincerity in sending me a letter and the many gifts.[15]

And Nichiren also feels eternally grateful to his own mentor, Shakyamuni Buddha, saying that the debt of gratitude owed to him is deeper than the ocean, weightier than the earth and vaster than the sky. In Western culture, the more we have, the more we seem to want. And the more we have, the less grateful we feel – typical of the Hunger state explained earlier. A self-centred and arrogant culture of entitlement means that 'thank you' is often forgotten or said as a cursory afterthought or a mumbled aside pronounced in the hope that the other person will give us more of what we want. Or sometimes it's uttered as an indicator of good manners and is therefore just a necessary social nicety, part of our daily 'to do' list. At other times we diminish gratitude as a stoic reaction to small mercies, or we are grudgingly grateful, a kind of 'could be worse' consolation.

Yet true gratitude can be a powerful attitude that truly enriches our lives. As Daisaku Ikeda states: 'No matter how much action people might seem to be taking outwardly, if they lack the spirit to repay their debt of gratitude, their arrogance will destroy their good fortune.'[16]

Spirit, rather than 'keeping up appearances', is the key word in this advice. It is the heart that is most important, character rather than reputation, or as Roman philosopher Cicero wrote, 'to be rather than to seem'. As we've seen, 'thanking the spoon' includes being grateful for things that bring the sediment in a glass to the surface of the water, a metaphor for the gratitude we can feel for events and people who stir up our own illusions from the karmic depths of our lives.

Difficult as it often seems, chanting Nam-myoho-renge-kyo means we can feel appreciation for those who hold up a mirror to our own negativity, that we might learn to transform it and thereby polish our lives. Gratitude is the Buddha's answer (i.e. your own inner answer) to the sufferings of despair and arrogance. Your gratitude can create an oasis of hope and joy where others can seek refreshment. Remember, you can only really feel this degree of gratitude and appreciation when you know in your heart that life is precious (see Chapter 2). I have a friend (not a Buddhist) whose daily mantra is 'I see beauty everywhere', and he is one of the happiest people I know, despite no shortage of challenges in his life.

Cycling in the countryside near my home recently, it occurred to me that when things are going well, we rarely notice the helpful tailwind behind us. We are much better at moaning about the headwinds we face when life is difficult. Yet of course it is only the headwinds that make us stronger.

Be neither elated by prosperity nor grieved by decline

Here's one more quote from Nichiren to help you master your mind, rather than finding yourself buffeted by changing fortunes and letting your mind master you:

> Worthy persons deserve to be called so because they are not carried away by the eight winds: prosperity, decline, disgrace, honour, praise, censure, suffering, and pleasure. They are neither elated by prosperity nor grieved by decline.[17]

— ✦ —

Mindset mantras for mastering your mind

Everything I am begins in my mind. Therefore I treasure, nurture and master *all* of my thoughts and feelings.

Everything I am looking for I already have inside me.

I choose how I feel about what people say to me and about everything that happens to me.

I feel expansive and perfectly serene about every challenge I face.

I created this situation, therefore I can create the solution.

Every problem is a gift in disguise.

When faced with obstacles, I rejoice instead of retreating.

I say YES when my life is asking to grow.

I face whatever it takes to fulfil my personal mission in life.

I only create value with my anger, using it with wisdom and compassion.

I say goodbye to my angry victim and make room to feel empowered and grateful instead.

I use my anger to fight for the dignity of life instead of to protect my smaller self.

I am angry with the right person, to the right degree, at the right time, for the right purpose and in the right way.

I compare myself only to my own potential or to inspirational mentors.

More and more I am discovering the transformative and enriching powers of hope and gratitude in my life.

I see beauty everywhere, I see the Buddha in me and the Buddha in you.

When I am brave I am everything.

Journal exercises

1. When did you last stop and make a list of what's important to you in life?

2. How can you use every experience you have had to fulfil your life purpose?

3. When you are totally honest with yourself, where in your life do you feel that you may be 'shouting at the shadow' instead of taking responsibility for your own happiness?

4. When you develop more courage in your life, what will you be able to do that you currently stop yourself from doing?

5. What habits do you have that you think will make you happy, but don't really? (Such as getting too angry, being jealous, holding grudges, comparing yourself to others, being unable to apologise or complaining.)

6. How many 'conflict stories' do you think you absorb in a typical week from the media and TV programmes? What emotional rewards do you get from this and could you find such rewards in a more constructive way? Or find different and better rewards elsewhere?

7. Who are the 'muddy potatoes' you have attracted into your life? What can you learn from them?

8. Which of the eight winds are most apt to 'carry you away'?

CHAPTER 13

HOW TO CHOOSE
A GREAT MENTOR

As a topic, life is bigger than any single individual, and even the most brilliant person can eventually come to an impasse without a great mentor – someone wiser who can temper any potential for arrogance and the complacent stagnation it brings. That's why it's important to choose a mentor who has been and remains a brilliant pupil/disciple themselves and who:

1. inspires you to rediscover your brilliance and determination when you cannot find it any more;

2. has strong enough self-esteem and humility to celebrate your abilities rather than feel threatened by them;

3. will know *he* has won when he sees you outperform him;

4. knows your weaknesses and will therefore stretch you to your limits and beyond;

5. knows life is precious and will therefore support you to the maximum;

6. can see when you're beating yourself up and help you get over yourself;

7. will recognise when you're being arrogant and help you get over yourself;

8. has overcome his own 'S-O-S' mindset;

9. shares a powerful mission and sense of purpose with the people who follow him;

10. works, often unseen or in the face of adversity, to protect his followers, taking action even when nobody is watching;

11. does not want to be deified, knowing that disciples stagnate and stop taking responsibility when they put the mentor on a pedestal.

For 12 million SGI Buddhists, Nichiren Daishonin and Daisaku Ikeda are such mentors, because they have been brilliant disciples themselves and they both fought relentlessly for other people's happiness before most of those people even realised such happiness was possible. And on a local face-to-face level, the Buddhist leaders who've inspired me most also behave in the ways described above. The most inspirational leaders in the worlds of business or public service also exhibit these traits. As do parents at their best.

A great mentor is both strict and compassionate

Compassion without strictness is comforting, but ineffective. Strictness without compassion is disrespectful. As Nichiren wrote:

> Even though one may resort to harsh words, if such words help the person to whom they are addressed, then they are worthy to be regarded as truthful words and gentle words. Similarly, though one may use gentle words, if they harm the

person to whom they are addressed, they are in fact deceptive words, harsh words.[1]

Likewise, to stretch someone without supporting them is a recipe for disappointment; but to support them without stretching them doesn't get the job done. A great mentor, like Nichiren, places equal emphasis on you achieving your full potential while reminding you of your personal accountability when you fall short of what you know you can achieve. This is also my philosophy as a coach and quite often my role is to help a client remove their subconscious excuses for under-performance. We don't always like our mentors very much, but we can see that what they say is true.

Why some small companies fail

How many brilliant small companies fail to grow because their founding leader lacks the true self-confidence to develop capable successors? Or the humility to have his own mentor? Far too many. And yet it all started so well. The leader is usually inspirational, charismatic and highly intelligent. He (or she) has launched their business on a very helpful belief that they are the best at what they do. Here is a CEO who is several steps ahead in every strategic or tactical conversation. Clients love his brilliant insights, employees feel safe (S-O-S mindset) around his macho energy and the business would be lost without his vision and originality. He becomes very wealthy (treasures of the storehouse) and is influential in the social and business circles that matter to him (storehouse again ...).

As leadership expert David Taylor points out, the three most difficult words for a leader like this to say are 'I don't know'. Why so difficult? Well, it's another leftover from our Neanderthal brain. Imagine the scene: Cave-child says: 'Daddy, is that a bison or a sabre-toothed tiger out there in the bush?' Daddy replies: 'I don't know, son, let me think about it.' Does he heck ... Caveman Dad 100 per cent instantly knows the difference between dinner and being dinner, and his ability to know and decide quickly is the difference between life and death. The corporate jungle is not so different, however plush the carpets in our boardrooms ...

Anyway, thanks to our CEO's sense of certainty, his company has now grown so much that he's working seventy-hour weeks and still dealing with phone calls and emails on holiday and at weekends. Clients insist on dealing with him and him alone – which is wonderful for his ego but less marvellous for his family. He becomes a stranger to his children (who admittedly have every toy and treat they could wish for) and meanwhile his concerned wife urges him to spend less time at work. Eventually and reluctantly he gives in to her pleas and decides to appoint a Number Two, someone who might one day succeed him at the helm. He warns her that it may not work out – after all, can't she remember what happened the last time he tried to 'let go' of the business? Nevertheless, she breathes a hopeful sigh of relief.

Without a mentor you cannot raise capable successors

The would-be successor (perhaps a former client who reveres our leader) starts work and all is rosy for a few weeks or months. Our leader has chosen someone who shares his vision and values, someone who can be moulded in his own impressive image. The new Number Two makes some early mistakes but then begins to take the initiative, to impress clients, to win new business, to get buy-in from employees and other stakeholders. He even dares to try and tinker with the company's products or services. Our alpha male founder begins to feel threatened, to feel slightly less adored, needed and indispensable; he wonders, when he looks in the 'mirror mirror on the wall' if he is still 'the fairest of them all'. In short, he is stuck in his S-O-S mentality.

He starts to find fault with his would-be successor, to nitpick the small stuff. He even worries that this upstart wants to usurp him and take over the company! In short, the new Number Two cannot be trusted, clients might be let down – after all, how could he really be as good as the man who has his name above the door? (How indeed ...) The belief that he is the best – though handy in the early days of the company – is no longer serving him so well.

After a disagreement, he reluctantly decides he has no alternative but to let his latest Number Two go. And who will come riding to the rescue, so that any disasters can be averted? You guessed it, our heroic leader, who goes home and announces to his wife: 'What did I tell you, the new guy turned out to be hopeless!' Yet the mistake is his alone, for not having his own mentor, not having someone in the wings who can candidly tell him to 'get over himself'. And because our leader has never been a 'disciple', he has never learned how to raise his own capable successors. From a Buddhist perspective, the first job of a leader is to make you feel amazing about yourself and other people.

A mentor succeeds when his disciples outgrow him

By contrast, a great mentor is able to appoint successors who will one day outperform him and he will do everything in his power to help them succeed, including giving praise where it is due. Nichiren said that when we are praised highly by others, we feel that there is no hardship we cannot bear and that courage springs from such words of praise.

You will also fast-track your connection to your full positive potential if you can find such a mentor and look at yourself through their eyes. As I once said to a friend of mine: 'With my mentor's mighty heart next to mine, I feel twice as brave and that the mission we both share can definitely be achieved.'

In Buddhism the mentor-disciple relationship is sometimes compared to a needle and a thread. The mentor is the needle and the disciple is the thread. When sewing, the needle leads the way through the cloth, but in the end it is unnecessary, and it is the thread that remains and holds everything together.

Mindset mantras for choosing a great mentor

When I look at myself through my mentor's eyes
I can see my full potential more clearly.

I choose a mentor who will stretch me to the limit
and support me to the maximum.

I choose a mentor who helps me discover my bigger self.

I choose a mentor who inspires me with a powerful sense
of purpose and mission.

I choose a mentor who is compassionate yet strict.

I choose a mentor who fights for my happiness.

I become a brilliant mentor myself, nurturing people
who will outperform me.

Journal exercises

1. Who in your life do you most admire and why?

2. Do you have a mentor in your life? What difference do they make to you?

3. If you do not have a mentor, how could you benefit from having one?

4. Who could you choose as your mentor and why?

5. Could you be a great mentor one day and what would it take for you to become one?

CHAPTER 14

SMALL SELF, BIG SELF

One of the biggest challenges we face is: 'How can I truly be myself as an individual, yet also belong in the group around me?' This struggle is perhaps most visible when children are maturing into adults, though for some, the dilemma seems to last long beyond the teenage years. And here's another knotty but related problem: How can you achieve your personal success whilst living in harmony with others and your surroundings?

Buddhism seeks to resolve these difficulties, just as many social and political philosophies have grappled with similar questions. For example, it could be said (simplistically perhaps) that Communism has emphasised the collective, but at the expense of the individual; while Capitalism emphasises the individual, but at the expense of the collective. Both systems have had strong supporters, but neither has taught people to be happy based on the 'treasures of the heart'.

One of the benefits of spiritual practice is that you gradually come to see how the unique individual melody of your life is part of the greater cosmic symphony of all Life. This is what it is to be a Buddha and this is what makes you a truly complete human being.

Learning to gaze at other people's navels

From one perspective, chanting Nam-myoho-renge-kyo can look like an introspective and self-centred experience; after all, part of its power is that it delivers insights into who you are so that you can more easily 'master your mind'. Indeed, when people first start chanting, it is perfectly natural do so, without realising it, from an S-O-S state of mind. But although Nichiren wrote some of his most powerful letters while alone in exile, his is not a teaching that encourages solitary navel-gazing. We are only really unlimited beings when our life becomes big enough to go *outwards* and embrace others, to look at other people's belly-buttons (if you will) as well as at our own. A process that starts when we bust through the limitations of the small ego, when we reach *inside* to discover our own Buddhahood and with it our intrinsic shared humanity. This is not easy. For the 'absolute happiness' taught in Nichiren Buddhism includes tuning into the lives of other people and connecting with them at this deeper level, a place where differences of race, gender, sexuality, politics, class, profession and religion gradually become little more than dust before the wind. We find this concept difficult because it is not the route to happiness that we are S-O-S hardwired to pursue. It is the path of the 'bigger self' and, as Shakyamuni said, it takes courage to 'discard the shallow' and 'seek the profound'. As Professor Lou Marinoff points out, in a dialogue with Daisaku Ikeda: 'Biologically, humans are one species, but for a long time, natural selection favoured human dispersion via competitive and often hostile tribes.'[1]

Break free from your small tribal circle

Stuck in our small and narrow survival mentality, we prefer to surround ourselves with people who are 'just like us'. People of the same colour, sexuality, accent or football fan club, people who share our own language, values and temperament. We might even instinctively avoid others based on a split-second appraisal of their weight, tattoos, jewellery or hairstyle. We probably do this even more as we reach middle age and beyond. Life is definitely easier this way; it feels safer and more comfortable. There are fewer problems. Indeed the experience of shared laughter or debate with close friends is one of the great joys of life – and one that Buddhists treasure as much as anyone else. Yet even the closest relationships can disintegrate. Just as strangers slowly become old friends, so it is that old friends can gradually (or suddenly) become strangers.

Likewise serious rifts can emerge in a marriage where none were apparent before. Gradually we forget what we had in common, lose respect for each other and focus much more on perceived differences that were not even on the radar when the relationship was rosy. We focus on the flotsam and jetsam – the arguments and wreckage – on the surface of life, instead of on the common stream we swim in and the energy we share.

Daisaku Ikeda paints an eloquent reminder of our shared humanity:

> Each of us is born as a precious entity of life. Our mothers didn't give birth to us thinking, 'I'm giving birth to a Japanese' or 'I'm giving birth to an Arab.' Their only thought was 'May this new life be healthy and grow.'[2]

A sentiment echoed (in a more scientific context) by Professor Brian Cox: 'Every piece of you and me was forged in the furnaces of space, every atom in my body was once part of something else.' Physically we are visibly very separate from each other, emotionally we feel strongly connected to some people and not others, but at the deepest spiritual level, Buddhism says, we are all connected.

When locked in our S-O-S, we are blind to this bigger picture. This is the powerful illusion of separateness and another example of FD in action. It is the opposite of seeing the Buddha in you and the Buddha in me. It is the cause of prejudice, intolerance and war. It could be said that the definition of evil is, in fact, the illusion of separateness.

Why you cannot change other people

We might sometimes try (albeit subtly and subconsciously) to make others 'more like us', so that they become part of our own safe little tribe. Indeed we have evolved all sorts of techniques for trying to modify others' behaviour and these include:

- the icy stare of disapproval and long stony silence
- a disappointed tone of voice
- the sceptical raised eyebrow
- giving or withdrawing affection as a reward or punishment
- acting all cool and detached
- giving off a whiff of 'burning martyr'

These do not work – not in the long term anyway – because the Universe responds to the intentions in our heart, not to superficial mind games. Such techniques are based on a mindset that says the other person 'should be more like me' and therefore create a fragile and conditional happiness reliant on how other people behave. As Dr Olivier Urbain says in a fascinating book about dialogue called *Daisaku Ikeda's Philosophy of Peace*:

> The small ego, the smaller self, finds evil outside, creates some abstract idea explaining all the wrongs of the world, and is ready to sacrifice countless people considered as embodying this evil, convinced that in doing so it is fighting on the side of justice or 'good'.[3]

Trying to make others more like us is an ego-driven route to temporarily higher self-esteem, whether in the home, in the office or when invading a foreign country. For example, if your partner's behaviour is failing to follow the exact specification that you arrogantly demand, you might need to get over yourself. Indeed, the best thing you can do in this situation is to stop 'shouting at the shadow' and become a brilliant spouse, not just on the surface, but deep down in the core of you. That way your relationship will naturally become more harmonious. In his book *The Undefeated Mind*, my fellow SGI Buddhist Alex Lickerman describes how he chanted in earnest for a relationship and finally had his lightbulb moment: 'And in that moment I realised what my million-daimoku campaign had actually been about all along: not finding a wife, *but turning myself into a person who could have one.*'[4] (A 'million daimoku' means chanting Nam-myoho-renge-kyo one million times, usually in a period of just three months, equivalent to three hours of chanting per day.)

It's the same in the world of business. I have coached managers complaining about their suppliers until they have slowly realised that they might just be difficult clients to work for. And that they will only get the best from their supplier when they become the best client they can be. I was once that kind of manager myself.

And so it is that when we let go of our judgemental prejudices and allow others to express their own unique talents and personalities, we most often discover the treasure of our shared humanity. Even racists have to admit that if you go back far enough up the family tree of a 'pure Englishman', there is no such thing as a pure race, for we are all immigrants.

Forced marriages are a tribal version of S-O-S, brides apparently bring 'dishonour' if they marry someone outside their religion, but the real problem is that they are going *outside their tribe* and the parents are terrified of losing face, being seen as failures and then being rejected by other tribe members, to the point where they would rather disown their closest flesh and blood. So it is that prejudice is based less on fear of others' differences and more on fear of rejection from our own tribe. Presumably this tribal loyalty was valuable when we lived in caves. Incidentally Buddhist organisations are not exempt from such tribalism, but chanting naturally brings individual and collective flaws to the surface so that we might better transform them. Thank you, Spoon.

Individual talent, shared humanity

Whether struggling to connect with a person we instinctively recoil from, seeking to repair a broken relationship, overcoming ingrained prejudice or working with someone we do not like, transformation becomes possible when we discover our common core. Buddhism teaches that chanting Nam-myoho-renge-kyo and sharing dialogue with others are the tools for achieving this. Tools that promote understanding, tools that, step by step, hack out a route to greater harmony. This journey – strewn with obstacles of the ego such as stubbornness, prejudice and revenge – can feel slow and it can feel difficult. It is, after all, a struggle with our FD and a part of the joyful (mostly) combat of human revolution.

'Shared humanity' sounds all very lovely, but is it really achievable? In the throes of lovemaking we may have no trouble feeling it and in drunken camaraderie many of us think we definitely know who our mates are. In intellectual debate, we can forge deep mind-to-mind bonds and when an orchestra or band is in the zone or 'in flow', truly wonderful connections can happen with the audience. Likewise, dinner with friends, building a tree-house with your child or swimming in the ocean with a loved one. Simple.

But what about when facing a persecuting boss, dealing with an anti-social neighbour, talking to someone who holds beliefs that are the polar opposite of ours, or even meeting someone who has taken the life of a loved one? How do you find the shared humanity then? My fellow SGI Buddhist David Hill, an ex-coal miner from Derbyshire, can tell us how:

Some nineteen years ago I was discharged from hospital with a life-threatening illness and the advice to get my affairs in order. My chances of survival were slim, I was weak and frail and did not really want to carry on with my life. While in hospital and without realising it, I had been introduced to Buddhism by a visiting volunteer worker who chanted to me while I fell asleep. I was not in much of a state to take it in at the time and didn't start to practise myself until many years later.

I returned home to my small homophobic racist town and found my house had been sprayed with graffiti, saying 'Gay with Aids lives here'.

This further lowered my already low life state and I was very scared. I removed the graffiti several times and put up a board saying this was their problem not mine, they were cowards, get over it. So they started putting faeces through my letter box, but at least a litter tray to catch it was cheaper than having paint removed! Eventually my tormentors got bored and the harassment stopped. But my hatred and anger toward these people stayed with me and caused me to stay indoors and be really bitter and twisted for many years to come.

Some fifteen years after my first encounter with Buddhism and with my immune system deteriorating, I went on a weekend respite break. I heard this chanting from the room next door and recognised it was the same as the one I had heard from the health worker in the hospital. This intrigued me, so after much discussion with the man from the next room on Buddhist philosophy, I realised this was the piece of the jigsaw I had been looking for in my life.

Back to my fifteen years of bitter twisted anger and hatred. It was really hard to chant for my persecutors' happiness or see their Buddha nature, but when I did, I realised this hatred was mine ... I had created the cause and had reaped the effect. Once I realised this, my anger and hatred for these people dissolved and changed to a feeling of sorrow and even compassion.

I had always isolated myself from my community out of fear. Eventually I decided to integrate with these people, so where better than at the pub! I experienced homophobic remarks when I went, with the local racist men singing 'Puff, the Magic Dragon', but I ignored them. Then I found out the landlord was a racist and was always referring to 'poofs and darkies and sooties', which really infuriated me.

One day I went to the pub and he looked really worried. I asked if he was OK and he explained that his daughter was in hospital with suspected meningitis. I told him I used to work at the hospital and there were some very good African, Asian and Polish doctors, so she was in good hands! I think he knew that I was empathising with him whilst also challenging his racism.

As time went by, I eventually got talking to him about my hobby, fishing, as I knew he was a fisherman and I challenged him to a match, which he accepted.

While fishing we discussed our different philosophies and I revealed I was a Buddhist. This made him think I really was a freak – a gay and a Buddhist! He asked me why my head was not shaved and I didn't wear robes but he also showed interest in where I was coming from. We discussed life experiences, my work in the coal mines and Buddhist philosophy such as energy never being created or destroyed, karma and so on.

And I listened to his outlook on 'immigrants taking our jobs'. I said that although I respected his views, I did not agree with them, and did not expect him to totally agree with mine. Since then we have had lots of dialogue and developed respect for each other, and recently I was invited with my partner to go on a fishing/caravan holiday with him and his wife and parents. We accepted and had a great time, talking late into the nights.

And things have changed at the pub, the men that sang the homophobic songs have been banned by the landlady (she is the boss really!) They now have an African lady behind the bar and a Hungarian chef working in the kitchen. I still get comments when I go there such as 'Have you been chanting, Dave?' I reply: 'Yes, I am chanting for you lot to accept all people as human beings.' They reply that they do and then I say: 'And I'm chanting for you all to come back as black lesbians in your next lifetimes!'

I remember reading that in the 1970s Daisaku Ikeda was criticised by some people in Japan for visiting Communist regimes when he went to talk to leaders in China and Russia. When asked why he was going, he replied: 'Because there are human beings there.' That's why I kept going to the pub and I now see these people as human beings with Buddha nature, not with anger or hatred any more but with compassion. If it was not for my illness and my persecutions I would not have become a Buddhist or developed compassion. Thanks to the practice I have turned poison into medicine.

For more inspiring stories of people transforming hatred into harmony, visit: www.theforgivenessproject.com

The Buddha in me is the best of me

Ultimately, this battle to connect with others, this ongoing duel with your FD, is the daily fight to lose your ego, to overcome your lesser self, to release your attachment to the illusions of your limited karmic identity. Your S-O-S. The self that sees itself as separate from others. And the self that thinks life ends when you die. As a coach, I encourage my clients to overcome limiting beliefs and the negative effects they have on their lives. The two limit*less* beliefs taught by Nichiren Buddhism are:

1. Our life energy is eternal – we stretch forwards and backwards in time.

2. Our life energy is inseparable from the web of life – we stretch 'sideways' into space.

For most people, these two concepts are hard to understand using intellect alone, but as discussed earlier, Nichiren Buddhists believe that prayer can help transform a heart, and through chanting it is possible to feel this liberating sense of fusion, freedom and timelessness. To reach a place that feels like the effervescent epicentre of everything, of life itself. What Deepak Chopra calls 'the field of all possibilities'. There is a sense of losing who you are yet feeling whole, of being totally free yet also belonging, of being utterly relaxed yet totally focused, like your whole life has hit a sweet spot and is in the zone. And chanting in rhythm with other people can be especially powerful.

Personally, I can also often achieve this feeling through twenty minutes of Qi Gong, a physical meditation similar to Tai Chi which improves health and vitality.

The Buddha in you is the best of you

So why on earth would I bother chanting for an hour and a half every day as well? It's because the goal of chanting is not only to bring out the best of me but to draw out the best from you as well. This Buddha state is a place where the petty concerns of the ego dissolve and where other people's goals and sufferings become as important as your own. A place also where you look in the mirror and realise that the faults you perceive in others are traits you very often share, albeit usually wrapped in different clothing. What we dislike in others is very often what we sub-consciously dislike in ourselves.

When you perceive your shared humanity with others, you can even chant, like Dave Hill, for the true happiness of people who have hurt you. That's the fastest way to develop your own humanity in a situation that you find painful. (That means chanting for their Buddha nature to emerge, rather than for them to seek happiness by harming more people.) You'll get control back over your own life much more quickly. Or rather you'll realise that you've always been in control; remember, whatever happens in your life could not occur if you had not made the cause, if your own little bubble of karma had not attracted it. Thank you, Spoon.

Here's a quick recap of how the lesser self (ego or S-O-S) looks and sounds. This ego which can, interestingly, deliver a high degree of individual wealth, success and status, this ego that often evolves in response to rejection, this ego that also produces the worst aspects of what we call 'office politics', this ego that starts wars with other nations, this lesser self who:

1. needs to look good all the time;

2. needs to be right all the time;

3. constantly seeks approval, reassurance and applause;

4. blames others for their unhappiness;

5. negatively focuses on differences;

6. 'writes a script' for exactly how other people 'should behave';

7. tries to control every eventuality of an evolving situation instead of trusting life;

8. only feels safe in its own tribe (religious, family, political, sporting etc ...);

9. fears rejection;

10. fears failure.

As William Woollard says: 'We tend to have this powerful and instinctive need to place ourselves at the centre of our own universe, and we hear loud and clear the inner voice that shouts out our own needs and wants.' From this comes the tendency to build a great towering edifice (such as career, status or wealth ...) upon our fragile egos. If you are lucky then the edifice may come crumbling down at some point, opening the door to your true self and the chance, if you choose to grab it, of absolute happiness.

When the ego succeeds, humanity fails

Numbers 1 and 2 on that list explain why many people have such a deep-seated fear of public speaking or of making presentations, for it is in these situations that we are most scared of looking bad, being wrong and having nowhere to hide – our survival feels threatened. We are equally embarrassed when our children let us down in public, fearing we will be judged a bad parent.

We use our ego, our lesser self, to build high walls around our low self-esteem and our past hurts, walls designed to protect our illusions and keep us ignorant of other people's Buddhahood. In such ways do some people rise to positions of power in business and politics. In such ways do some of the rich and famous make it to the top. In such ways do we start wars and desecrate our planet. In short, our S-O-S is one hell of a powerful beast and it has shaped the civilisation we live in and the trappings of success that we aspire to. But when the ego succeeds, humanity fails. And will continue to fail for as long as we worship the self that puts conflict, comparison and jealousy above harmony, confidence and compassion.

But just as the gifts life brings you come disguised as problems, so can the desires of your S-O-S masquerade as happiness. Such is the power of our illusions. That's why you need wisdom to master your mind and discern the truth of your life. It can take a high level of humility to surrender to your bigger self. To abandon the comfort zone of very powerful but nevertheless partial teachings such as the pursuit of materialism or the belief that everyone should practise the same religion as you. Or that it's your partner's job to make you happy. Humility that often only happens when your treasures of the body and storehouse run out. But it is through the sometimes difficult experience of humility that you discover your true authenticity. It is only by letting go that we may ultimately connect with the heartbeat of the cosmos.

Commenting on his approach to dialogues with people of different countries and faiths, Daisaku Ikeda says:

> Choosing dialogue is the key to building peace and achieving a victory of our inner humanity ... I have met and spoken with thousands of leaders and thinkers of every nationality, ethnic background, religion, and ideology. In each of those encounters, the greater the differences between us, the more I concentrated on trying to understand as deeply as possible the other person's thoughts and feelings.[5]

In a similar vein, French philosopher Joseph Joubert said: 'The aim of an argument or discussion should not be victory, but progress.' Next time you're in a conflict situation at home or work or in the pub, have a go at understanding as deeply as possible the other person's thoughts and feelings – it's not always easy, but it's the fastest way to find a win-win way forward.

In my Buddhist practice, I have often discovered (always with some reluctance) that, deep down, and beneath a protective layer of ego, I share the same pain or suffering as the people I consider to be the most awkward/difficult/annoying. Lots of people are like this. Men especially tend to cover their emotional pain in layers of anger, arrogance and resentment, of bitterness, bravado and booze. Of prejudice and feigned perfection. They then go out into the world and perpetuate their own and others' suffering. So if you find yourself in this situation, instead of fighting each other, develop utter determination for the other person to become absolutely happy. With this approach you can both declare: 'Fellow Buddha, let's fight our negativity together! Let's both win in front of the Gohonzon! Together let's transform our shared poison into medicine!' For when we win together based on the supreme life state of Buddhahood, we can begin to change the consciousness of the whole world.

Lose your ego and connect with your brilliance instead

For the status-driven man, ego is nearly always the biggest obstacle to genuine happiness. When he gets obsessed with climbing the greasy corporate pole, he gains a feeling of self-importance but risks disconnecting from what really is important – for example, family and friends or other 'treasures of the heart'. And often it is ego that makes a man suffer in silence rather than risk losing face by sharing his troubles with people who might support him.

Too many men don't find the strength to be vulnerable when it would help them. In fact the greatest weakness of the alpha male is his S-O-S need to look strong all the time.

So it is that our well-intentioned ego-based S-O-S comes at a heavy price: disengagement. From our true potential, from self-respect, from our life purpose and from deep respectful connections with other people. Much better, says Buddhism, to connect with your brilliance instead. As we saw earlier, in the words of Nichiren: 'Worthy persons deserve to be called so because they are not carried away by the eight winds: prosperity, decline, disgrace, honour, praise, censure, suffering, and pleasure.' In Buddhism 'worthy persons' are those who have mastered their minds – their lesser selves or ego.

Only connect

The most crucial moment of transformation in Nichiren's own life was in 1271, when at the age of forty-nine he survived an attempt by government soldiers to behead him at Tatsunokuchi beach when a bright comet in the sky sent the soldiers running for cover. Sensing perhaps that his life could end at any time and believing it was his Buddhahood that had put him in such rhythm with the Universe, Nichiren began teaching others with more urgency and fervour. And he started to inscribe the scrolls that his followers chant to, the Gohonzon, which, he taught, reflects our inner Buddhahood. In a sense, his life became even bigger post-Tatsunokuchi and he dedicated the rest of his days to helping others become happy in this lifetime; in fact some of the aforementioned soldiers even began to chant. Exiled to the bleak island of Sado after the failed execution, he said that the person named Nichiren had been beheaded and that it was his soul that had come to the island.

By 'soul' he means his *true identity*, and the Tatsunokuchi experience is described as the moment when Nichiren 'cast off the transient' and revealed his true mission as a Buddha. Most of us are unlikely to face the horror of decapitation but there are make-or-break moments in every lifetime, moments when each of us will face our own personal 'Tatsunokuchi'. Be it battling through depression, facing persecution from homophobic racists, losing a job or loved one, handling a divorce, learning to forgive, challenging our money karma, finding value in a severe illness, bonding with our children or 'just' profoundly changing the soundtrack of our mind.

The temptation in these difficult situations is to disconnect from others and take refuge in an S-O-S safety zone – men are especially bad at 'sharing'! The less happy we feel, the more we separate ourselves. As Alastair Campbell says in his book *The Happy Depressive*, 'Whenever I am going through a depressed phase, I feel less desire to connect with other people.' Addictions to drink and drugs are an effective way to disconnect from others, be it behind a smokescreen or an alcoholic haze. But the more we separate ourselves, the less happy we will ultimately become. It is a vicious circle. The time to reach out is when you least feel like it. Feel the resistance and touch someone anyway.

We can learn quite a lot about togetherness from the way that a flock of geese flies. As each bird flaps its wings, it creates an uplift for the bird following. By flying in a V formation, the whole flock adds a 71 per cent greater flying range than if a bird flew alone. The geese in formation honk from behind to encourage those up front to keep up their speed, and each goose takes it in turn to face the most wind resistance at the front of the V. What a team!

This One Life

Whatever their personal growth challenge, Buddhists invariably find that the victory is bigger and better when they expand their lives to embrace others. This may seem paradoxical – after all, when we're in the depths of suffering, our S-O-S will be screaming things like: 'I need all my energy and compassion for me right now! How on earth do you expect me to chant for or support other people?'

Yet this self-pitying attitude is part of the problem, not part of the solution, and when we embrace others, when we live with the belief that everyone has the unlimited life state of Buddhahood, we truly bring our lives into harmony and can begin to bloom in our own unique way. In the early years of my own practice, my mindset for fifty minutes of my daily hour of prayer was almost exclusively: 'I chant to solve this problem in my life'. Then for ten minutes at the end, I would chant for others' happiness – this was an effort at first and did not come naturally. Often I just forgot. Ever so gradually, I found myself chanting more often and more naturally for others, even people I did not like very much, but still this was sometimes an afterthought, despite knowing that Nichiren taught that the most important thing is to 'continually strengthen our wish to benefit others'.

Then grindingly, begrudgingly, after twenty years and many personal 'Tatsunokuchis', practising for others came much more naturally. After winning my major battle with depression, I now find myself simply chanting every day for Life itself to be fulfilled. This eternal 'One Life', this precious cosmic heartbeat that, for 28,000 days (or so) at a time, expresses itself as you and as me and as seven billion other people on this beautiful planet. This 'One Life' that Nichiren called Nam-myoho-renge-kyo. I start to feel that I am casting off the transient and revealing the true, discarding the shallow and seeking the profound, and doffing my hat to the many people I know (Buddhists and non-Buddhists) who seem to have cracked this one much faster than I managed to, sincerely embracing others' lives for many years already.

Get obsessed with your Buddha self

So it seems to me that since we are naturally self-obsessed beings, spending 100 per cent of every day and night in our own heads, the main question of Buddhist practice becomes: 'Which self am I obsessed with? My lesser 'survival' ego-driven self? Or my greater, interconnected, all-embracing Buddha self?' Do I lead a self-centred life? Or a 'centred-self' life?

My fellow SGI member Sharon Holding once shared an experience of a tricky situation at work where her prayer began with feelings of indignation towards a colleague, her constant thought being: 'How dare she treat me like that?' Applying all the principles we have been discussing, her chanting gradually brought her out of her S-O-S and into a place where she felt: 'How dare *anyone* treat *anyone* like that?!' And it was from this 'bigger self' moment that her personal situation began to change for the better. As mentioned earlier, one of the messages of hope from the Lotus Sutra is the promise that you can transform 'poison into medicine', change your karma and accomplish your human revolution. But the most important thing about medicine is that you don't just keep it to yourself, you can share it with others and help them heal their lives as well.

Daisaku Ikeda eloquently captures our shared humanity:

The misfortune of others is our misfortune. Our happiness is the happiness of others. To see ourselves in others and feel an inner oneness and sense of unity with them represents a fundamental revolution in the way we live our lives. Therefore discriminating against another person is the same as discriminating against oneself. When we hurt another, we are hurting ourselves. And when we respect others, we respect and elevate our own lives as well.[6]

Perhaps the uniqueness of Nichiren Buddhism is that it encourages us to flower as unique individuals while also making us aware of our shared humanity and how we connect with the whole Universe.

Get excited about Respect

'Respect' has become a much diminished word. In some inner-city areas, it's what you get from other people because you carry a knife. In too many contexts it's a poor relation to liking someone: 'You don't have to like him, just respect him.' And of course we 'pay our respects' to the dead. Might it be time to start paying some more respects to the living? (Genuine respect, that is, not just the respect we fake for as long as it takes to get what we want from another person.)

Respect also has connotations of being a boring old-fashioned word, but in reality a life based on respect is a very exciting way to live, because it means finding the brilliance in everyone, irrespective of where they sit in society's hierarchy. We are all magnificent works in progress. When a manager inherits a team that at first sight seems a bit mediocre, the manager who has deep respect for each person's potential to improve will bring out the best in them and realise that they had as much untapped potential to be amazing as they did to be average.

In the title track of his album *Ordinary Heroes*, my fellow SGI Buddhist and singer-songwriter Howard Jones celebrates what he calls 'the courage and fighting spirit of people in their ordinary lives. It is never reported in the press but is the thing that holds society together'.

There is a story in the Lotus Sutra about a Bodhisattva called 'Never Disparaging'. He was a disciple of Shakyamuni. He was originally a very wealthy man, but he was very unhappy. When he converted to Buddhism, he decided that he would completely respect every person he came across and so he bowed at every person he saw. People couldn't understand this behaviour from a complete stranger. So they started cursing him and he just kept on bowing. And then they started stoning him wherever he went. And as he fled from the pelting stones, he just kept bowing and saying, 'I deeply respect your life.'

This was in no sense a 'turn the other cheek' or martyr's response, it represented the strongest possible desire for people to connect with their full potential, just like the approach taken in the pub by my friend David Hill. This attitude is reminiscent of the 'unconditional positive regard' made famous by humanist therapist Carl Rogers who believed that such a level of respect was key to the personal growth of his patients.

Respect is also needed to:

- see the world through someone else's eyes, rather than just your own;
- overcome personal prejudices;
- be a strict but compassionate mentor;
- nourish goodwill in professional relationships;
- keep a marriage alive once the honeymoon days are over;
- listen to another person properly.

Real listening comes from the heart

I used to think listening was just a skill that can be easily taught, but real listening goes much deeper and comes from the heart. Of course, there are behavioural techniques we can use, such as nodding, making appropriate noises, resisting the urge to interrupt, not looking too obviously at our watch, summarising what people have said to show understanding etc ... These are all the usual skills taught on training courses. But if in your heart you are judging, disparaging or disrespecting the other person then your skills training will be worth a hill of beans and no connection will be made, especially if you are under pressure or in a low life state. When I trained as a coach I was given the beautiful explanation that listening is 'the highest form of hospitality'. Interestingly, the Chinese character for 'ear' is central to the meaning of the character for 'sage'. So when we listen closely and humbly to the words of another, we are wise.

The Buddha in the bedroom

When I first wrote about love on my blog (www.thanking thespoon.com) on 14 February 2013, Valentine's Day, the post received more views than any other topic, showing that the search for fulfilling relationships is one of our most profound desires as human beings. That particular blog post still gets around twenty hits every day. So, what does Nichiren Buddhism say about the search for love? First of all, love is not about walking into the sunset with the man or woman of your dreams, even though a whole advertising industry has been built up over decades to make us believe that Love with 'The One' – complete with a cottage and a rose garden – is the answer to all our problems. Because of this powerful myth, for some people Valentine's Day and similar occasions can feel like a dream come true, while others may feel their hearts have been broken because they didn't receive any attention at all.

Love – looking together in the same direction

Buddhism encourages individuality, and there are no tribal or moral rules about things such as sex before marriage, fidelity, homosexuality or divorce. Instead, there are guidelines to create greater harmony.

1. Because life is precious, nurture a deep desire to respect unconditionally the eternal core of your partner's life – and your own. Ultimately, a current of deep respect is more important than the surface waves of romantic love. When contempt replaces respect, goodwill quickly ebbs away and the relationship suffers.

2. Love in Buddhism is all about personal growth, human revolution and making the world a better place. I love these words by Kahlil Gibran in his bestselling book *The Prophet*: 'And stand together yet not too near together: [for the] oak tree and the cypress grow not in each other's shadow.'

3. Do not make your partner your religion or your object of worship; your happiness is ultimately your own responsibility, not theirs, so do not burden them with this expectation.

4. Your partner is not there to make you complete, even if you do call them your 'other half'! As Antoine de Saint-Exupéry wrote: 'Love is not two people gazing at each other, but two people looking ahead together in the same direction.' That means two people coming together to foster each other's spiritual growth and happiness and move together towards shared goals in life.

5. Real love is not one person clinging to another; it can only be fostered between two strong people secure in themselves.

6. Both of you need to feel like deserving winners in your relationship, not needy victims.

7. Don't commit to being with someone just because they have qualities that you don't feel you have, such as strength or joy or proactivity. You *do* have all these attributes yourself, in a latent state – draw them out from within. If you just look outside yourself for these qualities, placing huge expectation on your partner, you risk devouring and destroying the things you most admire in them.

8. Don't try to write a script for your partner, they are not a project for you to work with. Such an illusion stems from arrogance. Understand that you will never change your partner's behaviour. Or that if you do, it will be at the cost of their own self-respect and then you will respect them even less.

9. Always put more energy into changing yourself than into trying to change the other person. Remember that your partner may stir up stuff from the depths of your life, so be grateful – thank the spoon! Move your own life instead of 'shouting at the shadow'.

10. Don't use the words 'always' or 'never' when criticising your partner. They're almost always never true.

11. Argue with a view to progress rather than to proving that you are right.

12. Talk openly and maturely about the difficult stuff, rather than 'painting over the rust'.

13. Learn to laugh about and treasure your differences more than you argue about them. In happy relationships, this is known as 'domestic banter'. Remember to hear your partner's nagging as the sweet song of a bird.

14. When you feel hurt by the ending of a relationship and your S-O-S wants to build a wall of protection around you, remember that when you lock the world out, you lock up the love inside you too.

15. End it or mend it. Only leave a difficult relationship once you have grown as much as you can from it and changed the karma that first attracted it into your life; otherwise the same pattern will repeat itself in the next phase of your love life. As Joe Vitale says, 'Get the lesson and you no longer need the experience.'

16. Cultivate the treasures of the heart.

Mindset mantras for discovering your connection with all of Life

I am unique. I am also interconnected with all of Life.

I let go of my smaller self. I am an unlimited being.
I am overcoming the limitations I have accepted in my own heart.

I connect, at the deepest level, with the lives of other people.

I break free from my tribal limitations and discover our shared humanity.

The Universe responds to the intentions in my heart.

I spend more energy changing myself rather than trying
to change others.

When I let others express their own unique qualities,
I discover the treasure of our shared humanity.

I release my small ego and live in greater harmony with
those around me.

I release feelings of prejudice and revenge. I choose
dialogue as the way forward instead.

My life energy stretches forwards and backwards
in time forever.

I find the humility to surrender to my bigger self and
discover true authenticity.

I cast off the transient and shallow, I reveal what is most
true and profound in me.

I feel grateful to the people I instinctively recoil from,
for they often hold up a mirror to my own pain.

I work to understand as deeply as possible the thoughts
and feelings of people I disagree with.

I release the need to look good and be right all the time.

I discover that respecting others is a truly exciting way
to live.

Journal exercises

1. Reflect on the times when you have consciously or subconsciously tried to change other people. What can you learn from these experiences?

2. Think about the times when you have managed to form a connection with someone whom you did not initially like. What was the key to your change of heart?

3. Of the 16 points made about 'significant other relationships', which ones strike a chord with you? What are you already good at? Where could you make a step forward?

4. Can you think of any relationships where what you have disliked in someone else is what you subconsciously dislike in yourself?

5. Think of times when you have fallen out with a close friend and then repaired the rift at a later date. What were the lessons for each of you?

6. If people showed greater and deeper respect in your world, what could change for the better?

7. How might your life be better if you let go of your 'small ego' and connected more often with your 'bigger self'?

CHAPTER 15

BEYOND THE OK SOCIETY

As we have seen, Buddhism teaches that the happiness of others is neither an afterthought nor a bolt-on optional extra. Nor is happiness something that we only start to seek for others once we've succeeded enough in our lives to give something back to society (laudable though philanthropy can be).

Moreover, in Buddhism the essential oneness of the individual and universal means, for example, that there's not much value in going on an anti-war march if you've refused to speak to your father for ten years – the angry vibe your heart is sending to the Universe adds to the problem rather than the solution, however powerful and eloquent the message of peace displayed on your protest banner.

A 'we' prayer, not just a 'me' prayer

But at the same time, Buddhism teaches that the deepest level of personal development only comes from a strong commitment to social transformation; you cannot do your human revolution alone in a bedsit. Instead, you chant for all of Life to be fulfilled – this energy that flows through you and me and the people we love, the people we don't yet know and yes, even the people we hate. In short, Nam-myoho-renge-kyo is a 'we' prayer, not just a 'me' prayer, and to persist with your human revolution is nothing less than the triumph of the big self over the ego.

Difficult as it is to quantify such things, it seems to me that personal development via Buddhism can be a slower path than more conventional routes to fulfilment (such as being coached, doing affirmations or meditating). I guess this is because chanting is deeper and more fundamental, coming as it does from our ninth rather than seventh consciousness; which means coming from that 'One Life' Buddha source expressed by Nichiren as Nam-myoho-renge-kyo. If the changes are slower, it is perhaps because on this path we are changing our karma, not just our subconscious. And we are bringing other people with us. In fact, we are each of us changing the destiny of the planet.

As the Lotus Sutra says:

> Buddhas wish to open the door of Buddha wisdom to all living beings ... That is why they appear in the world. They wish to cause living beings to awaken to the Buddha wisdom, and therefore they appear in the world.[1]

The Lotus Sutra even claims that in the distant past we all made a deep vow to become absolutely happy and to guide others to do the same, through overcoming our personal difficulties. Another teaching which, though very hard to believe, produces a valuable mindset for the challenges of daily life. And I do feel we only achieve our full potential when we surrender to the Light and Love at the source of all Life.

Millions of human revolutions

The inclusiveness of Buddhist teachings means that, as Daisaku Ikeda suggests, we can even consider a broader definition of the concept of 'home':

> Your home is where your loved ones live. Your home is the place where you work together with your fellow human beings

to build a paradise, a realm of peace and prosperity for all. When we are asked where our home is, we can answer: 'My home is the world. Everywhere in the world where my fellow human beings live, all of it, is my home.'[2]

My personal experience of practising with SGI leads me to believe that the movement's monthly discussion meetings provide a forum for developing this 'big self' spirit and this 'realm of peace'. Not least because the eclectic mix of people attracted to Nichiren Buddhism inevitably creates the sort of healthy (though sometimes difficult) friction without which 'muddy potatoes' cannot be cleaned. Clark Strand, author of a study on SGI called *Waking The Buddha*, describes these meetings as the place where the 'rubber meets the road', where the beliefs of Buddhism are put to the test.

And it seems to me that people often come to Buddhism to learn how to love again – or even to love for the first time. Love themselves and their lives. Love their partners, their children and their parents. Their achievements, their mistakes, their futures and, above all, their personal missions. They give themselves permission to honour their talents, gifts and values – sometimes for the first time ever, often for the first time in a long while. They come to confront the harsh realities of daily life and they leave with a sparkle in their eye, a joyful soundtrack in their minds, action plans for personal growth and the tools and courage to achieve what they truly deserve. They return a month later to inspire others with the victories they have had, the differences they have made or the struggles they have still not given up on.

SGI member and Hollywood actress Cathryn de Prume says in an interview on my blog: 'The SGI movement is set up brilliantly. It gives a person the opportunity to raise their life condition by chanting and supporting others.' She added that her favourite quote from Nichiren's writings is this one: 'A blue fly, if it clings to the tail of a thoroughbred horse, can travel ten thousand miles.' 'SGI is that horse,' she says, 'and we can travel so much farther than we could on our own. We can create peace right where we are with people whom we would not normally connect with. When one person becomes happy they influence those around them. Eventually our hope is that this will create world peace.'

So the overwhelming message of Nichiren Buddhism is that lasting world peace depends not so much on protests and politics but on personal development, on hundreds of thousands of individual human revolutions, on millions of people encouraging each other to discover and develop their wisdom, courage and compassion – to the point where these treasures of the heart become an ingrained everyday habit, just as conflict and wars are currently entrenched in the karma of humanity, in this ego-driven, S-O-S-dominated age of ours. That means relying less on politicians and scientists to drive change and more on building a humanistic network of people who are prepared to challenge their own and each other's FD. And prepared to melt the cold indifference in people's hearts. As Professor Lou Marinoff says: 'Our next major steps as a species will be neither biological nor technological but will entail an evolution (or revolution) in human consciousness.'

It is encouraging to see how, after centuries that saw a steadily overpowering emphasis on IQ, we are now in an age that sees the growing and welcome influence of EQ. Richard Dawkins (who I would guess has a higher IQ than many...) concludes *The God Delusion* with these words: 'I am thrilled to be alive at a time when humanity is pushing against the limits of understanding. Even better, we may eventually discover that there are no limits.' Hear, hear! Although Dawkins would probably not agree, surely the next phase of our development as a species, and one to be celebrated even more than IQ or EQ, will be the rise of our collective SQ – humanity's 'spiritual intelligence' – and the realisation that, as Dawkins suggests, there really are 'no limits'.

I can be me, you can be you

And this was nothing less than Nichiren's ultimate aim. The goal for which he risked his life, the cause in whose name he went through such severe persecution and exiles, was something called 'Kosen-Rufu', which we touched on briefly in Chapter 4. Often loosely translated as 'world peace', it is much more than just the absence of war. It describes a time in the future where individual hearts and minds are so enlightened by principles such as those taught in the Lotus Sutra that society as a whole becomes a much more harmonious yet no less dynamic place. A society where the positive rather than negative aspects of the Ten Worlds are revealed, where more people are more often in touch with their 'bigger selves', a world where the Buddha in me connects more often with the Buddha in you.

For this reason, sharing Buddhist philosophy and teaching others to chant is an integral part of following Nichiren's teachings. When interviewing Cathryn de Prume, who has brought a hundred people to the practice, I asked her: 'If you could teach anyone in the world to chant, who would it be?' I think I expected her to say 'Oprah Winfrey' or 'Tom Hanks' or some A-list director amongst her circle of friends. But her answer both surprised and moved me: 'It would be a teenage girl on the verge of making a big decision, someone at a fork in the road,' said Cathryn, 'because teenagers and youth are our hope. They can change the world. But they can also destroy themselves. There's nothing more exciting than introducing someone to the practice and watching them change their life.'

Nichiren's vision of course is not of a world without problems, any more than individual happiness is a life without difficulties. Kosen-Rufu is not a flower-power utopia or la-la land, nor is it some other-world paradise or nirvana; nor is it a static destination. It is a fast-flowing current where I can be me and you can be you and each of us is stronger for having each other in our lives. Buddhist scholar Clark Strand alludes to the dynamism of Nichiren's philosophy, pointing out that religious teachings 'rarely spark the fire of revolution'. He adds that 'societies prefer the elegant confinement of the candle on the altar over the open flame of reform'. We live in times where revolution and reform are urgently needed.

Incidentally, there is no expectation in Nichiren Buddhism that everyone in the world will chant – only that many people will, that many will follow other philosophies upholding the dignity of Life and that many others will support them from the sidelines. It's about reaching a healthy tipping point, not converting everyone to one religion; and indeed there have been, are and probably always will be people who oppose – in some cases very strongly – teachings such as those espoused by Nichiren.

Compassion and determination are nothing without each other

The biggest threat to the achievement of world peace (or any other ideal) is not of evil people being powerful, but of good people being apathetic; as philosopher and statesman Edmund Burke famously said: 'All that is necessary for the triumph of evil is for good men to do nothing.'

When people who care enough find it in themselves to stand up for justice and create momentum, selfish people will automatically feel uncomfortable and eventually vanish. Only people who deeply feel that life is a precious treasure are able to speak up, stand up and take action in such a way. It is not enough to be a nice but inoffensive person because compassion without determination gets nothing changed. Meanwhile, determination without compassion just produces autocrats. We need both of these qualities, in equal and harmonious proportions. And we must challenge our passive and pervasive acceptance of other people's unhappiness.

Perhaps the biggest obstacle to Kosen-Rufu is neither apathetic good people nor energetic evil people, but something in between that one might term the 'OK society'. Generally, in this society, it is quite acceptable for things to be 'not so good' or 'not too bad'. We do not seem to mind very much when we are just 'keeping our heads above water', when we are just 'getting by' or 'muddling through'. This is a familiar feeling for many people. Damaging symptoms of the 'OK society' are that we settle for 'that'll do' relationships, a 'good enough' job done, health that is 'not too bad' and a 'mustn't grumble' approach to daily life. All of this against a backdrop of a widely held belief that 'contentment' is achievable but happiness is not, at least not in this lifetime.

By contrast, Nichiren's message is one of constant growth rather than just S-O-S contentment; spiritual growth, that is, rather than the sort of economic growth that most governments around the world are obsessed with. Growing the treasures of the heart rather than just the treasures of the storehouse, developing absolute rather than just relative happiness.

Because you're a Buddha and that's what your Buddhahood wants

So, what is the solution to this widespread S-O-S mindset and the 'OK society'? First to be aware of our over-used survival mentality, second to feel that life is so precious that we want to live it to the full, and third to engage with the Buddha in ourselves and overcome the FD that pretends 'OK' and 'content-ment' are enough. It is a daily battle and can only be transformed by a daily victory.

When the volume is turned up on our FD, it is quite normal for Buddhists to think: 'Kosen-Rufu, why bother?' Or, 'Why be concerned with other people's desires and problems?' But the answer that emerges through prayer, through turning up the volume on the good stuff, through connecting with the bigger self, is this: 'It's because you're a Buddha and that's what your Buddhahood wants.' Buddhahood, remember, is the deepest wish held in your heart and the reservoir of all that is best in you and in me.

As Daisaku Ikeda writes, this battle is an incredibly rewarding experience:

> The fight to create a new life is a truly wonderful thing. In it you find for the first time a wisdom that causes your intelligence to shine, the light of intuition that leads to an understanding of the universe, the compassion that enables you to take upon yourself the sorrows of others, the sense of fusion with the cosmic source of life that creates a rhythm in the lives of all men. As you polish that jewel which is life, you will learn to walk the supreme pathway of true humanity. I myself think of this flowering of the creative life as a human revolution. This human revolution is your mission now as it will be throughout your lives.[3]

I hope that after reading this book, you feel more enlightened, uplifted and optimistic. More grateful, more confident and more determined. I hope you feel that Life is the most precious treasure and that we are all interconnected in the wonderful and mesmerising rhythm of the Universe. I chant each day to live with this wisdom, to accomplish my own human revolution and to help transform our planet. And, whether or not you practise Buddhism, I encourage you to discover and reveal the inherent dignity and nobility in your heart. Nurture and nourish your uniqueness. Have the courage to be true to yourself. Live a flourishing, magnificent and authentic life of absolute happiness. Win over your struggles and, through your victories, encourage others to do the same. Have no regrets on your passing from this existence. Revere your awesomeness. Treasure every moment. Life is precious, cherish it.

THE BUDDHA'S INVITATION

Will you come to eternity's tentative edge
Then teach the world of its unspoken power?
Will you plunge filthy waters with only your faith
Then fly to the heavens on hope's thinnest breath?

Will you squeeze yourself through to the middle of you
Yet still keep a space for those who might hate you?
Will you sit with the scream at the core of your soul
And then share your song with those who might love you?

Will you dive, will you run
Will you rise with the sun
Will you laugh, will you weep
Will you chant till you sleep?

Will you fashion your future from garbage and grit,
Yet keep one hand free for those who would hold you?
Will you bet all you have on an unfancied truth,
Then share your raw wisdom with those once were brave?

Will you cast off your shackles, your comforts, your props,
Will you scrap sweet illusions for a Law that could break you?
Will you trade your bravado for slivers of faith
Will you silence your mind just to follow your soul?

Will you give up your status, your perks and your pride,
Will you join me in exile, where many have died?
Will you strip bare the critic, the cynic, the fool,
All the roles you have played, all the clichés, the rules?

Will you sit with the tramp, and the thief and the whore,

Will you keep giving hope when they ask you for more?

And if I stand by your side on this grand Treasure Tower ...

Will you smile, will you shine

Will you say what you saw?

Will you dance, will you chant,

Will you promise me more?

Will you risk, will you write

Will you make a new Vow?

Will you stand, will you fight

Will you come with me now?

DAVID HARE

NOTES

1. What's it all about?

1. Nichiren Daishonin, 'New Year's Gosho', *The Writings of Nichiren Daishonin*, Vol. 1, p.1137.

2. Life is precious

1. Nichiren Daishonin, 'Regarding an Unlined Robe', *The Writings of Nichiren Daishonin*, Vol. 2, p.599.

3. Happiness is the soundtrack of your mind

1. Nichiren Daishonin, 'On Attaining Buddhahood in This Lifetime', *The Writings of Nichiren Daishonin*, Vol. 1, p.3.
2. Nichiren Daishonin, 'The Four Virtues and The Four Debts of Gratitude', *The Writings of Nichiren Daishonin*, Vol. 2, p.637.
3. Nichiren Daishonin, 'The "Entrustment" and Other Chapters', *The Writings of Nichiren Daishonin*, Vol. 1, p.915.
4. Nichiren Daishonin, 'The Unanimous Declaration by the Buddhas of the Three Existences regarding the Classification of the Teachings and Which Are to Be Abandoned and Which Upheld', *The Writings of Nichiren Daishonin,* Vol. 2, p.843.
5. Steve Taylor, *The Fall,* O-Books, (2005), pp.238-9
6. Jules Evans, *Philosophy for Life*, London: Rider Books (2012), p.124.
7. Nichiren Daishonin, 'The Gift of Rice', *The Writings of Nichiren Daishonin*, Vol. 1, p.1125.

4. The Ten Worlds – Buddhism's model of the mind

1. Nichiren Daishonin, 'Hell Is the Land of Tranquil Light', *The Writings of Nichiren Daishonin*, Vol. 1, p.456.
2. Daisaku Ikeda, *Buddhism Day by Day*, Middleway Press (2006), p.215.
3. Nichiren Daishonin, 'The Real Aspect of the Gohonzon', *The Writings of Nichiren Daishonin*, Vol. 1, p.832.
4. Nichiren Daishonin, 'Letter to the Brothers', *The Writings of Nichiren Daishonin*, Vol. 1, p.496.
5. Nichiren Daishonin, 'King Rinda', *The Writings of Nichiren Daishonin*, Vol. 1, p.989.
6. Alastair Campbell, *The Happy Depressive*, London: Arrow (2012), p.36.
7. Daisaku Ikeda, http://www.ikedaquotes.org/human-revolution

5. Karma – your whole life in your hands

1. Kahlil Gibran, *The Prophet*, London: Arrow (1998), p.20.
2. Nichiren Daishonin, 'Letter from Sado', *The Writings of Nichiren Daishonin*, Vol. 1, p.305.
3. Nichiren Daishonin, 'Reply to the Lay Priest Soya', *The Writings of Nichiren Daishonin*, Vol. 1, p.486.
4. Nichiren Daishonin, 'On Prayer', *The Writings of Nichiren Daishonin*, Vol 1, p.340.
5. Alex Lickerman, *The Undefeated Mind*, Deerfield Beach, FL: HCI Books (2013), p.38.

6. Everyone's a Buddha

1. Nichiren Daishonin, 'The Four Virtues and The Four Debts of Gratitude', *The Writings of Nichiren Daishonin*, Vol. 2, p.637.
2. Nichiren Daishonin, 'On the Treasure Tower', *The Writings of Nichiren Daishonin*, Vol. 1, p.299.
3. Nichiren Daishonin, 'The Object of Devotion for Observing the Mind', *The Writings of Nichiren Daishonin*, Vol. 1, p.358.
4. Marianne Williamson, 'Our Deepest Fear' in *A Return to Love*, London: Thorsons (1992), p.190.
5. *The Lotus Sutra*, translated by Burton Watson, Columbia University Press (1993), pp.287–8.
6. Quoted in Richard Causton, *The Buddha in Daily Life*, London: Rider Books (1995), p.51.

7. You have a problem? Congratulations!

1. Nichiren Daishonin, 'Happiness in This World', *The Writings of Nichiren Daishonin*, Vol. 1, p.681.
2. Lou Marinoff and Daisaku Ikeda, *The Inner Philosopher*, Cambridge, MA: Dialogue Path Press (2012), p.9.
3. Daisaku Ikeda, *Faith into Action*, World Tribune Press, Santa Monica (1999), p.37.
4. Nichiren Daishonin, 'The Three Obstacles and Four Devils', *The Writings of Nichiren Daishonin*, Vol. 1, p.637.
5. Nichiren, Daishonin, 'The Opening of the Eyes (I)', *The Writings of Nichiren Daishonin*, Vol. 1, p.283.
6. Daisaku Ikeda, Speech at April 1996 Leaders Meeting.

8.Beyond the survival mentality
1. Kazuo Fujii (lecture, 1993).
2. Daisaku Ikeda, *Discussions on Youth*, Santa Monica: World Tribune Press (2010), p.410.

9. Cultivate the treasures of the heart
1. Nichiren Daishonin, 'The Three Kinds of Treasure', *The Writings of Nichiren Daishonin*, Vol. 1, p.850.
2. Nichiren Daishonin, 'Earthly Desires Are Enlightenment', *The Writings of Nichiren Daishonin*, Vol. 1, p.318.
3. Nichiren Daishonin, 'A Sage and an Unenlightened Man', *The Writings of Nichiren Daishonin*, Vol. 1, p.106.
4. Oriah Mountain Dreamer, *The Invitation*, London: Element (1999). www.oriahmountaindreamer.com
5. Anon.
6. Kalle Lasn in interview with Jules Evans – http://www.philosophyfor life.org/kalle-lasn-founder-of-adbusters-on-the-coming-revolution
7. www.ikedaquotes.org/life.

10.Living in the moment – happiness here and now
1. Nichiren Daishonin, 'New Year's Gosho', *The Writings of Nichiren Daishonin*, Vol. 1, p.1137.
2. Nichiren Daishonin, 'On Attaining Buddhahood in This Lifetime', *The Writings of Nichiren Daishonin*, Vol. 1, p.4.
3. Nichiren Daishonin, 'Letter to Niike', *The Writings of Nichiren Daishonin*, Vol. 1, p.1027.
4. Nichiren Daishonin, 'On Attaining Buddhahood in This Lifetime', *The Writings of Nichiren Daishonin*, Vol. 1, p.3.
5. Photo-essay by Daisaku Ikeda, 'Scotland—The Land of True Humanity' (2004).
6. Daisaku Ikeda, Lecture on Nichiren Daishonin's writing 'On Prayer'.

11.Determination through the ups and downs
1. Nichiren Daishonin, 'Letter to Niike', *The Writings of Nichiren Daishonin*, Vol. 1, p.1026.
2. Nichiren Daishonin, 'The Third Day of the New Year', *The Writings of Nichiren Daishonin*, Vol. 1, p.1013.
3. W. Timothy Gallwey – quoted on http://theinnergame.com
4. Lou Marinoff and Daisaku Ikeda, *The Inner Philosopher*, Cambridge, MA: Dialogue Path Press (2012), p.78.

5. Nichiren Daishonin, 'The Selection of the Time', *The Writings of Nichiren Daishonin*, Vol. 1, p.558.

6. Linda Johnson, public talk.

12.Become the master of your mind

1. Viktor Frankl, *Man's Search for Meaning*, London: Rider Books (2011), p.53.

2. Josei Toda, *The World of Nichiren Daishonin's Writings*, Soka Gakkai Malasia, Vol. 3, pp.18-19.

3. Daisaku Ikeda, 'On Attaining Buddhahood in This Lifetime'. Lecture on Nichiren Daishonin's writing.

4. Nichiren Daishonin, 'On Attaining Buddhahood in This Lifetime', *The Writings of Nichiren Daishonin*, Vol. 1, p.4.

5. Nichiren Daishonin, 'Reply to Kyo'o', *The Writings of Nichiren Daishonin*, Vol. 1, p.412.

6. Quoted on Words of Wisdom website. http://www.ikedaquotes.org/success/success890.html

7. Nichiren Daishonin, 'Persecution by Sword and Staff', *The Writings of Nichiren Daishonin*, Vol. 1, p.962.

8. Quoted on http://www.ikedaquotes.org/human-relationships/human relationships253.html?quotes_start=14

9. Nichiren Daishonin, 'The Actions of the Votary of the Lotus Sutra', *The Writings of Nichiren Daishonin*, Vol. 1, p.764.

10. Ibid.

11. Robert McCammon, *Boy's Life*, London: Pocket Books (1999). Quoted on http://www.robertmccammon.com/2011/05/19/boys-life-quoted-on-one-tree-hill

12. Nichiren Daishonin, 'Winter Always Turns to Spring', *The Writings of Nichiren Daishonin*, Vol. 1, p.536.

13. Mariane Pearl, http://marianepearl.com/articlesEssays.php?pressId=5

14. Quoted on Words of Wisdom website. http://www.ikedaquotes.org/hope/hope219.html?quotes_start=7

15. Nichiren Daishonin, 'The Person and the Law', *The Writings of Nichiren Daishonin*, Vol. 1, p.1097.

16. Daisaku Ikeda, *The Wisdom of the Lotus Sutra*, Santa Monica: World Tribune Press (2000), Vol. 6, p.13.

17. Nichiren Daishonin, 'The Eight Winds', *The Writings of Nichiren Daishonin*, Vol. 1, p.794.

13.How to choose a great mentor

1. Nichiren Daishonin, 'The Tripitaka Master Shan-wu-wei', *The Writings of Nichiren Daishonin*, Vol. 1, p.178.

14.Small self, big self

1. Lou Marinoff and Daisaku Ikeda, *The Inner Philosopher*, Cambridge, MA: Dialogue Path Press (2012), p.205.
2. Daisaku Ikeda, http://www.ikedaquotes.org/stories/arnold_toynbee.html
3. Olivier Urbain, *Daisaku Ikeda's Philosophy of Peace*, London: I.B. Tauris (2010), p.156.
4. Alex Lickerman, *The Undefeated Mind*, Deerfield Beach, FL: HCI Books (2013), p.66.
5. Daisaku Ikeda, New Year's Message, 2009.
6. Daisaku Ikeda, *The Wisdom of the Lotus Sutra*, Santa Monica: World Tribune Press (2000), Vol. 1, pp.149-50.

15.Beyond the OK society

1. *The Lotus Sutra*, trans. Burton Watson, Columbia University Press (1993).
2. Daisaku Ikeda, Photo-essay on the Makiguchi Memorial Garden, Tokyo.
3. Daisaku Ikeda, 'To the Youthful Pioneers of Soka', address to Soka University Student Union (2006).

GLOSSARY

(dedicated to my mum, who noticed this book needed one ...)

Buddha: a person who has become awakened to the true
nature of life and who strives to lead others to the same
state of enlightenment. **Buddhahood** is characterised by
joy, wisdom, courage, compassion, gratitude and optimism.
Nichiren Daishonin taught that it is a state achievable by
common mortals in this lifetime.

Coaching: a goal-focused, forward-looking talking therapy
that uses listening and questioning techniques to help
clients discover their own unique answers to their challenges
and achieve breakthroughs in their lives. More here: www.
thankingthespoon.com/coaching

Daimoku: 'to chant daimoku' means chanting the mantra
Nam-myoho-renge-kyo and is the main morning and
evening practice of Nichiren Buddhists.

Daisaku Ikeda (b.1958): third and current President of Soka
Gakkai International (SGI), who has pioneered the worldwide
spread of Nichiren Buddhism. Widely respected as a philosopher, peacebuilder, educator, author and poet, Ikeda was
shortlisted for the Nobel peace Prize in 2015 and has held
dialogues with the likes of Nelson Mandela, Rosa Parks,
Arnold J. Toynbee, Chandra Wickramasinghe, Norman
Cousins, Linus Pauling, Mikhail Gorbachev, Joseph Rotblat
and André Malraux.

Fundamental Darkness (FD): the innate ignorance that stops
you seeing your own Buddhahood and fulfilling your full
potential. FD can manifest as 'negative self-talk' (to use a
coaching term). However, when we accept our FD as part of
our precious lives and harness it as an impetus for spiritual
growth, it becomes a springboard to enlightenment.

Gohonzon: literally the 'object of devotion for observing your

Buddha mind', this paper scroll is a tool for revering your life and embodies the Mystic Law in physical form, with the mantra Nam-myoho-renge-kyo inscribed in big and bold calligraphy down its centre. It serves as a reminder that we all have the power within us to become happier when we put Buddhahood at the centre of our lives.

Gongyo: literally 'assiduous (constant) practice', gongyo means to recite two short portions of the Lotus Sutra and is a fundamental daily practice for Nichiren Buddhists.

Gosho: literally 'honourable writings', this term describes Nichiren Daishonin's legacy – the hundreds of letters he wrote to his followers, as well as treatises presented to the government of his time.

Josei Toda (1900–1958): succeeded Tsunesaburo Makiguchi (1871–1944), to become second President of Soka Gakkai. An educator, businessman and peace activist, he did more than anyone else to bring Nichiren Buddhism to the masses amidst the nuclear devastation of post-war Japan.

Human revolution: a personal transformation of the heart aimed at creating a more vibrant, respectful and peaceful world. Describes the process of transforming karma into mission through Buddhist practice.

Karma: a fundamental teaching in Buddhism that helps explain how life works. Can be summarised as the future we create for ourselves in every moment of every lifetime through the 'causes we make' in thought, word and deed. Sometimes used to describe the deep patterns that repeat over and over in your life. An understanding of karma sets you free and simultaneously gives you total responsibility for transforming your life.

Kosen-Rufu: a time in the future where individual hearts and minds are so enlightened by principles such as those taught in the Lotus Sutra that society as a whole becomes a much more harmonious yet no less dynamic place. Kosen-Rufu is the ultimate goal of Nichiren Buddhist practice and means raising the life state of the whole planet through individual human revolutions that reveal the dignity inherent in every life.

Law of Attraction (LOA): a new-age teaching which asserts that your thoughts and your feelings create your life, including the events and people that you 'attract' into it.

Lotus Sutra: a scripture formulated and taught by Shakyamuni, the Lotus Sutra was revolutionary in its insistence that common mortals could attain Buddhahood in this lifetime. As such, it became the inspiration for Nichiren's life and teachings.

Mystic Law: the fundamental life force governing the workings of the Universe. Sometimes compared to 'gravity', it acts on all of life, all of the time. Nichiren Buddhists chant Nam-myoho-renge-kyo to put their lives 'in rhythm' with it. Described by Buddhist author Eddy Canfor-Dumas as the 'mystical, invisible thread between the churning, inner reality of my life and the great outdoors of the rest of the world'.

Nam-myoho-renge-kyo: the title of the Lotus Sutra and the mantra chanted by Nichiren Buddhists. Literally means 'I dedicate my life to the Mystic Law of cause and effect' and can be interpreted as the voice of the Buddha in you, the rhythm of life, and the Law of the Universe.

Nichiren Daishonin: a revolutionary Japanese monk (1222–1282) and bold reformer of Buddhism, he based his philosophy on the Lotus Sutra, the ultimate scripture taught by Shakyamuni Buddha. Persecuted by Japan's rulers, he survived repeated exiles and attempts on his life to successfully propagate the teaching of the mantra Nam-myoho-renge-kyo.

Nine consciousnesses: a multi-layered model of the mind that comprises our five senses, rational mind and subconscious, but also includes karma and reveals that you can make profound and lasting changes in your life by accessing your Buddhahood – your ninth layer of consciousness.

NLP (Neuro-linguistic Programming): a popular approach to personal development created by Richard Bandler and John Grinder in the 1970s and still used by many life coaches and therapists. Its central principle is that we can change our behaviour by using resourceful language to re-programme our minds.

SGI (Soka Gakkai International): a global lay movement of more than 12 million socially-engaged Buddhists who follow the teachings of Nichiren Daishonin. More below and at www.sgi.org

Shakyamuni: also known as Siddhartha Gautama, Shakyamuni lived in India around 3,000 years ago and is the founder of Buddhism. Originally a prince of the Shakya tribe, he renounced a life of luxury to embark on a spiritual quest and relieve the fundamental causes of human suffering.

S-O-S (Survival-Obsessed Self)*: fashioned by 14 million years of primate evolution, this is the hardwired (and originally well-intentioned) instinct within us that is rooted in 'Animality' state and wants us to steer clear of problems, challenges and growth. Useful in terms of avoiding danger (e.g. when crossing a busy road), its downside is that it separates you from the universal human race. Buddhists sometimes use the term 'small self' as our S-O-S comes from our ego and is therefore also a source of arrogance, 'office politics', anxiety and other aspects of our Fundamental

* Note: Survival-Obsessed Self is not a term that is widely used in Buddhist circles as it is an expression coined by the author while writing this book.

Darkness. The Survival-Obsessed-Self lies at the root of our attachments to comfort zones, to money, status and fame and to self-protecting prejudice of any kind, often manifesting as destructive tribalism.

Ten worlds: the concept Nichiren Buddhism uses to explain many of our individual differences and the constant flux in the 'soundtrack of our minds': Hell, Hunger, Animality, Anger, Tranquillity, Rapture (also called 'Heaven'), Learning, Realisation, Bodhisattva and Buddhahood. Also often referred to as 'life-states'. **Mutual possession of the ten worlds** means that each of these apparently separate ten life states 'contains' all the others, in a latent or potential state, illustrating how, in every situation, we can strive to reveal our Buddhahood and create value for self and others.

Thanking the Spoon: an attitude of being grateful for people and situations that cause us to suffer, seeing them as a source of spiritual growth. Also the name of my blog.

ABOUT SOKA GAKKAI INTERNATIONAL

For the record, and for anyone interested in learning how to chant with other Nichiren Buddhists, I am a member of Soka Gakkai International (SGI, www.sgi.org), a lay religious movement that has grown out of the atomic devastation of post-war Japan. In its early days SGI was routinely derided as a movement for the 'poor and the sick' but has now become a global movement with 12 million members in 190 countries.

SGI provides a network where people from all walks of life can meet, chant together and support each other with the challenges of daily life. There is a big emphasis on dialogue, on personal growth and on social transformation. Meetings of different kinds are held several times a month in members' homes and bigger events can take place in village halls up and down the country or at the UK national centre in Taplow, Berkshire. The biggest surprise to social scientists and experts in comparative religion is SGI's diversity. Unlike other Buddhist movements that tend to be predominantly white middle-class and intellectual, Nichiren Buddhism has attracted people from right across the spectrum of social class, education, racial background and sexual orientation.

Most people come to Buddhism via personal one-to-one friendships as my fellow SGI member – singer-songwriter Howard Jones – explains: 'I met Buddhism through my friend Jeff Banks and I loved the way he was as a person, always really respectful to other people and full of energy and life. And I thought, "I want to be like that."'

The leader of this movement is Daisaku Ikeda, a man who has overcome major obstacles and challenges to spread this teaching around the globe and who is frequently quoted in these pages. SGI has been described as an extraordinary movement of 'ordinary people leading ordinary people to enlightenment'. When receiving an award from SGI (on 22 March 2003) for his contribution to world peace, Mikhail Gorbachev, former President of the Soviet Union, said: 'President Ikeda is a philosopher, a thinker, and a poet with a grand vision and a big heart. He is working not only for Japan but for the sake of the entire world. I am very proud to accept this award, and I hope to continue to work even harder to contribute to the world.' Philosophy Professor Lou Marinoff describes Ikeda as the 'most accomplished Buddhist leader of our age' who is 'truly working for the happiness of all human beings', adding that his 'achievements in propagating Nichiren Buddhism ... deserve special note in modern history'.

To find contact details for your nearest national SGI centre, go to: http://www.sgi.org/contact-us/ then scroll down to 'SGI Centers Worldwide' and enter your country name.

SELECT BIBLIOGRAPHY

I express my deep gratitude to these authors whose work has profoundly influenced my life, and whose books and websites I heartily recommend.

Nichiren Buddhist

The Writings of Nichiren Daishonin, Soka Gakkai, 1999

The Quotable Nichiren, World Tribune Press, 2003

Edward Canfor-Dumas, *The Buddha, Geoff and Me*, Rider Books, 2005

———, *Bodhisattva Blues*, Rider Books, 2014

Richard Causton, *The Buddha in Daily Life*, Rider Books, 1995

Martin & Morino Hochswender, *The Buddha in your Mirror*, Middleway Press, 2001

Daisaku Ikeda, *A Piece of Mirror and Other Essays*, Soka Gakkai Malaysia, 2004

———, Buddhism Day by Day, Middleway Press, 2007

Alex Lickerman, MD, *The Undefeated Mind*, hcibooks.com, 2012

Lou Marinoff & Daisaku Ikeda, *The Inner Philosopher*, Dialogue Path Press, 2012

Duncan Pow, *In Between Jobs*, Duncan Pow 2013

Chandra Wickramasinghe & Daisaku Ikeda, *Space and Eternal Life*, Journeyman Press, 1998

William Woollard, *The Reluctant Buddhist*, Grosvenor House Publishing, 2007

Shin Yatomi, *Buddhism in a New Light*, World Tribune Press, 2006

Other Buddhist

Danielle & Olivier Follmi, *Buddhist Offerings 365 Days*, Thames & Hudson, 2003

Hermann Hesse, *Siddhartha*, Penguin Classics, 1922

Dalai Lama, *Daily Advice from the Heart*, Element, 2003

Other spiritual

Paulo Coelho, *The Alchemist*, HarperCollins, 2012

Viktor E. Frankl, *Man's Search for Meaning*, Rider, 2004

Kahlil Gibran, *The Prophet*, Pan, 1991

Bradley Trevor Greive, *The Meaning of Life*, Random House Australia, 2002

Oriah Mountain Dreamer, *The Invitation*, Element, 2003

James Redfield, *The Celestine Prophecy*, Bantam, 1994

Robin Sharma, *The Monk who sold his Ferrari*, Element, 2004

Eckhart Tolle, *The Power of Now*, Hodder, 2001

Steve Taylor, *The Fall*, O-Books, 2005

Personal Development and Coaching

The Barefoot Doctor, *Liberation*, Element, 2010

Rikki Beadle-Blair, *What I Learned Today*, team angelica books, 2011

Alastair Campbell, *The Happy Depressive*, Arrow, 2012

Andy Cope & Andy Whittaker, *The Art of Being Brilliant*, Capstone, 2012

Stephen R. Covey, *The 7 Habits of Highly Effective People*, Simon & Schuster, 2004

Myles Downey, *Effective Coaching*, Texere Publishing, 2003

Byron Katie, *Loving What Is: How Four Questions Can Save Your Life*, Rider, 2002

Nancy Kline, *Time To Think: Listening to Ignite the Human Mind*, Cassell, 1998

Roy Leighton, Emma Kilbey & Kristina Bill, *101 Days to Make a Change*, Crown House, 2011

Paul McKenna, *Change Your Life In Seven Days*, Bantam Press, 2010

Pam Richardson, *The Life Coach*, Hamlyn, 2004

David Taylor, *The Naked Leader*, Capstone, 2002

Joe Vitale, *The Key: The Missing Secret for Attracting Anything You Want*, John Wiley & Sons, 2009

Academic

Jeanane & Merv Fowler, *Chanting in the Hillsides, The Buddhism of Nichiren Daishonin in Wales and the Borders*, Sussex Academic Press, 2009

Richard H. Seager, *Encountering the Dharma*, University of California Press, 2006

Clark Strand, *Waking the Buddha*, Middleway Press, 2014

Olivier Urbain, *Daisaku Ikeda's Philosophy of Peace*, I.B. Tauris, 2010

Bryan Wilson & Karel Dobbelaere, *A Time to Chant: Soka Gakkai Buddhists in Britain*, Clarendon Press, 1998

Websites

www.thankingthespoon.com

www.sgi-uk.org

www.sgi-usa.org

www.nichirenlibrary.org

abuddhistpodcast.com

www.transcend.org

theforgivenessproject.com

www.marianepearl.com

www.actionforhappiness.org

www.happinessinthisworld.com (Reflections of Buddhist physician Alex Lickerman)

www.mancroftinternational.com

www.nakedleader.com

ACKNOWLEDGEMENTS

My sincere thanks to all the friends, clients and Buddhists who have helped me to develop and express the ideas in these pages.

My heartfelt thanks first to Christiane Alix who in 1983 kept talking to me about Buddhism long after less compassionate and determined people would have given up. To Daisaku Ikeda, President of SGI, whose attitude and heart have taught me everything. To Mum for her great love of literature and for spending many hours encouraging me to read and write from an early age. To Dad for buying lots of self-help books and nurturing my interest in psychology. To my sister Alison for introducing me to the outstanding Winning Edge personal development programme, just when I needed it most. And to Richard Jackson and Barry Stiff for having the courage to create and launch it (back in 1984, when courses on happiness were viewed with some scepticism). Winning Edge provided a huge impetus to finally get this book out of my head and onto the page.

To Anna Golden, Marc Warburton, David Rowe and David Wright, who read early drafts of the book and shared with me their honest and insightful comments. To Stephanie J. Hale and Leigh Ferrani at Oxford Literary Consultancy, who read the finished draft and provided professional expertise and warm encouragement, as did fellow Buddhist writer Kelly Lawrence, singer-songwriter Meri Everitt, Naked Leader author David Taylor and my wonderful literary agent Susan Feldstein.

To my fellow SGI members who have generously contributed their experiences of practising Buddhism. To the hundreds of readers from 151 countries who have engaged with me on social media (extracts from this book were first posted on my blog: www.thankingthespoon.com) and in particular to Mel and Susan Turcanik for their wise insights and to Melson Diniz of Brazil for translating my blog posts into Portuguese. Also to Duncan Pow for his encouragement and Eddy Canfor-Dumas for warm support and thoughtful comments. Also to William Woollard, Roy Leighton and Lorraine Debnam for helping me over the finishing line when my many and versatile gremlins were urging me to give up. To Joan Anderson and the Publications Committee at SGI's Tokyo headquarters for giving me permission to quote from the writings of my mentor, SGI President Daisaku Ikeda, and from the SGI translations of Nichiren Daishonin's writings. To my editor at Rider, Sue Lascelles, for believing in a manuscript from a first-time author and for her deft and elegant touch making suggestions at final draft stage.

My sincere appreciation also to Tim Jones, a great friend and client who disagrees with almost all of the ideas in these pages and sincerely believes them to be 'hippie voodoo liberal nonsense' (polite translation). His scepticism has been truly inspirational.

And finally my sincere thanks to the many Buddhist leaders in SGI who have supported and stretched me in my faith and practice since 1985, including Jean-Marie Alix, Marc Tardieu, Annick and Andy McKenzie, Colin McEwan, Norma Cockburn, Paul and Robert Samuels, Richard and Maggie Norwell, Paul and Sharon Holding, Tanya Myers, Steve Lowe, Roy Marshall, David Woodger, Ken Muir, Robert Harrap, Robbie Lockie, Jason Jarrett, Jim Cowan, Stuart Barton, Yas Hirayama, Fabienne Schiess and David Ginns. And finally to Liliya H.B. Kenzhebayeva, whose pure seeking spirit and noble wisdom have inspired me to start writing my second book, and to the late great John Delnevo of SGI-UK, whose warmth, wisdom and gentle humour touched too many hearts to mention.

Parts of this book were first posted on my Buddhist blog – www.thankingthespoon.com – where you can still find spoonfuls of good stuff. And stir up discussions.

INDEX

ability 162
Abutso-bo 84
actualisation 122
affirmations xxiv–xxv, 35
agitated states 38
alcoholism 32, 58, 116–18, 218
alpha males 217
American New Thought movement 22
Amida Buddha 139
anger 17, 78, 174–6, 178–84, 229
anorexia nervosa 116–17
anxiety 187
apathy 234
apologies 178
approval-seeking 146
Aristotle 184
Armstrong, Adam 68
arrogance 87–9, 102, 110, 192–3, 198
Atkinson, William Walker 22
attachment 15
Auschwitz 169
authenticity 186–8, 216
autopilot mode 24
'away from' motivations 112

Baggio, Roberto 125
black-and-white thinking 57–8, 84–6
Blake, William 30
blame 43, 67, 78, 147, 180, 184–5
Bloom, Orlando 125
bonding 163–5
Boy George 125, 169
brilliance 55–6, 103–4, 147–9, 166, 186, 197, 217
Buddha 2, 3, 73, 139–40, 153
  definition 1
  in everyone 5, 26, 46–52, 68–9, 82–93, 101–3, 118, 146, 148, 155, 166, 188, 191, 206, 212–15, 220–1, 233, 235–6
  as a god 146
  see also Amida Buddha; Siddhartha Gautama

Buddhahood 17, 26, 28, 41–2, 49, 50–1, 54–7, 59–60, 68, 205, 217–19, 235–6
  and anger 184
  and chanting 38
  defining xiii, xxi, 170–1
  denial of 185
  and determination 156
  growth in everyday life xxv
  and happiness 143
  and karma 68, 73–4
  and problems 96, 98, 102
  underestimating the power of our 166
  voice of your 18
  within us/latent 5, 56–7, 82–6, 88–90, 147, 215
bullying 76–8
Burke, Edmund 234
business 199–200, 208

Campbell, Alastair 60, 218
Campbell, Joseph 104
cancer 8, 33–5
Canfor-Dumas, Edward 23
Capitalism 204
cause and effect see Mystic Law of cause and effect
challenge 113–15, 163, 172–3
change 95, 102, 113–14, 176, 207–8, 225
chanting xvi–xvii, 3–4, 55, 116, 117, 163–5, 212–13, 219–20, 233–4, 236
  affirmations to guide 35
  and calmness 38
  and determination 156
  different effects on different people 39
  first experiences of 77–8
  for a higher life state 130
  how it works 39
  and karma 66, 73
  and latent states 54

positions for 37
practicing with others 39–40
and problems 99–101, 103–4
and treasures of the heart 132–3
struggling with 28–9
what to think about 38
for what you want 37–8
see also 'Nam-myoho-renge-kyo'
children 40, 64, 163–5, 215
choice 46, 65, 70, 169, 181
Chopra, Deepak 213
Christianity 69, 145
Cicero 193
clarity 162
Cognitive Behavioural Therapy (CBT)
xix, 54
coincidence 73
comfort 128, 140–1
Communism 204, 212
comparison-making 178, 185–6
compassion xiii, 182, 198–9, 234–5
complaining 184–5
confidence 87–9, 174–6
connectedness xx, 4, 5, 23, 205–6,
212, 218, 226–8, 236
conscious mind 24
consolation 140–1
consumption 112–13
Cook, Rob 20–2
Cooper, Tommy 43
coping mindsets 113–15
cosmology 20
courage xiii, 162, 165, 170, 174,
176–7, 182
Covey, Stephen 88, 127
Cox, Brian 206
Creator 145

daily practice 37
Dale, Patti 75–6, 179
Dawkins, Richard 71, 232
de Prume, Cathryn 4, 130, 231–2,
233
de Saint-Exupéry, Antoine 224
death xxii, 2, 7, 8, 24–6, 63, 65, 99,
112–13
defeat 177–8
Delnevo, John 94, 105
depression xix, 7, 100–5, 133, 179,
188, 218, 220

desire 123–5, 134, 162
destiny 24, 26–7
determination 153–68, 234–5
disconnection 217, 218–19
drug addiction 58, 155
DuMont, James 26–7, 157–8
Dyson, James 155

Edison, Thomas 155
ego 88, 147, 161, 186, 213–17, 220,
230, 232
see also self, small; Survival-
Obsessed Self
'eight winds' 194
Einstein, Albert 50
Ema, Lord 136
Emerson, Ralph Waldo 74
Emotional Intelligence (EQ) xx, 31,
32, 48, 232
emotional reactions 46
empathy 162
emptiness 128, 186
energy 63
enjoyment 96–7
enlightenment xiv, xxi, 54–5, 83,
125, 146–7, 160, 236
entitlement culture xviii, xx, 113,
150, 192
equality 84
Evans, Jules 32, 149
Everitt, Meri 132–5, 180
evil 84–6, 89, 140, 188, 206–7, 234
evolution 3, 232

failure 56
faith xxi, 148, 150–1, 161, 177
father-infant bond 163–5
Ferrani, Leigh 33
fibromyalgia 133, 134
focus 160, 160–1
Frankl, Viktor 169
freedom 66–9
friendships 206
frustration 174–6
Fujii, Kazuo 113–14
Fundamental Darkness (FD) (inner
gremlins) xx–xxi, 8, 55, 69, 90,
99, 101–3, 111, 136, 157–60,
162–3, 166, 176, 178, 180,
189–90, 206, 209, 212, 232, 235

Gallwey, W. Timothy 162
Gandhi 9
Gardner, Howard 31
Geldof, Bob 135
Gibran, Kahlil 64, 65, 224
goals 15, 17, 37, 155, 162–3
God 145–7, 149
'Gohonzon' (scroll) 27–8, 37–8, 134,
    160–1, 188, 217
'gongyo' ceremony 37
good 71–2, 84–6, 89, 140, 188, 234
Gore, Al 72
'gosho' 40
gratitude attitude 192–3
Gröbler, Jürgen 155–6

habits 178
happiness xx–xxv, 26–7, 157, 166,
    221
  absolute 16, 17, 205, 215, 217, 236
  and affirmations xxiv
  definition xix, 13–14, 94, 97
  and external factors 15, 50, 128–9,
    149
  focusing on 160
  and the here and now 139, 141–4
  and IQ 31
  and the Law of Attraction 22–4
  mantras for 6, 18–22
  and money 125–6, 129
  of others 4, 14, 38
  relative 16–17
  as the soundtrack to your mind
    13–40
  and treasures of the heart 122, 125
harmony 209, 219, 224
Hawking, Stephen 111–12
heart xxi, 26, 28–9, 58–61, 175, 223
  see also 'treasures of the heart'
heaven xxi, 42, 139–40, 143, 145–6,
    149
heaven mindset/myth 143–4
Heaven/Rapture state 15, 41, 44, 47,
    50, 52, 55, 57, 59
hell xxi, 42, 139–40, 145
'Hell state' 7, 41, 44, 47, 52, 54–5, 57,
    59, 68, 100, 101, 147
hierarchy of needs 122, 123
Hill, David 209–10, 213, 222
Hillgruber, Jan 144

Hobbes, Thomas 109
Holding, Sharon 220
homes 230–1
homophobia 210–11
honour 157
hope 188–92
Howell, Ryan 130
human nature 51–2
human revolution 2, 5, 10, 74, 103–4,
    116, 131, 220, 229–32
humility 215–16

'iceberg' diagram 24
idolatry 27, 28
Ikeda, Daisaku xvii–xviii, 43, 60–1,
    97, 103, 117–18, 135, 141, 148,
    170, 175, 178, 191, 193, 198, 205,
    206, 212, 216, 221, 230–1, 236
illusions 2–3, 57, 104, 116, 160, 170,
    206, 215
individual differences 41
intangible rewards (inconspicuous
    benefits) 129–30
intelligence xx, 31–2, 48, 232
Intelligence Quotient (IQ) 18, 29,
    31–2, 48, 232

Jackson, Richard 7, 46
Jackson, Tim 128
Japan xiii–xv, 10, 82–3, 139, 146,
    154, 182–3, 212
Jazz, Maxi 125
jealousy 110, 178, 185–6
Jeffers, Susan 160
Jesus 9, 145
Johnson, Linda 165–6
Jolie, Angelina 190
Jones, Howard 5, 67, 221–2
Joubert, Joseph 216
journal exercises xxiv–xxv, 12, 36,
    62, 81, 93, 107, 120, 138, 152,
    168, 196, 203, 228

Kankucho bird, story of 144
karma 4, 24–6, 63–81, 99, 104, 143,
    164–5, 220, 230, 232
  attachment to 72, 170
  bad 170
  changing your 26–7, 71, 156
  definition 24, 71

fairness 65–6
and freedom 66–9
karmic Achilles heels 26–7
and life states 46
and personal responsibility 66–9
and problems 73–4
transforming into mission 74–9
and the Universe 64–6
'Kintsukuroi experience' 104–5
Kipling, Rudyard, 'If' 131

labelling 55–6, 57–8, 86
Lasn, Kalle 128
latent states 53–4, 56–7, 175
Law of Attraction (LOA) xxii, 22–4,
    26, 145
Laws of Life 23, 27
see also Mystic Law of cause and
    effect
leadership 199–201
left-brained people 18
Leighton, Roy 170
Lickerman, Alex 75, 208
life 8, 97, 204
    eternal nature xxii, 113, 115,
        140–1, 149, 212
    preciousness xx, 7–12, 34, 43, 104,
        165, 177, 193, 236
    rhythm xxiii, 18
    web 212
life force 38, 63
life purpose xxii, 18, 19, 75, 79, 183,
    198, 217
listening from the heart 222–3
locus of control
    external 44, 147, 149
    internal 147, 213
logic 29–31
Lotus Sutra xiii, 2–3, 18, 20, 37, 53,
    70, 82–4, 87, 90, 154, 156, 177,
    183, 189, 220, 222, 230, 233
love 89–90, 223–6, 231
Ludlum, Robert 64–5

magic 187
Mandela, Nelson 9, 86, 155, 157
manifest states 53–4, 56–7, 58–60,
    175
mantras see mindset mantras;
    'Nam-myoho-renge-kyo'

Marinoff, Lou 97, 162, 205, 232
marriage 206, 207–8
Maslow, Abraham 122
materialism 112–13
McCammon, Robert 187
media 60
mentors 197–203
Milton, John 42
mind
    and death 25–6
    mastering your 38, 169–96, 205,
        217
    nine levels of consciousness model
        23–6, 25, 29, 41, 65
    'set' 42
    soundtrack 13–40, 14–16, 42, 127
    see also subconscious mind; ten
        worlds model of the mind
mindset mantras 6, 11, 35, 61, 80,
    92, 106, 119, 137, 151, 167,
    194–5, 202, 226–7
mission 74–9, 156, 158, 183, 198
'mojo', mislaid 53–4, 187
money 125–6, 127–9
morality 69–70
Motson, John 155
Myers-Briggs profile 86
Mystic Law of cause and effect xxii,
    19–20, 22, 60, 66–75, 79, 96, 143,
    145–7, 149, 156, 174, 185
mysticism 29–31

'Nam-myoho-renge-kyo' xiii, xxiii–
    xxiv, 18–22, 53–4, 116, 117, 220
    and the 9th level of consciousness
        26
    and authenticity 188
    changing ourselves through 176
    and compassion 182
    daily practice 37
    and Fundamental Darkness 160
    'Gohonzon' (scroll) 27–8
    and gratitude 193
    and harmony 209
    and hope 191
    introspective nature 204–5
    meaning 18–21
    and problems 96, 100–1, 103
    for revenge 124
    and sex 125

to beat illness 34–5
and treasures of the heart 132
as 'we' prayer 229–30
National Health Service (NHS) xix
nature nurture debate 70
needs, hierarchy of 122, 123
'Never Disparaging' 222
Nichiren Buddhism xiii–xv, xviii,
    xxii–xxiii, 4–5, 221
  awakening the Buddha in others
    90–1
  defining 1
  and determination 154, 156, 157
  and Fundamental Darkness xx–xx
  and happiness 13, 15, 205
  and human revolution 131
  and karma 63, 69–70
  limitless beliefs of 212–13
  and living in the here and now
    142–3
  model of the mind 23–4, 25
  and overcoming the self 1–2
  and reframing 43
  and romantic love 223
  and treasures of the body 126
  and wealth 125
  and the wonderfulness of people
    148
  and world peace 232
Nichiren Daishonin xiii–xiv, xxi, xxii,
    xxiii, 1–5, 9, 56–7, 60, 77, 114,
    116–17, 126, 185, 205, 217, 220,
    230–1, 233–4
  and anger 180–4
  and authenticity 187–8
  and the Buddha within us all 82–6
  and chanting 18, 19, 37, 54, 219
  and courage 176, 177
  and desire 125
  and determination 153–4, 161
  and enlightenment 137, 146
  exile xiv, 10, 153–4, 183, 205, 218,
    233
  and Fundamental Darkness 55
  and 'gosho' 40
  and gratitude 192–3
  and happiness 17, 18, 19
  and heaven and hell 124, 139–41
  and honour 157
  and idolatry 27, 28

and karma 66, 68, 70, 71, 73
and latent states 54
and the Law of Attraction 23
and the Law of cause and effect 145
and mastering the mind 169–70,
    176, 194
and material well-being 123
as mentor 198–9
model of the mind 26
mysticism of 30–1
and optimism 188–9
persecution xiv, 10, 153–4, 183–4,
    205, 218, 233
and personal growth 235
and personal responsibility 67
and the preciousness of life 34
and the present moment 139,
    140–1
and problems 96–8, 100–1
and the profound 165
quoting of T'ien'tai 88
and spiritual intelligence 32
and the ten worlds model of the
    mind 41–2
and treasures of the heart 121–38,
    131
ultimate aim 233
Nin, Anaïs 46, 99
ninth consciousness 156, 174
nirvana 124, 139, 140, 143

'OK Society' 234–5
optimism 114, 188–92, 236
Oriah Mountain Dreamer, The
    Invitation 126–7

paradigm shifts 2
Parks, Rosa 135
peace 2, 5, 166, 231–5
Pearl, Mariane 190–2
perception 46
perfectionism 145
permanence, illusion of 57
personal growth 95, 106–7, 135,
    229–30, 235
personal responsibility 66–9, 78–9,
    147, 165, 181
pessimism 57, 114, 188–91
Plato 1, 129
pleasure, pursuit of 128

positive potential 61, 160–1, 186
positive psychology 1
potential 53–4
Pow, Duncan xvii
Practical Intelligence (PQ) 48
pragmatism 156
prayer 28–9, 38, 148–9, 154, 156, 229–30
pregnancy 83
prejudice 206, 208, 209
present moment, living in the 15, 139–52
previous lives xxii, 24–5, 51, 63–4, 67
problems 94–107
procrastination 8–9, 143–5
profundity 165–6
psychology 24, 27
Pure Land Buddhism 139

Quantum Physics 20

racism 76–9, 208, 210–11
randomness 73
recession 129, 169–70
reframing 42–3, 53–4, 56, 60, 95, 169–70
reincarnation xxii, 24–5, 51, 63–4, 67
rejection, fear of 208
relationships 46, 50–1, 206, 207–8, 223–6
resilience 153–68, 191
respect 221–2, 224
revenge 74
revolution 234
'rock bottom' 99–101
Rogers, Carl 222
Rotter, Julian B. 44
'rust, painting over' 172–3

sadness 15, 78
Sado 153, 218
'scarcity sell' 109
scepticism 28–9, 66
Secret, The 22–4, 26
self
  being yourself 186–8
  'big' 44–5, 115, 116, 119–20, 122, 125, 204–28, 230, 231, 233
  see also treasures of the heart
  getting over yourself 1–2, 11, 102
  giving up on yourself 177–8
  small 100, 112–13, 124–5, 147, 161, 186, 204–28, 230
  see also Survival-Obsessed Self
self-belief 162
self-esteem 87–90, 186, 207, 215
self-help 4
self-judgment 188
self-love 89–90
self-pity 219
self-talk, negative 58
Seligman, Martin 1, 57, 130
Seneca 174
senses 24
separateness, illusion of 2, 206
sex 125
shallowness 165–6
shared humanity 209–12, 221
Shaw, George Bernard 175
Shijo Kingo 121, 136
Siddhartha Gautama (first Buddha, Shakyamuni) xiii, 3, 9, 42, 68, 71–2, 84, 90, 105, 139, 144, 146, 151, 165, 171, 183, 192, 205, 222
signature strengths 130
sin 146, 148
society, fabric of 141
Soka Gakkai International (SGI) xv–xvi, xvii–xviii, xxiv, 2–5, 26, 40, 52, 68, 75, 89, 102, 113, 116–17, 130, 141, 144, 154, 157, 165–6, 170, 179, 190, 198, 208–9, 220, 222, 231–2
Speed, Gary 16–17
spirit 8, 111–12
spiritual growth 235
Spiritual Intelligence (SQ) 31, 32, 232
Spokes, Caroline 116
Strand, Clark 231, 233–4
String Theory 20
subconscious mind xxiv, 3–4, 24, 109–11
successors 200–1
suffering 2, 96–7, 99–100, 104–5, 117–18, 123–4, 135, 140, 153, 160, 171, 173, 216, 219
suicide 16–17

supporting others 4, 5
survival ladder 16, 129
survival mentality 108–20, 171, 185, 190, 205
Survival-Obsessed Self ('S-O-S') 2–3, 5, 50, 86, 88, 90, 97, 108–12, 131, 140, 161, 170, 187, 190, 198, 200, 205–6, 208, 212–15, 217–20, 226, 232, 235
  see also ego; self, small

talent, individual 208, 209–12
tangible rewards (conspicuous benefits)) 129–30
Tatsunokuchi beach 121, 217–18
Taylor, David 54, 199
Taylor, Steve 31
Ten Commandments 69
ten worlds model of the mind 41–62, 51–61, 70, 85, 233
  Anger state 41, 44, 46–7, 51, 53–4, 59, 68, 85, 88, 89
  Animality state 41, 44, 46–7, 50, 55, 59, 111
  Bodhisattva state 41, 48, 59, 68
  Buddhahood state 41, 49, 50–1, 54–5, 56–7, 59–60, 68
  dominant life states 46, 50, 57, 60
  Hell state 7, 41, 44, 47, 52, 54, 55, 57, 59, 68, 100, 101, 147
  Hunger state 41, 44, 46, 47, 59, 143, 147, 192
  Learning state 41, 48, 51, 59
  Rapture/Heaven state 15, 41, 44, 47, 50, 52, 55, 57, 59
  Realisation state 41, 48, 59
  as reframing tool 42–3, 53–4, 56, 60
  Tranquillity state 41, 44, 47, 52, 59, 68
Thoreau, Henry David 111
Tibetan Buddhism xii, 38
T'ien'tai 88
Tiro, Ramothibi 157
Toda, Josei xv, 141, 170–1, 182
Transactional Analysis 66
'treasures of the body' 122–3, 126,

131, 134–5, 216
'treasures of the heart' 121–38, 143, 204, 226, 235
'treasures of the storehouse' 122–3, 125, 127–9, 131, 134–5, 216, 235
tribal circles 2, 205–8
Tsunesaburo Makiguchi 141

unconditional positive regard 222
uniqueness 221, 236
universal life force 145, 147, 150
Universe 8, 24, 104, 149, 175, 207, 218, 229, 236
  essential vibration of xxiii, 18
  gears of the 73
  and karma 64–6, 67–8, 73–4
  multi-layered 20
  thanking the 74
  trusting in the 114
Urbain, Olivier 207

victims, angry 179–80
virtues 1, 129–30, 146
visualisation 37
Vitale, Joe 2, 226

war 88, 112, 179, 206, 215, 232
Wilde, Oscar 188
'will there be enough?' mindset 109
Williams, Betty 135
Williams, Steve 155–6
Williamson, Marianne 86–7
wisdom xiii, xxv, 75
Witherspoon, Reese 4
Woodger, David 76–9
Woollard, William 3, 15, 23, 28–9, 214
works in progress, magnificent 56
world, changing the 58–61, 95, 102, 156
world peace ('Kosen-Rufu') 2, 5, 166, 232–5

Yatomi, Shin 89

Zen Buddhism xii, 38